Aloha Valerie,

Blessings to you in your journey of Love. You are amazing!

Always in Love,

Cindy Matedani Sellers

1

I ask that you not go out and try to do any liver cleanse with out making way for
the particles to get out. I ask my Angel Graduates to not share the information
I give them here at Angel Farms because we all have no nerve endings in our
digestive tract. You have no idea the kind of things including ropes, worms, and
pockets that can catch things and not allow particles to be released from your body
safely. Our Cleanse program does not even consider emptying the liver until the
seventh day, only if they are clear. Therefore, I am not including the Liver Cleanse
program so as not to cause harm to those of you who are not willing to do all the
deep work first and be educated so you do not cause harm to yourself or others.

This information from the Cleanse Program was compiled from over 20 years
of my personal experiences. This is not a colon hydrotherapy program down
the street. We are a complete physical, emotional, mental, and spiritual
program. I really suggest you learn all you can about the different types
of colon hydrotherapy and choose the most gentle and cellular intelligent
program that allows your body to release at it own will and not someone elses.

Published by Cindy Sellers/Angel Farms Publishing
www.angelfarms.com
Editor: www.writementor.com
Layout/Design: www.soulsecretservice.com

You Don't Have To Hurt Anymore

Cindy Mahealani Sellers

 # Contents

 **Contents**

 **Contents**

Feel free to visit www.angelfarms.com for more
information on Angel Farms, CDs, DVDs and Charts.

This book will challenge your beliefs and perceptions
about life and who you are!
Are you truly ready to
change your life and not hurt anymore?

I have a question for you and I promise it will
not be the last time I ask this question.

On a scale of 1 to 10,
10 being the highest,
how much do you love yourself?
On that scale of 1 to 10,
10 being the highest,
how much does God love you?
10 of Course!

There are only 2 things as human beings
we can be addicted to and be healthy.
WATER and LOVING!
All the rest in moderation.

Always in love,
Cindy Mahealani Sellers

What Is An Angel?

Throughout this book, I refer to each and every one of you as an "Angel", because that is how I know you! What is an Angel? A celestial being with all the knowledge of the universe! I truly believe that all things are possible and that is why I am a Miracle Junkie. I know that you have loved even when it has been hard. You are an Angel! I know what your love is worth and how important you are. I know the absolute good that you are. I know the wisdom you carry, 100%. I know why you are here. I know how many walk with you and how honored they are to do so. I know how bright you shine. I know how powerful you are. I know that you are safe and wanted in this world. I know you are a seed of God walking on earth, blessing it with every step you take and every breath you breathe. I have witnessed many people literally transform their body, mind, and spirit over the years. What amazing miracles I have been able to witness! I am educated mostly by God and by life and by listening, although I absolutely have had many great teachers! I am honored to know where their work has blossomed through me. This book is to help you know what I know about how very special you are to the Creator and to the World. Bless you and your Great Love.

Throughout this book, I will be referring to an Angel "tool box". If you choose to use your tools on a daily basis they will become a part of you. They REALLY work. They are easy to practice. Be open to the possibility of health and freedom. Let go and let God! Every step in your journey is divinely perfect, so allow for a change in perception. "A miracle is a change in perception."

Letter From Cindy Sellers

I wish to deeply acknowledge my beloved husband and best friend of 30 years, Larry Sellers. I also want to thank Shara, my beautiful daughter, for her ancient wisdom and all she has done to help me with this book. I couldn't have done it without her. She is the first human I have known who did not have to have a trauma to bring her to her intent. I thank Anthony, our son, who has been a master teacher for me and is the cook at our facility. To their partners, Jim and Amy, who are my family too, and my beautiful grand children, Mikayla, Dustin, and Jacob! To my teachers who found me and to my students; for all of you awaken me. Gratitude to my Grandmother, Fern Manning, as a master teacher and poet. To Dr. Liz Atchison, my sister Vickie Sorensen, Heidi Rose Dane, Julie Christensen, White Eagle, Jim and Big Hal, Deepak Chopra, Marianne Williamson, Neil Donald Walsh, Dr. Wayne Dyer, Greg Bradan, Abraham Hicks, Satyen Raja, and to Sophia and Jewel for their music which soothes my soul. To my little dog, Shilo and our beautiful cat Orion, who have been by my side these past 12 years, thank you! You have helped many in their transformations with your unconditional love and forgiveness.

Also thank you Beah for your transcribing, editing, friendship, and your ancient wisdom. This book is enriched by you. My best friend forever, Shalona for your help in editing, your laughter, and your Light. Thank you to my team at Angel Farms who make my life better and everyone else's also. To all the worldwide Angels that have found their way to Angel Farms and made me a miracle junkie. Many of you are in this book as master teachers; your journey is worthy of being shared!

I am honored to be a part of the Nation of Hawaii and for her help in bringing me home, and thank you to Goddess Pele who reminds me to flow. To Kaliko, my brother and true strong friend who chose to walk with me as a miracle junkie. Kahu for your infinite wisdom, teachings and passion for life. And most of all, to The God of Love who inspires me to wake up and love, and be a part of the awakening of the world to heaven on earth, as love is remembered in every particle on this beautiful planet.

So much Mahalo to Teri Hitt for her great wisdom and knowledge of computers and how to lay out a book. To Wanda Webster, Shalona Clark and Tammy Walker, Amy Altman, and Sarah Barrington, for their help in editing.

A Note From Larry Sellers

When Cindy asked me to write a note for her book, I was first of all honored. Our wonderful marriage of 32 years, our two children, and having the opportunity to grow in a true healing center have all been very enriching. We have all heard stories about places like Angel Farms and when needed they might have been hard to find or were not as great as we might have heard. I'm telling you this, Angel Farms, is one of those magnificent places and we are those people who have made it their life's mission to give back to humanity the truth about health in an easy to understand way, and to therefore help people get back to the basics of life.

In return our family has been blessed with the Light that this work has given us; namely the miraculous healings that we have witnessed in the 5000+ lives that have been touched here at Angel Farms Cleansing and Rejuvenation Center, all in the name of Love. At Angel Farms we ask one question; on a scale of 1 to 10, how much do you love yourself and others? Everyone always answers 10! Cindy says it is the 10's that will change the world.

What is my part in this? When you're really ready to relax, I am honored to help you with that. Relaxing is an art. We all have a different definition of relaxing and I believe we forgotten how. I help you remember; my touch helps you relax. When a stiff joint relaxes, the pain goes away. How can it be hurting if it's relaxed?

I personally have witnessed every type of miracle {a change in perception] that this book and its teachings have recorded, and in every form of wondrous possibilities. It has taken a lifetime to compile this book in an easy to read and understand manual that will have you crying and laughing, so bring a box of tissues. When you realize how simple it is, and that it's all up to you, you will wake up with a smile and a positive attitude. Very soon you will be used to it being that way.

—Always with love, Larry

Aloha Angels

I have a few questions for you. What would your life be like if you could live in complete and utter bliss, full health, and love for the rest of your life? What if you didn't have to die to do that? What if you just had to wake up? My intention for this book is to help you come into a state of full knowing of your physical, mental, spiritual, and emotional bodies. What if you could wake up healthy, happy, and grateful for life? What if you could wake with the anticipation of another glorious day in physical form?

Life is unique. Have you ever seen identical snowflakes, leaves, flowers, or even faces? Everything is unique. Our uniqueness makes the world far more interesting! True appreciation of the individuality and variety of interests and talents of others keeps us free of comparison, judgment, and sadness. May you find the balance in these words. Find your bliss and follow it! Spirit is trying to get your attention! Be still and listen.

There are two main reasons for disease and illness: first, people do not understand the meaning of their lives and feel disconnected from Spirit, and second, they don't have a full knowledge about how they can change themselves in order to overcome life's challenges. We are Spiritual Beings first. We have always been, are now, and always will be! We cannot change that because we did not create that. We just have to remember what is already within us. This book will help you understand your physical body temple and how it works and will assist you in establishing an ever stronger connection to God which will allow you to walk peacefully through the world. Inner knowing will answer the questions we all ask ourselves: Why am I here and what am I going to do about it?

Throughout this book I will be giving you very workable tools for you to take with you into every day life, creating the peace and joy you deserve as your constant companion, under any and all circumstances. When you find yourself at work, with family, or in relationships, the tools I will teach you in this book can show you how to peacefully deal with all of these aspects of your life.

This book is presented to you to remind you that "If you hold on to anything, it hurts". Relax, breathe, and just let go of everything. I am so excited to share my 20 years of experience with you, about how the organs and systems of the body work, how they are nourished through the large intestine (colon), and the best ways to clear your organs of physical, emotional, and spiritual pain.

In this book, you will learn how the organs and systems of the body work, how they are nourished through the large intestine (colon), and the best ways to clear your organs of physical, emotional, and spiritual pain.

I'm the Boss

When God made man there was only one, and the various parts of the body argued about who would be boss. The hands said they should be because they did the work. The feet said they should be because they took man to where he could do the work and get the food. The stomach thought it should be because it digested the food. The heart thought it should be because it pumped the blood that allowed the food to be digested by the stomach and reach the body. The brain said, "I have to send all the signals to get each of you to do your job, therefore, I am boss." The colon said, "I'll show you who is boss," and clogged up and would not let anything pass. After a few days the stomach ached .... The hands were practically helpless ... the feet could not carry the body .... The heart was ready to stop pumping blood .... The brain's signals were being ignored. To all this there is a moral... —Author Unknown

Our bodies are phenomenal events. We have this amazing gift built within us called grace, and whatever has happened to you in your life can be moved and released from your body. You are not punished for your beliefs, perceptions and mistakes, only by holding onto them. Ultimately, you will know the greatest thing you will ever learn, and that is "YOU DON'T HAVE TO HURT ANY MORE!"

Life is about BALANCE. Our life is like four legs of a chair: one Spiritual, one Emotional, one Mental, and one Physical. Each leg has equal importance and if one leg of your chair is out of balance your whole chair will fall over.

We each have our natural strengths; areas we tend to focus our attention and our energy on a daily basis. Some people work on their physical bodies every day. They have awesome physiques. Some people meditate daily and work on their spiritual selves. Some people have been doing therapy and emotional release work. Some people are professional students, really mental, mental, mental and on their computer every moment that they can be. I honor each of these folks. I have found, though, that to have a happy productive life, we must balance our time and energies among all 4 categories: all 4 legs daily.

You will learn that when the physical, mental, emotional, and spiritual bodies are balanced, food will be your medicine, and your medicine will be your food. You can assimilate your food properly, so that even the need for supplementing will be rare. You can feel younger, happier, more energetic, calm, and at peace with and in appreciation of yourself; you can feel better than you've ever felt before.

Did you know that the digestive tract is the first organ to be created in utero, in the umbilical cord? It then connects from the mouth to the anus and buds are formed to create your different organs: spleen, liver, heart, lungs, pancreas, kidneys, and etc. This is why it is so important to understand the functions of the colon and how it feeds the body and assists in regeneration. Many doctors believe the colon is not that important and only necessary for waste removal. This is incorrect!

I have had 20 years of watching people look and feel younger, as well as heal all kinds of diseases. Wrinkles disappear and even 'natural' face lifts happen in front of me, including hair turning from grey to its original color in 10 days. When I was young I learned in school that hair is dead. How can that be when it changes in 10 days? That means it is not dead, it just does not have nerve endings in it. Doing my work for over 20 years has shown me that many teachings and perceptions we were taught in school are not true! Anything is possible!

It is time now, beloved Angel, to wake up and honor your body, mind, and soul. You are the one we have been waiting for! Feeling alone, often from our first breath, plays a big role in keeping us stuck in the past traumas and negative life stories. This "shit" literally manifests in the body preventing us from absorbing the nutrition and information. Dis-ease does not allow us to hear Spirit's guidance and find our purpose, which is to Love! The body, mind, and spirit work so perfectly and effortlessly together.They crave balance like the 4 legged chair! We can have joy and happiness rather than illness, dis-ease, and pain.

When you are ready, you can let go of all the past experiences: flush out of your organs, body, and mind, all those on-going soap opera-like dramas and traumas that can seem so real that we keep projecting and re-experiencing them. Remember when you think about what is, you get more of what is. This form of 'drama' comes with a high price to pay-- adrenal and physical stress on organs and glands of your body. Each distressed organ of the body, each medical condition, is an indication of the specific types of issues that need to be released and the emotions that need to be refocused or retrained. Are you courageous enough to choose joy over pain? Is it possible for you to drop your old shitty stories to create and embrace some happy new ones—dreams of joy, love and peace instead of recurring, all too familiar, life nightmares? BE the Divine Being you were born to be! I hope I can help you find the balance in these words.

Throughout this book, I will be referring to an Angel "tool box". If you choose to use your tools on a daily basis they will become a part of you. They REALLY work. They are easy to practice. Be open to the possibility of health and freedom. Let go

 ## Your First Angel's Toolbox!

Make your morning prayer be "Thank you for this day and all the beauty and love I can taste, smell, see, hear and feel. Thank you for all the opportunities I have to love this day."

The word heal has a common origin with words whole and holy; pointing to the relationship between body and spirit. All emotions bring us closer to our true nature and powerful creative capacity whether we call it consciousness or God.

1 John 4:8
Whoever does not love does not know God, because God is love.
1 John 4:18
There is no fear in love.

Let's get to the first judgment of an Angel! Yes You!! Did you notice the word "God" in the last paragraph? You may have a mis-perception of the word God. Get over it! You are not the first or the last Angel to have a judgment on that word! I am in full agreement with John 4:8, God is Love. If you just substitute any word you have for God, Creator, Source, Goddess, Mohammad, Jehovah, Ra, Is, Great Spirit, Krishna, or whatever, we are all on the same page. We are all from Love, whatever the definition.

20

God is Love, and this love is very different from human love. God's love is unconditional. God doesn't love us because we're lovable or because we make God feel good; God loves us because God is love!

Many people have come to Angel Farms stating 'I don't believe in God.' I ask them, "Do you believe in love?" By definition, God is love. If you love anything, then you believe in God (Love). Do you love anything in your life right now? Do you love a dog, cat, butterfly, friend, partner, yourself, the sunrise, sunset; then you believe in God. I have seen many go from pure atheists to lovers of God and themselves! You are a spiritual being first. You just misinterpreted God—and you have just rejected a definition of God that is other than love. With this understanding of the definition of God, you find you are really great and powerful LOVERS! Loving is innate to our nature. 'We practice but an ancient truth we knew before illusion seemed to claim the world. And we remind the world it is free of all illusions when we say God is but love and therefore so am I.' A Course in Miracles

Within these pages, I will educate you on how you can feel younger, more energetic, happier, calmer, and more in love with yourself than you've ever felt before. Do you know that you not only absorb nutrition from your food, you also absorb information from the environment you live in? The sun, rain, earth, bees, flowers everything around us is emanating information. You've been searching for "You" all your life, for that "wondrous self" that has been, is now, and will always be! You have been searching for the knowing that you are the light unto the world, the love of God made manifest into physical form. Do you know how important that makes you? Perhaps your consciousness has been focused in the past or the future; that you think you should change, but you can't. You can change your judgment of the past. You can change your now, by letting go of your attachments to the past, the judgments of times when you think you didn't love enough, or do enough, or that you made the wrong choices. Judgment is often holding your self to a perception or reality of who you should have been, or how you should have done something or been something different, according to other people's projections or societies' standards. How does your past define you? What would it mean to totally let that go? Are you really ready to not hurt anymore? Do you want to be right or do you want to be happy and healthy?

I'm a spiritual healer first. I just happen to use the colon as the doorway to God. This method works very fast. 10 days isn't long to wake up an Angel, even though they've been on all kinds of journeys. When it comes right down to it, everyone makes their purpose so hard...it's not hard at all, and it's the same for everyone... to love, and to drink a gallon of water a day!!! That's it! Love is unlimited, so if you love all you can and drink a gallon of water every day, you are living your purpose! People are on the verge of waking up, rising to their greater awareness. This planet has great hope.

What is the definition of FEAR?
Fantasized Emotions Appearing Real.

Maybe you have been taught that fear means
False Evidence Appearing Real.
This still is a judgment.
Be careful because your kidneys are asking
you to release all judgment.

Chapter 1
Water & Kidneys
How does Judgement And Criticism Affect Your Kidneys and Your Life?

I am safe. I am open. I am whole. I am complete.

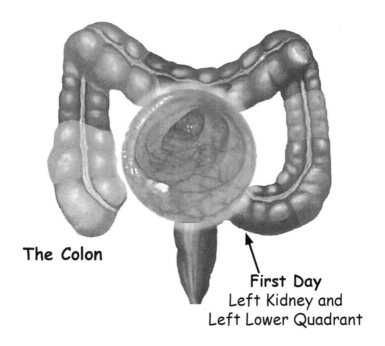

The Colon

First Day
Left Kidney and
Left Lower Quadrant

Water

Let's talk about the magnificence of WATER. Without water we would not even be here in our bodies and Mother Earth could not exist as herself! For this reason, I have a very deep and profound respect and honor for the element of water. Over the years, I have witnessed the miracles of water as the baptism from within to awaken Angels here on earth. Water holds a major place in nature's cycle. Life on this planet and species reproduction could not exist without water. Water is the most important ingredient required by your body on a daily basis. It is the primary transporter of nutrients throughout the body. Water is responsible for and involved in nearly every bodily process including digestion, absorption, circulation and elimination. To keep the body functioning properly, a gallon, or 8- 8 oz glasses each day are necessary for your body to stay healthy. In my 20 years of experience, I have witnessed how very important water is for our overall health and happiness.

The human body can only live healthfully for a few days without water because our bodies rely on water to filter, move, and get rid of toxic and foreign particles that accumulate in our system. Your body's cells cannot communicate with each other without the conduction of water. You are an electromagnetic being, or as I like to say, a battery in a bag. When you do not drink water, your body attempts to get some fluids from what you eat by sucking dry what food comes in to the body. This creates many problems in your body including constipation, hard stools, hemorrhoids, and bowel upset, and is the number one cause of chronic health conditions.

Our bodies are 80% water and 20% mass just like the Earth herself. Our brain is 93% water. It weighs three pounds and when dehydrated it weighs just a mere eight ounces. Amazing! Even our eyeballs are 96% water. We need 80% more water than food. A couple of symptoms or signs of dehydration are dry lips and being able to smell or see your urine (unless you are on B vitamins).

If you put anything in water, it is no longer water. It is not even spelled water anymore. Your tongue is really smart and can tell if you put lemon in water. It is then no longer assimilated as water but as a lemon. Tea and juice are not water and neither is coffee. I have had people come in for an Angel Farms 10 Day Cleansing Program and I ask them when they last drank some water. They reply: I drank my tea, I drank my juice, I drank my coffee, etc— they don't get that those are not water. Through the tongue, the body registers the tastes of bitter, sour, astringent, salty, pungent, and sweet. The tongue registers water as the only neutral substance. It is not positive or negative, it is neutral. It allows the body's cellular intelligence to use it for whatever the body needs.

It is easy for your body to drink a full glass or more of water at a time, because the taste buds do not have to "catch" the information. Any other drinkable liquid, however, has to be processed by the taste buds for the information transfer between brain and organs in order for best assimilation of nutrients. Your taste buds turn on the information of how to process anything that touches them. It all begins in the mouth!!! So chew your liquids and drink your food. This means that if you swallow something that is not fully liquefied, like applesauce, the food will not digest properly, which causes gas, indigestion, and mal-absorption. Keep chewing your wonderful food and then you can swallow!!! You only have teeth in your mouth! And don't forget to give your juices and other drink-ables a swish before you swallow! Get those taste buds working! Remember this for healthy digestion and absorption! I believe this is one of the keys to good health.

The first drink of water in the morning is called brain food. Enjoy! It bypasses the whole system and goes directly to the brain. Your brain has to have water to function, even if it is old stagnant pond water, it will hold on to every drop it can. Flushing out the brain first thing in the morning, keeps the entire body communicating properly. Remember your precious brain is 93% water. Can clearer thinking really be this easy? Yes!

Here are some immediate and life-long benefits that you can experience from upping your intake of water: it will change your cell structure, affect the way your body moves, you will stand taller, wrinkles will disappear as the skin renews itself to vitality and elasticity, the whites of your eyes will get whiter due to an increase in oxygen, and your eyesight will improve; your hair gets softer, joints become more flexible, thinking becomes clearer. What amazing miracles your body can experience just from re-hydrating yourself daily. Remember this Angel! It matters. You are a "water being" moving around this Earth!

As Dr. Emoto states in his book, The Hidden Messages in Water, "Water is life force." Understanding that we are essentially water is the key to uncovering the mysteries of the universe. The more you understand water, the more difficult you will find it to deny the existence of God. Water can align itself with the consciousness of human beings. Dr. Emoto did an experiment that convinced him that 'love and gratitude' form immunity. Because you are 80% water, whatever you feel, think, say, or do affects you on a cellular level. For instance, when you hate, have unloving behaviors or fear, it affects your water molecules by not allowing cell to cell communication and therefore affects your health. Just remembering that you are a being of light and love, and mostly water, affects the health and happiness of yourself and ultimately the world.

When I discovered Dr. Emoto's work, I became so incredibly excited. I have found after working with over 5000 people in 20 plus years that it takes 200 gallons of water to sprout an Angel and that is not including what they drink! I watched how the water literally wakes up Angels. Dr. Emoto's work has been my validation of the way The Cleanse works by bringing the body with all its wondrous organs and systems back to full hydration. Very exciting! I was in love with him the moment I read his work. I had the opportunity to meet him in Hilo, Hawaii for a talk he did to honor Hilo as a place that has been blessed by water, even by a tsunami! He is a very special person on the planet today. Daily, I send Love and Gratitude to the water on our planet, our oceans and in our body temples.

These implications create a new awareness of how you can positively impact the earth and your personal health. What has put Dr. Emoto at the forefront of the study of water are his findings that thoughts and feelings affect physical reality. By producing different focused intentions through written and spoken words and music and literally presenting it to water, the water "changes its expression". Imagine what the water does inside your body! Amazing!

Snowflake

Due to the necessary requirement of permission to use other people's pictures or words, and time restraints for this book, I am asking all of you to imagine all water droplets looking like snowflakes. Follow up on Dr. Emoto's awesome work and you will learn so much about the power of water and intention.

I am so grateful for Dr. Emoto and all he does in the world.

Send your Love and Gratitude to every drop of water within you. It will change into healing water, and everythingand everybody will be filled with a vibration of Love and gratitude because that is what you are sending out now.

Studies show that 75% of Americans are chronically dehydrated. That also applies to about half the world's population. In 37% of Americans, the thirst mechanism is so weak that it is often mistaken for hunger. If you want to lose weight try drinking a glass of water before you eat and you may not even be hungry! Even MILD dehydration will slow down one's metabolism as much as 3%. One glass of water shut down midnight hunger for 100% of dieters in a University of Washington Study.

My experience indicates that 8-8oz glasses of water a day can significantly ease back pain. The number one trigger of daytime fatigue is lack of water. A mere 2% drop in body water can trigger fuzzy short term memory, trouble with basic math, and difficulty focusing on the computer screen or on a printed page. Studies show that drinking 5 glasses of water daily decreases the risk of colon cancer by 45%, decreases the risk of breast cancer by 79% and one is 50% less likely to develop bladder cancer. If you are not drinking up to a gallon of water a day, you are not drinking enough water.

Because your brain is 93% water, if you never want to get Alzheimer's or senility or dementia, never ever let your brain get dehydrated! I have seen many Angels regain full brain function after The Cleanse because they are hydrating their brains again! You may believe that too much water can harm you; if you are 80% water, how could this be so? Please, Angel, find your own understanding about the absolute necessity of daily water so you do not have to hurt anymore!

Many have difficulty in remembering and relearning how to drink water. I suggest these easy steps to incorporate more water into your daily routine. Try initially removing everything from your drinking regimen except for the water. Just keep trying until you become addicted to water like me. This is a good time to give up that caffeine or soda attachment you may have! You can slowly add your favorite beverages back in to your daily regimen. I remind my Angels that you know you will be doing only two things if you wake up in the morning. Drinking water and loving. The rest is gravy. Water is the foundation to all healing!!!!

Let me now give you my tried and true ways of increasing your water intake to a gallon a day! I recommend you carry a gallon of pure, clean water with you every day to see how much you are drinking. The first quart of water in the morning-heat it up like it's a warm yummy tea in a glass and drink it . When you go out to eat, it is best to order water without ice. It is very difficult for your body to warm up water in your body during digestion. Place a 5 gallon water dispenser at room temperature with easy access for everybody to hit the water first, not the fridge to find juices or soda. It is nice to incorporate a little bowl underneath your water dispenser for the dog or cat, so they always have easy access to water.

When you first significantly increase your water intake, you will pee A LOT. Keep drinking your water and your body will find its balance. Sometimes it takes about a week before you feel like you don't have to pee all the time, as your kidneys trust that you are intent on giving them plenty of water. When you feel thirsty, your brain is telling you to get more fluids to keep your body as balanced as possible.

If you don't have enough fluids in your body, the brain communicates with the kidneys by sending out a hormone that tells the kidneys to hold onto some fluids. This is when we notice swelling of the body or edema. When you drink more, this hormone level goes down, and the kidneys will let go of more fluids. Rejuvenation of the kidneys happens between 3-6 PM and 3-6 AM. You should be peeing most during these times. Another thing, the kidneys won't reset themselves if you only give them just a day or two of adequate water, they don't know if you are going to keep it up. I have heard many times my Angels say, "I peed all night, I didn't get any sleep." I always tell them, "Good for you, they will find balance. They always reset themselves. Don't you dare stop drinking water!"

Distilled Water

Allow me to explain something important: the difference between clean natural spring water and distilled water. Distilled water has been processed so the minerals from the water are removed by steam. The body requires natural minerals to process water. The body will pull excess minerals from the joints to process. I recommend that if you have joint pain, you may use distilled water temporarily for up to 2-3 weeks. When the joint pain subsides, go back to natural spring water. If you do not have relief of the joint pain within this time, please stop using the distilled water.

I have had many Angels with home distillers come in with their muscles literally falling off their bones. They were only able to reverse this painful journey by doing The Cleanse and thoroughly re-hydrating themselves with mineral rich water. Natural spring water, water that rises naturally to the earth's surface from underground reservoirs that has been bottled with the naturally occurring minerals still intact, is the best choice for daily drinking. Those naturally occurring minerals are beneficial to the body and that is why it tastes so good!

Remember the high school chemistry charts? We are

made up of all those elements! What are the elements in the human body? Most of the human body is made up of water, H_2O, with every cell consisting of 65-90% water by weight. Carbon, the basic unit for organic molecules, comes in second. 99% of the mass of the human body is made up of just six elements: oxygen, carbon, hydrogen, nitrogen, calcium, and phosphorus. **Here's the breakdown of the percentages:**

Oxygen (65%)
Carbon (18%)
Hydrogen (10%)
Nitrogen (3%)
Calcium (1.5%)
Phosphorus (1.0%)
Potassium (0.35%)
Sulfur (0.25%)
Sodium (0.15%)
Magnesium (0.05%)
Copper, Zinc, Selenium, Molybdenum, Fluorine, Chlorine, Iodine, Manganese, Cobalt, Iron (0.70%)
Lithium, Strontium, Aluminum, Silicon, Lead, Vanadium, Arsenic, Bromine (trace amounts)

Reference: H. A. Harper, V. W. Rodwell, P. A. Mayes, Review of Physiological Chemistry, 16th ed., Lange Medical Publications, Los Altos, California 1977.

Isn't it amazing that we are
the same elements as Mother Earth?
It is very important, Angel,
to know this and understand you
and your cellular makeup are all of this!

The main chemical needs of the body organs are:

Thyroid	Iodine
Bowel	Magnesium
Brain and Nervous System	Phosphorus & Manganese
Heart	Potassium
Kidneys	Chlorine
Skin and Circulation	Sulphur, Silicon, Oxygen
Nails and Hair	Silicon
Spleen	Fluorine, Copper
Teeth & Bones	Fluorine, Calcium
Adrenals	Zine (trace)
Liver	Sulphur & Iron
Pituitary Gland	Bromine
Stomach and Digestive Sys-tem	Chlorine & Sodium Potassium & Chlorine
Tissues and Secretions	Oxygen & Iron

Thus we have the 16 chemicals as found in man, largely from the work of Dr. W. G. Rocine, In his words, "A well-chemically balanced body is a healthy body."

Something to practice daily:
Take your water container into your hands, send it Love and Gratitude.
Perhaps you wish to write LOVE AND GRATITUDE on your container. Imagine snowflakes in your mind and run rainbow colors of light through your hands into your Sacred Water. Do you understand that you are the Angel who transforms the water into absolute goodness? Take a delicious drink and feel the water in your mouth. As you swallow, feel the water enter your temple and know this water is now sacred because it is now in a temple of love. God dwells within.

As you love anything today, and you will, the fluid in your body now releases blessed water. This blesses Mother Earth and the environment.

This consciousness will clear the septic systems and help the county systems. Your consciousness is the Key to transformation! That is how I help people get through bladder infections and interstitial cystitis and kidney disease. Your water is blessed because you have loved today. Even this fulfills your purpose on earth. You are awesome!

Miracle Story

This is Brian's story.

Brian had cancer for the second time in his life. On the 6th day of the Cleanse, I asked him what was pissing him off and making him angry. Instantly he went back to when he was 17 years old and he had cancer for the first time. The doctors told him that he would never leave the hospital and that he only had 2 weeks to live. He had a girlfriend at the time who was only 16 years old. She overheard the doctors say that he was dying and she disappeared out of his life. A couple of days later one of his friends came to visit and let Brian know he had seen his girlfriend with someone else. He was very upset and angry with her for leaving him, and he said, "I will show her! I am not going to die!" And guess what? He didn't. He lived on and loved a great lady whom he was with for 20 years. Sadly, they were in a car wreck in which she was driving and she was killed. This is what might have brought back the cancer. Angels, this is a karmic wheel. He had unhealed abandonment issues and so they were up for him again.

I said, "Brian, don't you hear the miracle? Somehow your girlfriend had the guts to walk away and because of that, you lived and you loved for 20 years. What a miracle!" He was on the board cleansing and he said to me, "Oh my God, what have I done?" I said "It's okay, Brian. We have this beautiful thing within us called grace. There's nothing that we have ever done wrong. We have always been doing the best we could with the wisdom we had. You didn't know who you were. So it's okay. She gave you the gift of life for 20 years and all this time you have been angry at her? Isn't that interesting?"

One of the things I was taught by my Native American teachers is that when you step into someone's shoes and you walk in their journey, then you can't judge them. I asked myself, would I have been able to walk someone across when I was 16 years old? My answer immediately was that I wouldn't have been able to do it either. I would have walked away too.

I said, "Wouldn't it be amazing if you could get her on the phone and let her off the hook?" (Because somewhere in us we carry the "coulda, woulda, shouldas"- the feelings of regret, disappointment, shame). "That's not possible" he said, "I haven't seen her in 20 years. That was back in Michigan and we are in Utah!" "Well, I know that", I said, "but wouldn't that be really cool?" "Yeah," he said, "that would be really cool."

So he comes in the next day and he says excitedly, "Cindy, you won't believe what happened! I got home from doing the Cleanse last night and my godmother tracked me down via my parents. I haven't talked to her in 15 years. She was in a mall going up an escalator in Michigan and met and recognized my ex-girlfriend from 20 years earlier. She is now 36 years old." That's a miracle right there!

So his godmother asked for her phone number, tracked Brian down in Utah and gave it to him that night. Brian called her up that very night and thanked her for his life. They had a 2 hour conversation about their lives and about how she had always felt terrible that she hadn't been able to stay there and watch him die, but she just couldn't do it. He said," I am so thankful that you did it just the way you did." And she said," I am so thankful that you called to tell me that because I have always felt badly about that." She healed what had held her down with regret over this life experience.

The miracle of this story is, at the exact time he was doing the Cleanse and having his miracle, remembering his whole-ness, his godmother and ex-girlfriend were meeting on the escalator in Michigan. Miracles have to come full circle for every party involved; that's how the 144,000 works. It isn't necessarily anyone you know, the miracles just happen when one person lets something go completely. In our oneness, every one then becomes clear. That's the day his cancer disappeared.

Another story on how we are connected to each other: There was an experiment done by the US Government. They swabbed the inside of the mouths of 500 military men to obtain their DNA. Heavy duty soldier types: Green Berets, Navy Seals, Special Forces, Delta Force. They swabbed the inside of each of their mouths and put the DNA into individual Petri dishes and drove those dishes 500 hundred miles away. In the rooms where they were training these men, they showed them very violent scenes of killing and maiming, scenes with guns and fire. 500 miles away, the DNA responded in each dish. Next they showed these men pictures of waterfalls, sunsets and babies and kittens, etc. 500 miles away the DNA responded in every petri dish.

Did you know, Angel, that each cell in your body has an estimated 6 to 8 feet of DNA?

If the DNA will respond 500 miles away, what is going on with our everyday DNA? What is going on in our cells when we speak or think negatively of ourselves or others? We are all the Christ and the Buddha. Stand in the good that is God. We are awakening to the Divinity that is God, and that is US. I speak it into the Universe! I remind people every chance I get! We are the ones we have been waiting for.

Left Kidney

Now, Angel, let's talk about your wonderful kidneys. In Traditional Chinese Medicine, the kidneys are known as the Mother of All Organs. Kidneys were once popularly regarded as the seat of the conscious reflection, and a number of verses in the Bible (Palms 7:9, Rev. 2:23) state that God searches out and inspects the kidneys, or "reins", of humans. Kidneys relate to judgment and criticism of self and others. You will find that people with kidney disease are very judgmental and critical. Just ask them about politics or

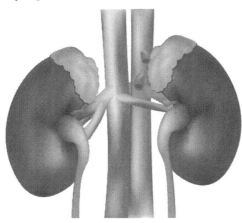

religion! Remember that judgment has created a world that is now in a war-like state. Haven't we all hurt enough? Judgment is what I believe is the first sign of separation and illness. The kidneys are the first to show problems, and it is really easy to see the kidney

lacunas in the iris of the eye.

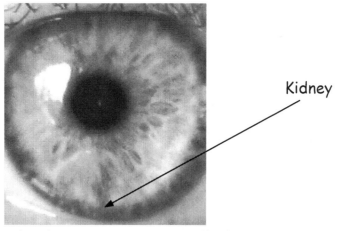

Kidney

So, Angel, right now go to a mirror and look at the colored area of your iris. Now see them as a clock; the topmost area is 12 o'clock, middle right is 3 o'clock, bottom most is 6 o'clock, and middle left is 9 o'clock. Notice the hair-like connective tissue. It can also look like fibers that go from the pupil to the outside of the iris. If you see a split or opening in the connective tissue, or fibers, you have a tendency to have a weakness in that area. The kidneys are located in the iris at around 6 o'clock. If a weakness, or lacuna, shows up in the iris in that area, you could have a tendency to carry judgment on yourself or others. I will be going into more details on Iridology in chapter 2.

What is Judgment? We all have our own definitions of what words mean. I have found Judgment to be an attachment to an outcome. We get angry or sad that someone or ourselves did or did not do or say something the way we think it should have, could have, or would have been. Then we begin projection. This is where we project into our tomorrows that which we have experienced in our past. Judgment is the journey of who we are not. Sometimes we have to know who we are not before we can know ourselves like God knows us. God wanted to know itself experientially through us! We agreed! The journey would be worth it! Truly knowing God is being free of judgment.

The kidneys are twin bean shaped organs and are the size of your own clenched fist. Kidneys are always busy filtering the blood and balancing fluids every second during the day. The kidneys remove wastes from the blood in the form of urine, and conserve water and maintain necessary fluid balance. Water makes up approximately 95 percent of the total volume of urine, with the remaining 5 percent consisting of wastes (i.e. urea, creatinine, and uric acid.) Did you know, Angel, that your kidneys process 1/4 of your body fluid every 15 minutes?

Amazing Human Fact!!! The kidney processes 50 gallons of fluids every 24 hours. That doesn't mean we pee that much, it just means that is how much fluid your kidneys process!

They are also the last filtration system of blood to the heart through the largest internal vein, the aorta, which is the diameter of a garden hose! Pretty amazing! Kidneys even make some of their own hormones. Working with the heart, the kidneys produce a hormone that tells the body to make red blood cells and they also help regulate the body's blood pressure. The brain is constantly sending messages to the kidneys to keep vital hormones communicating. Are you beginning to understand the importance of water and your brain, kidneys, and life?

When your kidneys are working well, the tiny filters in your kidneys keep protein inside your body. You need the protein to stay healthy. Kidney weakness begins long before you notice any symptoms. An early sign of kidney issues can be dark circles and puffiness under the eyes, swelling in the neck, shoulders, legs and arms.

The number one contra indication of most prescription and over the counter drugs or medicine is kidney dis-ease. Did you read the contra indication of your prescribed medication, Angel? The outside ventricles of the kidneys are a minute filtration system in the body and they can get plugged up with particles. Imagine how long your car would run without cleaning the filter! It is also easy to "overdose" even on supplements when your body has enough of the supplement and cannot use what is constantly being taken in. Please use your food as medicine and remember your daily intake of water.

Kidneys measure out chemicals like sodium, phosphorus, and potassium and release them back to the blood to return to the body. In this way, the kidneys regulate the body's level of these substances. The right balance is necessary for life, but excess levels can be harmful.

Kidney stones are hard, stone-like masses that can form from our hard stone like behaviors and control of others. The pain becomes agonizing when a stone breaks loose and begins to work its way down from your kidneys to your bladder. This can be your last chance to release your judgment of your parents or your neighbors, your children (you know the shoulds), even George W. Bush or other political or corporate figures! It is much easier to understand and forgive than to hurt yourself because you are taking other people's journeys personally. The judgment you are holding is a huge factor in kidney dysfunction.

The last step of kidney dysfunction in western medicine is to put the patient in a dialysis program. Doctors often tell patients that kidney dialysis is temporary. Please go and check this out for yourself before you ever consider it. Did you know that kidney dialysis centers are called the House of the Living Dead? Once the kidneys get on those machines they just dry up and shut down, so the person is on the machine until they are dead, unless they have a kidney transplant. We have to understand the absolute importance of returning to love and truth of our divinity or we are creating a way out. In this way, we will return to the Love and the Truth and the Peace! God is Love and you are it!

The following suggestions are to re-balance and re-nourish the kidneys.

Come to Angel Farms to Cleanse the body, mind, and spirit! Get that gallon of water down daily; eat more fiber, vegetables, and whole grains. Foods that are great for your kidneys are kidney beans, kiwi, celery, and bananas. Reduce your intake of sugar, refined foods, animal products, caffeine, alcohol, soda, and salt and reduce all corn sugars and corn syrups in products. Always dilute all your juices to lessen the sugar content.

Cranberry juice has been shown to reduce the amount of ionized calcium in the urine by over 50% in patients with recurrent kidney stones. But, be aware, I have found it is best not to drink cranberry juice in high concentration if you are under an attack from kidney stones. Beloved Angel, please be aware of choosing organic products and produce to help the kidneys in not having to filter toxic substances out of your beautiful body that are overwhelming and overworking them. Dairy and eggs need to be organic and cage free for the health of your body and our planet.

In the bible, Genesis, it says, God/Love created Heaven and earth. Have you ever heard that before? Which, translated, really means: Love created Heaven and earth. Because God is Love! Now, count 31 lines down, and it says, All that God/Love created is good. That would mean you and every blessed thing in the universe. Don't judge anything as less than God/Love and your kidney's will love and serve you well!

Remember, Angel, the words in this book are meant to bring awareness to your behavior and lifestyle and how easily we can correct imbalances and mis-perceptions. Anything that has happened in your past is part of who you are and is not to be judged

38

or criticized. You have been and always will be the best that you can possibly be, with who you know you are today and so is everyone else. Every step of the journey is exactly as it should be. Any "damages" or dis-eases (or as we like to call them, lessons) you might have in your body can be so effortlessly shifted to full health once a change in perception is made, when you are ready to accept yourself as a whole and loving child of God!

A miracle is a change in perception — A Course in Miracles.

Getting appropriate rest, regular exercise, and using relaxation techniques are other ways of improving kidney function and overall health. Remember to be gentle with your body as it heals; gentle walks and swimming, lomi-lomi massage, energy work,acupuncture and applying local heat and cold packs to help relieve pain and inflammation are wonderful therapies to incorporate into your healing experience. All in all, just remember- when you are IN pain, do only things that ease and keep you OUT of pain! Be gentle with yourself and forgive yourself and others, now! An awesome cleanse for the kidneys: purchase cut and sifted 1 ½ cups hydrangea root and 1 ½ cups parsley root from your local health food store. Boil ¼ cup of each ingredient in 2 quarts water for 20 minutes in a covered pot. Strain through cheese cloth into 2 quart jars, making 2 jars of "tea" every other day. Drink 1 quart per day for 10 days. Aside from refraining from dairy products and alcohol, eat regularly and listen to your body. Take an emotional inventory to see if you are experiencing judgment and/or criticism of yourself or others. Your kidneys are asking you to let it go!

Miracle Story

Big Joe was very heavy and incredibly swollen, had a lot of pain, and could not sleep or urinate.

Big Joe was dying and so were his kidneys. He was very angry, judgmental, and very hard on himself for being a mercenary in the war. I told him to go to the emergency room because his kidneys were not functioning and he was in danger of a heart attack at any moment. He said

"No way! I will die first!"

I told him I could start him on the Cleanse but he had to follow my exact directions. On the third day, he told me he was MAD because he was up all night peeing! I said to him, "Yeah!!! Your kidneys are kicking!" He peed off 40 pounds during the course of the 10 days. During the Cleanse, he miraculously noticed how many times he did not die during his life and realized that he was important and he had many gifts to offer the world. Miracle!!

A few days following the Cleanse, we were at the hardware store together and we came across his best friend who had spent two tours of duty with him in Vietnam. His friend walked right past him and did not recognize him. Not only had he lost 40 pounds, but his hair had changed from grey back to his natural color of bright red and his bald spot had completely filled in with hair! His kidneys returned to their perfect health and he was free.

It is important, Angel, to remember that wherever you are, God is, and has always been. When you're judging your journey, you are also judging the journey of God through you. Is your journey bringing you joy or pain? Isn't it time to set yourself free, like Big Joe?

The emotions and behaviors that most affect the kidneys with pain are: trying to control, judge or criticize yourself or others. Do you know anyone who does that? Our criticism and judgments are learned behaviors. We did not come in with them. They always keep us comparing and analyzing what we think others are thinking. This is what I call insanity! How could we possibly figure out what another person is thinking and the neural pathways their brain is traveling when we can't even follow our own neural pathways?

Are you starting to see how necessary it is to release judgment and criticism from your life? I believe judgment in our lives begins the feeling of separation, and therefore is the beginning of the breakdown of health in the human experience. We see everything as either God/Love or a fear-based reality. This is written on the tomb of an Anglican Bishop (1100 A.D.) in the Crypts of Westminster Abbey:

"When I was young and free and my imagination had no limits, I dreamed of changing the world. As I grew older and wiser, I discovered the world would not change, so I shortened my sights somewhat and decided to change only my country. But it too seemed immovable. As I grew into my twilight years, in one last desperate attempt, I settled for changing my family, those closest to me, but alas they would have none of it. And now as I lay on my deathbed, I realize: If I had only changed myself first, then by example I might have changed my family. From their inspiration and encouragement, I would then have been able to better my country and who knows, I may have even changed the world."

Beloved Angel, it starts with you! You are here to change the world and the time is now! Change is the only real difficulty you will ever encounter in applying any form of knowledge. All "applied knowledge" requires changing old habits and methods, as does the knowledge you will obtain in this book. Make change a positive learning experience. The ability to change requires only attitude, not skill. Change just means being in the moment and remembering who you are!!! Every time you release just one judgment from yourself, you help 144,000 others do it too. If you can release your judgment of the president, think of the 144,000 others you are allowing to release their judgment too! Why are you hurting over his actions when he probably does not even know your name? Do you understand how important you are? You are awesome! The universe says what is empty must be filled. Fill your kidneys with love! Haven't you hurt yourself enough?

Always be honest. Count your blessings. Forgive and forget. Be kind and tender hearted. Comfort one another. Keep your integrity. Be proud of each other. Laugh! Be true to each other. Treat each other like you treat your friends. And most importantly, love one another and yourself deeply from your heart.

Female Reproductive Organs

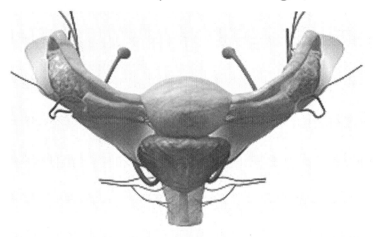

A woman has two ovaries. Their functions are to release egg cells and to produce hormones. They usually produce one to three eggs per month. The ovary produces two important hormones in a very unique way. For the first half of the menstrual cycle only Estrogen is produced but in the latter half the ovary also starts producing another hormone called Progesterone. These hormones protect against serious common dis-eases such as heart dis-ease and osteoporosis and they also contribute to sexual pleasure.

As a woman matures, the ovaries gradually reduce their production of hormones as the body shifts into menopause. Even after menopause they still produce small amounts of these necessary hormones.

The uterus or womb is another major hormone-responsive reproductive organ of the woman. One end, the cervix, opens into the vagina, while the other is connected to one or both fallopian tubes, depending on the species. It is within the uterus that the fetus develops during gestation. Women have issues in the uterus because of feelings of anger at male authority figures (often sexual abuse) and unloving feelings toward their mothers.

Premenstrual Syndrome

PMS is sign of self neglect. A woman will ease PMS symptoms by resting and creating something she loves. PMS panic attacks are the extreme of this: her body trying to get her attention that she is leading a life that has little to do with her, rather it is about everyone else's needs around her coming first.

How many of you Angels believe that you are responsible for another person's happiness? How many of you believe you have to sacrifice yourselves for others in order to be good enough to be with God? Get over it. You are not responsible for their happiness. They are responsible for their own happiness. You are responsible for your own. I see so many having terrible pain in their shoulders and upper back. Sound familiar? Ask yourself, If I am not happy, who is? When I am happy, who is? How would you like everyone on the planet to answer that question?

Foggy thinking, dizziness, heart palpitations, acne, headaches, stomach pain and pelvic pain are a sure sign a woman needs to let go of what she doesn't want in her life. It is time to face her innermost needs and if she is in non supportive situations, find her way back to God through meditation and nature. Women, remember your creative power and that this is your creative center. Your support comes from within and you just have to access it.

Angel's Toolbox

Practice your belly breath: Find a quiet place to relax for a few minutes. Pay attention to your senses. What do you hear, smell, taste, feel, and see? Exhale your breath and hum out on the exhale. What were you thinking? Nothing, right? The sound distracts the mind. Breathing deeply relaxes the nervous system. Put your hand on your belly, and raise your hand and belly with your breath. Counting slowly to 4, fill the whole lung cavity starting with the abdomen with your breath. Exhale in the same count. Do a few repetitions of these cleansing breaths. Listen to the quietness of the mind. Now feel the creative power of the universe in your belly. Breathe gratitude into it and let it flow. You are powerful beyond measure. Feel the power in the breath.

A wonderful, quick, and effective way to re-balance the female organs is to write down what you want. What if you could have everything you write on this piece of paper? Write down exactly what you desire. Align thoughts with inner guidance. This will create vibration to inspire creation. All women need to live for themselves and their passions. Make sure you aren't spending all your time and energy taking care of others and ignoring yourself. This is the creation of resentment and can get you out of balance.

One of my great teachers White Eagle called me to a sweat lodge one night. I told him I couldn't come because my moon cycle had just started. He said, "Who told you not to come because of that?" I said, "I thought it was the protocol." He said to come anyway and he would explain why. He said, "The way that protocol started was when women began their cycle the men felt they could take their power away in ceremony. Do you think you can take my power?" I said, "No, and why would I want to? I have God's power!" He said "Exactly. You cannot take another's power. You can only remember your own."

I learned to look at all rules, beliefs and protocols and ask, does this come from fear or from love? That moment changed my life. I found that all women have a creative energy before their cycles. If we focus that energy by creating something and then relaxing we do not have PMS symptoms. It is not a curse but a blessing. It is one of the reasons women live longer than men. We renew our red blood cells every month, which adds oxygen and strength. We can also bring forth life. What a gift we give to the God experience!

A great note about chocolate

Have you ever known a woman to crave chocolate? The University of Washington did a study on why women crave chocolate before their cycles. They used only organic, dark chocolate for the study. They had lots of volunteers! They found the cocoa had the highest form of bio-flavinoids than any other food which especially strengthens blood vessels. It also has a natural relaxant for nerve endings around blood vessels. Who knew!! Our intuition is so awesome.

Miracle Story ## Stephanie came in with cancer of the uterus.

She had 3 large tumors, one already perforating the wall. She had three young children. She started the Cleanse 3 days after her diagnosis. Her doctor called her daily and continually scared her. We asked her to please stop answering her phone until after her Cleanse. I told her to make an appointment right after she completed her transformation. She went in 5 days later and her tumors were gone. She told me she had not spoken to her neighbor for 9 years, because he was jerk! When I asked her why, she did not remember! I told her to take some bananas to her neighbor the next day and she said no way! I said then your choice is to die! She made another choice, and went to the neighbor the next day and forgave him. He was unaware of her hatred to him. She almost died over her idea of someone's old behavior. Are you holding anything unloving to anyone, Angel? Are you willing to die over someone's unconscious behavior? Stephanie is well today!

Do you want to help open your creative center (your belly)? Studies show that physical activity helps to relieve PMS symptoms by triggering the release of brain chemicals, including endorphins, which ease pain, relieve stress, brighten mood, and produce a sense of well-being. Exercise also relaxes muscles, which can ease aches. It also fights fluid retention which can reduce bloating and breast tenderness. Our lymph system moves when we move our bodies. Getting plenty of water to drink also helps to flush out anything that might cause "stagnant" feelings.

Eat healthy! Use the colors of the rainbow in your food. I recommend eating 7 vegetables, 2 fruits, 2 proteins, 1 carbohydrate/starch, and drinking a gallon of water a day. Add a lot of love and it is all you need to be healthy. Get more sleep. Being stressed out or sleep deprived is likely to aggravate many symptoms, including aches and pains, moodiness, and irritability. Use relaxation techniques as the period approaches, such as massage, meditation, yoga, and soaking in long hot baths. These great suggestions also relieve depression and post pregnancy hormonal shifts.

On Weight

Do you know, Angel, that obesity just took over heart disease as the number one cause of death in the US! Obesity is defined as being at least 50 pounds over your normal healthy weight. Estrogen and the liver have important roles in weight problems or obesity. Metabolism is mostly carried out in the liver. Sluggish metabolism due to sluggish liver and too much estrogen are contributing factors to weight gain. When the liver fails to eliminate estrogen efficiently, the excessive estrogen stimulates fat cell production, usually around the lower abdominal area and upper thigh where estrogen is more concentrated. Estrogen also binds to sodium which retains water and leads to weight gain.

Fat is lost only when energy is produced. It begins with falling in love with yourself! Weight cannot be taken off until fat is efficiently burned. Enjoy nature and go for a wonderful healing walk! Falling in love with yourself gives you the feeling of health, beauty, and vitality.

Here are some important facts in understanding weight loss. Stored fat cannot be changed to energy without Vitamin B6. If you lack any of the B vitamin family, it results in a lag in energy production. We know what that means! When people tend to have excessive blood fat and cholesterol, which indicates energy is not being utilized normally, the excessive blood fat leads to unnecessary fatigue - which then leads to obesity. If Panto-thenic acid is under supplied, fats burn at half their normal rate. Proteins are needed for energy producing enzymes. Fat is burned twice as rapidly when protein is adequate and thus calories are used. Plenty of Vitamin E foods allow for double the utilization of fats! Lecithin's major function is to aid in burning fats. Too little linoleic acid (one of two essential fatty acids that our bodies do not produce and can only be obtained in food) stresses the adrenals which then allows blood sugar to fall and make weight loss difficult. Linoleic acid can be found in most vegetable oils.

So, Angel, include healthy food choices to your diet. Find those wonderful vitamins and minerals in your food and enjoy them daily! Limit or remove processed, canned or boxed foods that are high in sodium and low in nutritional value. Spending 10 more minutes to whip up your own homemade creations are worth every bit! Include your kids! They love to learn about healthy choices and will enjoy them better if they get to help create! Love your food and it will love you!

I am sure you understand that weight and health go hand in hand. Obesity can be an unconscious defense mechanism indicating emotional misperceptions early in life. When such persons force themselves to reduce without having done sufficient transitional therapy to clear those early life issues, losing their unconscious defense mechanism can lead to emotional breakdowns, depression and even suicidal tendencies. One addiction replaces another and they take up addictions to cigarettes and coffee or even alcohol and drugs.

So the major issue is not the weight but rather self love and acceptance. Focus on gratitude for wholeness and health (rather than a self criticism concerning lack of perfection in your body image.) I have recommended to many Angels who are overweight to take a look at your body daily in the mirror without clothes on and repeat- I am the body of the Goddess! The Goddess is the female energy of the Mother Earth. Your particles in your body are the exact elements of the earth. If you can see beauty in the earth you can see it in yourself, too. It is all related! Fall in love with this body creation and it will find its own balance.

The problem with stapled bellies and lap bands are possible stroke. It is important to do your due diligence on any elective surgery. We must find a way to walk, swim, breathe, and get comfortable with loving ourselves. Weight is a protection device and helps us feel safe. If no one can get close enough -no one can hurt us. Right?

Soda

Mass soda consumption has increased dramatically since the 1980s. Children as young as seven months old are now consuming soda, even in their bottles! No wonder there is so much tooth decay so early in life! What is soda? It is a molecule of carbon and a molecule of sodium that explodes from your mouth to your butt! It is mostly toxic sugar water with no nutritional value at ALL! Why would you ever feed this to your child or yourself? Your body has to make it whole to process it otherwise it is stored as toxic because there is nothing good to regenerate on the tongue for the body to process.

How does obesity begin? A lot starts right in childhood! Uneducated food choices, lack of physical exercise, and emotional turmoil in early life begins a lifetime of health related issues. Childhood statistics indicate a steady increase in childhood obesity rates since 1980. According to the Centers for Disease Control and Prevention (2010), 6.5 percent of children aged 6 to 11 were obese in 1980. By 2008, the obesity rate for this group rose to 19.6 percent, meaning almost one out of every five American children are obese! Childhood obesity is the leading cause of pediatric hypertension, is associated with Type II diabetes, increases the risk of coronary heart disease, increases stress on the weight-bearing joints, lowers self-esteem, and affects relationships with peers. We know that social and psychological problems are the most significant consequences of obesity in children.

In general, children and adolescents are eating more food away from home, drinking more sugar-sweetened drinks, and snacking more frequently. Convenience has become one of the main criteria for America's food choices today, leading more and more people to consume "away-from-home" quick service or restaurant meals or to buy ready-to-eat, low cost, quickly accessible, low nutrition meals to prepare at home. More and more children and adults are spending more time in front of a screen, and less time in the sunshine and fresh air. Other studies indicate that children are not eating the recommended servings of foods featured in the USDA food pyramid. (Only 21 percent of young people eat the recommended five or more servings of fruits and vegetables each day and nearly half of all vegetable servings are fried potatoes!)

Americans tend to eat 80 percent of their food after 6 pm. One study of people who could not lose weight revealed that they obtained most of their food in the evenings and therefore had no appetite for breakfast. In the morning while their blood sugar was still high from the night before, will power to not eat was no problem. Perhaps even having lunch was not an issue. In the evening, the blood sugar drops and one can be irritable, exhausted and starved. The problem was not eating too much but rather too little.

In studies, many animals will become obese if forced to eat only two meals daily. When given small frequent meals of the identical food,however, their weight remains normal. Most of the food is converted into energy when small meals are eaten. Large meals overwhelm the body's enzyme systems so that food cannot be utilized properly and is then stored as fat.

I recommend always having breakfast to "break the fast" and eat your main meal in the middle of the day and eat light fruit or a smoothie in the evening. Kapha body types especially need to follow this advice to keep their weight in balance. We should not be trying to digest our meals and expect to sleep well because our bodies are busy digesting and not resting. Angel, please try to eat at least 2 hours before you sleep! It matters!

Many women are pleasantly surprised to find their weight reduced unexpectedly by doing daily morning exercise. When the liver becomes more efficient and bile flows better, the weight problem is usually helped significantly because the liver is the only organ in the body that produces the enzyme that breaks down fat. Love your liver and let go of your anger! Can you?

Consume daily-7 vegetables, 2 fruits, 2 proteins, 1 carbohydrate/starch, 1 gallon water and tons of love.
This is easy to do every day. The

Be mindful as you eat and really chew and taste every bite. Honor the food! You are also turning on information through your taste buds to let your body know what is on the way and to be ready! Sit down with your family every day and connect. Honor everyone and give each person some time to talk and express themselves. Listen, and thank them for sharing their day with you!

The Urinary/Bladder

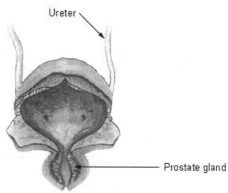

Ureter

Prostate gland

The urinary bladder is a hollow, muscular and elastic organ that sits on the pelvic floor. It can hold 17 to 18 ounces of urine. The urinary bladder changes shape according to the amount of urine it contains. It resembles a deflated balloon when empty but becomes somewhat pear-shaped and rises into the abdominal cavity when the amount of urine increases. Issues that create bladder problems are feeling "pissed off" at self or others and unable to release things or ideas no longer needed.

Miracle Story

Bobbi had interstitial cystitis-shredding of the bladder.

It is extremely painful. It took her days to get to us in Fort Bragg, California, a trip that would have taken others only hours. I helped her understand why she was so pissed off. Every time she peed she had to love her bladder. What an amazing Angel she is. She kicked it. She fell in love with her bladder and herself. Our love is the healer and the harmonizer in the physical body. All things are possible to reverse to wholeness when we are ready to not hurt anymore. Someone had to drive her to meet us but then she drove herself home. She is a great healer and has used her incredible journey to help many others.

About Abortion

When women come in to do the Cleanse or come across your path, part of their journey may have had an abortion or two in it. Women who have had abortions tend to beat themselves up very harshly. A woman then looks at that choice she made—whether it was when she made love and was not protected or con-scious of her choice to create this life; perhaps she needed to feel loved, and some guy put his arms around her and said 'I love you', so she melted into him and got pregnant. Things happen.

So these women beat themselves up mentally and emotionally. They may hurt in the middle of their back, and sometimes they hurt in their spirit area. Perhaps they have had intense cramps and bleeding monthly since the abortion(s) happened. First of all, you can't kill a spirit of God—no matter how hard you try. Even if you pull a gun on somebody and shoot them, you can't kill their spirit. The spirit always continues on forever into eternity, it always has been, is now and always will be. It's an unending eternal life always: That's not your stuff, that's God's stuff.

50

You have freedom of choice—and sometimes a woman can look at her life and say: 'If I do this, this, and this, then this won't work out.' It may not work out in her life at that particular time for her highest intended good or the child's. Abortion is the option available on the planet at this time. Perhaps having an abortion allows the woman to get into a safer place, and create a different journey-- then the child comes. The same child comes. Sometimes the soul of the child may try several times to come through.

Sometimes I have had situations where the woman has said, "Now I am 50+ and I can't have children, so how could this be?" I ask a woman to look into her life and see what child came to her with a message to her on a level that was so deep that it was like the mother and child anyway. Sometimes the woman will realize that even though she didn't birth that child, that child still found her in this lifetime and still got those things that it needed from her. They still connect regardless of whether she birthed the child herself or not. And always 100% of the time, when the woman looks back and remembers; she finds that there was some child there. 'Oh my little niece, oh this little girl that lived down the street and it comes to them, always.' No harm done.' Then, the woman is able to let that go and move on in the present unburdened by regret.

When women are able to really let that abortion go, to really get over it, their symptoms disappear. Perhaps their issue has been: 'How could I do this?' or 'I am this Bad person'—with all this guilt, shame and pain. There is nothing that the woman can do about it now anyway. These women are still loved and they are still treasured. They are still God stuff. Whether they chose to carry that life or not, they don't have to carry the guilt or regret anymore.

They have hurt enough for it and that's far too much. We are holding the intention for a healed planet and that requires letting go of pain and regret.

Now is the time to be done with it. Be thankful for your journey. You made the choice that was best for you at that time. Sometimes women say, 'Well, I didn't have the choice. I was young and my parents made me do it.' I tell them, "Well, again, are you going to stay in judgment and feel bad about yourself and about your parents or are you going to be over it? It's not happening now. It's over, it's a past life thing."

It does make a difference for the ladies to bring that to clarity. In women's bodies it shows up in the heart area because it is grieving; they are still grieving over this thing that never happened. It shows up in heart tissue and in the uterine area also as endometriosis. If you consider what endometriosis looks like, it is where you take a great big stick and keep beating the same tissue over and over again until it builds up a callused surface. It looks like this big lumpy safety net that keeps the woman from hitting herself more. The scar tissue is that they haven't let the journey go yet. Even if it's in their body somewhere else, if it hasn't been let go of, the scar tissue remains.

When they tell me that they have had an abortion(s), they cover up their mouth and whisper: ' And I have had an...' Their energy and posture indicates that they feel they did this shameful horrible thing; it is so intense that often they can hardly bring it out of their own bodies (mouths) to speak it. I gently pull the woman's hands away from her mouth and tell her she has never done anything wrong in her whole entire life. Then I ask the woman to repeat aloud for her:' I forgive myself for thinking that I ever did anything wrong in my whole entire life'. The woman has to repeat that 4 or 5 times until I know she has forgiven herself. 'Sweet Angel, it is just a journey. It's an old story and that child touched your life no matter what. It came through anyway. Whether the spirit came through you or another, it still got in and you still touched its life no matter what because it chose you. You didn't kill anything because you can't kill a spirit of God.'

And then the woman gets it. When a woman does, she responds often by saying, 'Oh my God, I have waited so many years to know that.' Then they are free of it. That is true of any of the journeys. The longer anyone carries the same issue, the more they have beaten themselves up for it.

Sex and Sex Drive

Sex after 40! Women who have gone through menopause or had a hysterectomy often struggle with hormone balance. Some lose their sex drive altogether. Well, if you don't use it, you lose it! Don't worry; you can get it back again!!! The same is true of guys who have had radiation pellets put in them for prostate cancer treatment. The doctor tells them they will never be able to perform sexually again. How sad! NOT TRUE! Women are now seeking relief with bio identical hormones. I have some more interesting information to share with you.

Unless you have had a lobotomy in the bottom part of your brain, you can still have sex and that 'loving feeling' come upon you. When you have an orgasm, you don't just feel it in your sex organs; you feel it all through your body because it comes from the brain. I believe it is the ONE time we feel the energy of God! All over! The left and right turns in the colon are the corresponding areas that your sex drive is stimulated and fed. If there are toxic pockets there or it gets plugged up and the body is not able to get clear nutrition to the blood vessels in those areas where the colon turns—it's not getting the nutrition or the sexual impulse message to the back part of the brain which manages that! Absorption of nutrition to the colon and brain equal a healthy body and thus a healthy sex drive.

Hepatic and Spleenic Flexture

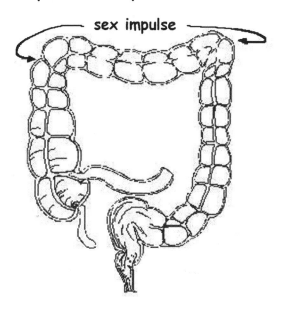

sex impulse

Keep in mind that the sex drive is stimulated by the 2 sides under the hepatic flexture and the spleenic flexture in the transverse colon.

If a client says to me that they just haven't had sex for a number of years, I remind them to be patient. So desire is definitely required. Both of you have to want to make love and share intimacy as part of your bond.

The Way of the Superior Man by David Deida is an

awesome book every man and every woman with a male partner should read! This book talks about how to keep the sex intimacy drive stimulated in your relationship. He talks about how to just start to tickle the brain to stimulate these nerve endings. If you saw What the Bleep, you may remember Ramtha saying that a man just has to have a thought to cause his member to have an erection. It all starts in the brain, not in the sex organs.

What turns you on physically? One lady told me a cute story about going out on a date with a guy to a fancy restaurant. She didn't think she still got hot for guys but when he pulled out a big wad of 100 bills, she said she got very hot!! Some types of foods turn on that trigger of a sensual almost sexual desire. Some smells ignite the senses. Did you know that some people go into color therapy to increase their sex drive? Remember the Adam's Family, whenever "Tish" spoke French, Gomez went crazy with passion and started kissing her, wild with ecstasy!!!

I know a sweet family with some great parents who were making love in their late 80's when he crossed over. What a wonderful expression of their love to leave in your sweethearts arms. I have always considered this a truly beautiful story of love! They had been married for over 60 years!

I had a beautiful Angel come in with fourth stage prostate cancer. He was given the radiation pellets and as everyone is told, you will not be able to make love again. NOT! When he and his wife came and told me this familiar story I had them immediately cancel that! His psa was at 38 and upon returning it was .001 ! He called me up two weeks later and in tears, guess what! The body does repair itself if given the chance. He is cancer free and playing an excellent game of golf! His doctors call him their miracle! Way to go Angel, and show them what is possible! We love you Alan and Cindy and family!

Let me tell you a secret. On the 9th day of her Cleanse, Joyce, one of our staff, called her husband and said "Get your butt home right now!" That was the first time in 7 years that she had felt like making love. Her desire had returned. Her husband signed up for the next Cleanse and said, "If that's going to do that for my wife, what is it going to do for me?" They reconnected and it's still all good for them! They are very happy and fulfilled completely as a couple!

For older couples, we have matured as people. We are not going after people for sex like we did when we were 20, right? We want heart connection and a conscious connection. We want to speak a loving language. We want a different kind of sex. We are not driven by the hormones to reproduce.

If there is love, there is always hope. Sometimes quickies are a gift you give your partner because it tickles them to be special; maybe you aren't in the mood but you honor your love for your partner and take a moment to show them an expression of that love! Love is about whatever it takes. Men taking the time to get their partner to the same plateau they are on, sharing the sexual experience. Intimacy is about sharing and caring with your best friend and partner through life's adventures!

I met a person at a business forum and SHE stood out in the crowd. I could easily see that although this person was born a man, he was now being a woman. I got to know and love this very special person. After the Cleanse this person went back to his home town and settled in to being exactly as he was born to be; honoring his choice as a man. Now he was comfortable with his sexuality and reunited with his partner and happy. Happiness works. I wanted to share his story because I so admire his courage to stand out and live how he feels. He was an inspiration in courage!

The Knee

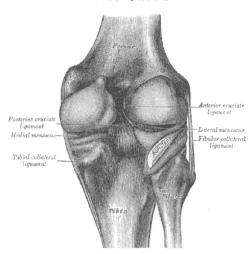

The knee is the lower extremity joint connecting the femur and the tibia. Since in humans the knee supports nearly the entire weight of the body, it is vulnerable to injury. The knee permits the following movements of flexion, extension, locking, unlocking, and slight rotation. The knee is a complex, compound, synovial joint which hovers.

There are more than 300,000 total knee replacements in the United States each year. The average age of the patient of knee replacement surgery is between 65 and 75. Of these surgeries, approximately 80% are unilateral (only one knee replaced) and 20% are bilateral. Women undergo the procedure more often than men, making up 60% of the patient population. Does that mean women are more stubborn than men?

So let's get into the emotions related to your wonderful knees. Knees teach us that being stubborn and inflexible and unable to bend and flow with life is not the way of an Angel. Ask yourself: "Would I rather be right than happy?" If you answered yes, you might have an issue in your knees!

Great Therapies To Aid The Knees
1) Apply local heat before and cold packs after exercise to help relieve pain and inflammation
2) Relaxation techniques- Deep belly breaths!
3) Catch when you are inflexible and go with the flow

The Hip

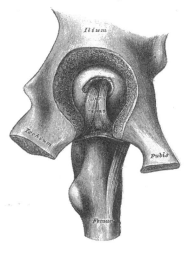

    The hip joint is the joint separating the thigh bone from the pelvis, and the surrounding flesh. The resulting ball-and-socket joint allows great latitude of thigh movement. Hip joints connect our upper and lower body. The hip joint is reinforced by 3 main ligaments. There are seven different kinds of movements possible in the hip area.

    Emotional connections of the left hip are fear of major change and movement (ex. Home, relationship, job) These are the big things in your life and many are afraid if I let this home, or relationship, or job go where or who will I be? Tune in deeper Beloved Angel and feel the guidance that is all around you. You are not supposed to hurt to move!

    Do you know, Angel, that the number one hip replacement is the right hip? Why? Because many have fear of major change in their lives and feel stuck and afraid to move. It is also the area where the small intestine empties into the large intestine at your iliocecal valve area which is right in front of your right hip. This is where we at Angel Farms say the "big boys" hang out. I have seen them six feet long! The worms eat the good food coming in from the small intestine and starve the hip to death. In the 20 years I have been doing this Cleanse we have had over 400 right hip surgeries become unscheduled and we have never lost a hip yet! We don't intend to either! The hip does come back when it gets nutrition and an Angel has released the fear of major movement.

The Feet

The human foot and ankle is a strong and complex mechanical structure containing 26 bones (some people have more), 33 joints (20 of which are actively articulated), and more than a hundred muscles,_____

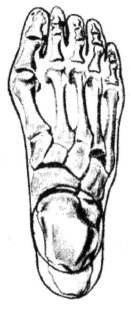

tendons, and ligaments. It is the lower extremity of the leg that is in direct contact with the ground in standing or walking and which bears weight and allows locomotion. One day an Angel (with severe feet problems) commented on how ugly her feet were. I immediately asked her to cancel that, and asked her where did she hear or start to believe that. She recalled when she was 7 her mother told her how ugly her feet were while walking across the yard! She believed that nonsense and judged her feet for 40 years. Every time she looked at her feet she saw only those words. No wonder her feet were screaming in pain for love and acceptance. I gave her an assignment to really, really love her feet and be very thankful for them because without them life is a whole different journey. Ask someone who doesn't have feet. Her feet completely healed and transformed to healthy beautiful feet! Love is the healer.

It is important Beloved Ones, to love every part of your amazing body and honor it. Watch your emotions and how they affect how you feel and how your body feels.

Miracle Story

Another miracle story happened with Raphael.
He had a scheduled hip replacement (right of course) and was going to take his daughter up the aisle for her wedding in a wheelchair. After his Cleanse he walked her up the aisle and in the video someone commented he was not even limping! Way to go Raphael!

Chapter 2

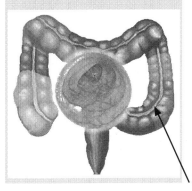

The Spleen

What Does Love Have To Do With A Healthy Immune System?

I am Loved. I am Loveable.
I am love. God is Love.

2nd Day
Spleen

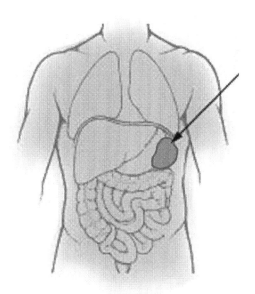

Spleen

Now I want to talk to you about your wonderful spleen. The feelings of forgetting your purpose, not allowing yourself to feel yourself or another person's love, feeling rejected, and a lack of present time awareness (worry) are the roots to a weak immune system. Let's get you to look at these emotions and how you can change your views on how much you love yourself! Do you know what the spleen does? Let me tell you how important it is to the marvelous body. The spleen is located in the upper left part of the abdomen below the bottom left ribcage, to the left of the stomach, and just below the diaphragm. The spleen is your immune system com-municator. It is a beautiful little sack that holds your red blood

61

cells and it is also your red blood cell counter. Did you know that blood is a liquid organ? If you get into an accident and cut a major artery in your body, you have a storage of red blood cells, an "emergency" supply with you in your spleen at all times. Isn't that nice to know?

The body of the spleen appears red and pulpy, surrounded by a tough capsule. The red pulp consists of blood vessels interwoven with connective tissue. The red pulp filters the blood and removes used blood cells. The white pulp that is inside the red pulp, consists of little lumps of lymphoid tissue. Antibodies are made inside the white pulp. Pretty cool, huh? The spleen also helps the body fight infection. The spleen contains lymphocytes and another kind of white blood cells called macrophages, which engulf and destroy bacteria, dead tissue, and foreign matter and remove these from the blood passing through the spleen.

Similar to other organs of the lymphatic system, particular immune cells (B lymphocytes and T lymphocytes) and blood cells are either made or matured inside the spleen. Blood enters the spleen via the splenic artery, which subdivides into many tiny branches. Each branch is encased in a clump of immune cells, which means every drop of blood is filtered for foreign particles as it enters the spleen.

If you get a cut or have an infection, or illness, the spleen, being the monitor of the immune system and red blood counter, senses when the infection or illness is over and then shoots instructions to the pineal gland, which sits in the middle of the brain. The pineal gland then shoots instructions to the adrenals which sit on top of your kidneys. The adrenals, beautiful little walnut shaped organs, put the sterol into the system to suppress white cell production.

After the infection or illness is over, your spleen gets busy with the liver and the bone marrow to produce more red blood cells. The spleen then releases all these new highly oxygenated blood cells into your system. That is the moment you say, my body is feeling better, but needs more rest. Remember to give your body the rest it is asking for at this point and send a grateful thank you to your spleen.

I have found in food signatures (the food looks like the organ it nourishes) that the spleen benefits from the nutrients found in coconut juice, celery, strawberries, onions, pomegranates, beets, garlic, potatoes, and citrus. Add these yummy foods to your diet when your spleen needs a little help recovering from an illness or accident. What a great way to say thank you to your wonderful spleen for the job it has done for you!

Beloved Angel, your spleen is your center of self love. So what are you doing to your own immune system if you are not really, really loving yourself? How important is it that we love ourselves and keep our immune systems healthy? Are you holding others responsible to love you so you will feel whole? No one can do this but yourself! You are responsible for loving yourself in order to keep your immune system strong. Only you! No one in your life can keep your immune system communicating properly but YOU! The way to heal your spleen: Love yourself more than you ever have in your whole, entire life! Even if it is for 10 minutes a day! Keep adding minutes every day! Self love test: ask yourself, on a scale of 1-10, 10 being highest, how much do you love yourself? On that scale of 1-10, how much does God love you? 10 of course! If you are not loving yourself at a 10, fake it till you make it! Your spleen and immune system are counting on your love!

"When we love ourselves, it generates loving words. How you love yourself and how you feel about yourself are directly proportionate to the quality and integrity of your word. When you're impeccable with your word, you feel good; you feel happy and at peace," says don Miguel Ruiz. You are here to awaken your Christed Self and to love. That's when you realize you only need to remember two things. It is not hard. Your loving purpose is about how you can take all your life experiences including the trauma drama that you drew into your life and use them in the highest service of another? How will you use them and be a master teacher, because of your journey and not despite it? Be the cause of it. If you really look at how purpose works, it is when you wake up and are tickled in your heart.

"Love is not a spectator sport," says Sam Keen, author of To Live and Be Loved. "You have to get off the bench, into the field, into the dirt, into the grass. It's time we all get messy, sweaty, heated, and lusty with celebration in the spirit and love of this timeless sport."

How To Get In The Now.

First put your hand on your belly and raise your hand with the inhale of your breath. Continue for five or six breaths, and understand that this relaxes the diaphram and therefore relaxes the nervous system. It stops the adrenals from running amuck. Then tune into your senses. Ask yourself 5 questions. What do I see? What do I smell? What do I taste? What do I hear? What do I feel on my body? Right Now! Then say this mantra "Where I am God Is and Where God Is I am". Now ask yourself, "What do I have to fear?" NOTHING right? How does that feel to be free of fear? Awesome isn't it? What would your life be like if you knew right now you would never again have anything to fear?

Auto Immune Affunctions

I want to explain to you about what I call auto immune system affunctions. You probably have never heard of that word. It is not a dis-function, as in weak, but it is overly aggressive, as in too strong! The immune system is so strong that it literally kicks your butt. This can show up in all diseases that have a very high count of white blood cells which means your immune system does not shut off. Many of our Angels have come with these very difficult journeys in their lives. Examples are IBS, Crohn's disease, ulcerated colitis, rheumatoid arthritis, cystic fibrosis, lupus, ms, Hashimoto's Thyroiditis, and any other diseases that the AMA uses steroids to suppress white cell production.

The real problem is that you are living too much in tomorrow and not enough in the now. Worry is the cause 100% of the time. Research has shown that guilt and worry damages your immune system by lowering your immunoglobulin levels. When you are trying to create a reality from something that is not there yet, (because you are not even there yet,) your brain creates a form of insanity. You are always in tomorrow and the body is trying to catch up, but it can't, because the molecules simply aren't created yet. Just try going into tomorrow and take a drink of water in it! You cannot because you are reading this book. Tomorrow does not exist, Angel. We need your love here, NOW! Each immune affunction is caused by worry!! The person with an affunction is throwing their attention/consciousness into tomorrow which does not exist!

People with immune affunctions have such powerful immune systems. They are immune to everything on the planet. They will never get SARS, or West Nile Virus, because their immune systems are constantly on and hyper vigilant.

Here are some diseases with immune symptom affuntions.

Cystic Fibrosis

Cystic fibrosis starts in the lungs, and impacts growth, breathing, digestion, and reproduction. CF often appears in childhood and early adulthood. Symptoms include continued problems with growth, the onset of lung disease, and increasing difficulties with poor absorption of vitamins and nutrients by the gastrointestinal tract. CF is a lung disease resulting from clogging of airways due to inflammation. Inflammation and infection cause injury to the lungs and structural changes that lead to a variety of symptoms. In the early stages, incessant coughing, excessive phlegm production, and decreased ability to exercise are common. Many of these symptoms occur when bacteria that normally inhabit the thick mucus grow out of control and cause pneumonia. In later stages of CF, changes in the architecture of the lung further exacerbates chronic difficulties in breathing.

Multiple Sclerosis

Multiple Sclerosis also known as MS, is an ulceration in the corpus collosum of the brain, the bottom grey part, which affects equilibrium and balance. MS is diagnosed with an MRI. If you have had such a diagnosis, I highly recommend you put up a picture of a healthy brain and visualize that several times a day. Tell your body/mind what you want! What we visualize and put our energy into comes about. Please learn about your immune system and how to keep in present time and out of the tomorrows.

Osteoarthritis

Osteoarthritis is the second leading cause of disability in the elderly population in the United States. It is a degenerative disorder that generally starts off mild and escalates with time and wear. As a person ages, first the water content of the cartilage decreases and then the protein composition degenerates, thus degenerating the cartilage through repetitive use or misuse. Angel, what does that tell you about the importance of drinking water? Sufferers find their every movement so painful and debilitating that it can also affect them emotionally and psychologically.

I have found that many older Angels have regrets of the past; regrets of failed marriages, regrets of not reaching their dreams, and feelings that they have not done enough. They also feel unsupported by God and by the world and this affects the skeletal structure of the body. Good news! The body regenerates the skeletal structure in only 3 months. You can have a whole new skeletal structure when you realize you are ALWAYS supported! What are you willing to let go of in the past? How are you willing to find more ways to stop judging along your sacred journey? Remember that God is always with you and so you are also judging the journey of God through you as bad. Do you really want to keep doing that and suffer pain in your very bones? Or, have you have enough?

Miracle Story

I would like to tell you about a sweet lady from California that had very bad arthritis in her hands and knees who came to do the Cleanse.

Pat's fingers were pulled to the side with a gnarly knuckle on her index finger. On her 3rd day of the Cleanse, when we were cleansing the part of the colon that feeds the hand, she cleared a pocket. The next day her left hand was completely normal. The miracle was that her body had even absorbed the calcium deposit on the knuckle; all her fingers on her left hand were straight and pain free. She asked, "Do you think it will happen with my right hand too?" And I said, "Around here all we do is expect miracles." So on Day 9, she got to the other side of the colon that feeds the right hand and sure enough, she cleared a pocket there that was preventing her right hand from getting nutrition. Again, overnight her right hand was completely normal.

Then I asked Pat, "What are you supposed to be using your hands for, but haven't been?" She replied, "Well you know, I have worked for the California school system for 30 years. I have sticky notes all over my apartment because I have always felt like I am supposed to write a book on a better way to educate children." I said, "Maybe that is what your hands want to do!" Two weeks after she finished the Cleanse, she called up and quit her job of 31 years. She is writing her book now!

The physical root cause of arthritis occurs as the immune system attacks joints in response to an injury or antigen or a substance it doesn't recognize such as trans fats or microbic toxins. Additional cells arrive and begin secreting peptides, bringing about an inflammatory cascade that causes swelling and inflammation.

Daily meditation, silence, quiet time with God, and inspirational readings are required to center the person in the NOW. Gratitude lists are important too. Einstein said there are 2 choices-either nothing is a miracle or everything is a miracle! By seeing everything as a miracle and counting one's blessings, the body and mind can come out of 'survival', it can stop worrying!! Retrain the brain and the body will follow! My grandmother used to remind me to put more gratitude in my attitude and I always felt better when I did it.

There is a miracle for all of you with these powerful immune systems. You have such a powerful immune system that the only thing that can cause you harm is yourself! You are immune to everything on the planet. You will never see illness like many others, because your immune system kicks butt on everything. In my experience I have found every person who had any kind of immune system affunction was a lactose intolerant baby. They all had a difficult time breaking down milk including mother's milk, and many can only tolerate goat's milk because the milk molecules are already predigested and feel really good on a babies belly.

Bromelain from pineapple enzymes reduces toxic build up. If your hands are already deformed due to arthritis, start with a 10 day Cleanse! Stop worrying and get in the Now! You can do a temporary therapy of distilled water for about 2 weeks . This is de-mineralized water and your body will pull excess minerals out of your joints to process. This can sometimes relieve joint pain. Do this for 2 weeks only. Any longer is still pulling minerals from your joints and it will hurt you!

Breasts

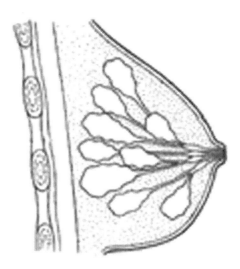

The breasts are located on the front of the chest and specifically hold the mammary glands. The word "mammary" comes from "mamma," the Greek and Latin word for the breast, which derives from the cry "mama" uttered by infants and young children sometimes when they are hungry and want to be fed breast milk.

Although the primary biologic function of the breast is to produce milk to feed a baby, the breast has been a symbol of femininity and beauty for many centuries. There is no single model that is the ideal breast. The appearance of the normal female breast differs greatly from one woman to the next. The breast of any given woman normally differs at various times during a woman's life-before, during and after adolescence, during pregnancy, during the menstrual cycle, and after menopause.

Inside each breast, there are mammary glands. Men and Women both have mammary glands. In women, the mammaries are milk-producing glands that are composed largely of cells that store fat. The fat deposits are laid down in the breast under the influence of the female hormone, estrogen.

In my experience, you'll never meet a woman with breast cancer who doesn't have issues with her mother. These issues are usually not having loving feelings toward their mother and sometimes even hating her. How do you let go of mother issues? First of all, recognize that you chose her! Own it, and then you can change it. She showed you who you didn't want to be. Thank her for showing you that. You are not a victim! You are power-ful beyond measure! Forgive her for having a contract that was very difficult for her to hold, just so she could show you who you are not. Then you can forgive, and have compassion for your mother's pain, because you understand that pain. Forgive yourself for not thinking you were/will be a great parent. This is the time to be self-loving. Nurture yourself like you never have before!!!

By letting go of hateful negative emotions toward your mother or your own mothering abilities, you can change your body's energy frequency. Doing this makes it impossible for breast cancer to even take root. In this sense, taking care of your emotion-al health is the most effective form of breast-cancer prevention. Few of us would consider ourselves angry or sad people, yet many of us waste our energy dwelling on events that upset us long ago. The event happened in the past, yet we spend our precious energy reacting to them and thus retelling ourselves and others our war stories thus reliving/re-experiencing them again and again and again in the present. If you hate your mother you may very well develop breast cancer. Why would you do that to yourself, Angel?

You know you are love, joy, peace and happiness. Look at a baby and know that is true. You can "pretend" you are not joy, love and happiness, and be sad, and angry and put things in "boxes". You'll choose to try to turn your boats the hard way and push them "up-stream", or against the flow. Sooner or later, you'll finally decide it's much easier and more fun to let go and go "downstream" with the flow and forgive your dad, your mom, and your perpetrators and know that you chose your entire experience, and it was all for your develop-ment and expansion. Beloved Angel, how many lives have you touched because of your journey not despite it? Congratulations, you made it.

We can choose love instead; it's more fun, less painful. Why choose a painful hell story when you can have Heaven now? When you choose love, the brain becomes quiet, creating more things in the NOW moment instead of trying to figure out how to do it in the past where you are directing your attention, or in the future where you might think your attention belongs, and it does not. Remember Angel, there are only two things you will do when you wake up tomorrow morning: Love and drink water. The rest is gravy!

Controlling mothers can create children who have anorexia/bulimia. Are you controlling of your daughter? Be aware of this. If you have a mother like that, forgive her for she does not know who she is. I like to say, when we think we have control, God laughs! Let go and let God have it, and the journey is much easier.

Whenever you start thinking about the past, just remember: You don't have to hurt anymore. There are other parts of your life that are more deserving of your energy and attention, right here, right now. Choose JOY now. Fibrocystic dis-ease, a condition rather than a dis-ease, is characterized by non-cancerous lumps in the breast. Many women with fibrous breasts have to be careful about their caffeine intake. If they drink too much caffeine, their breasts become tender and have painful lumps. This can happen in women of all ages. Should you notice these symptoms, I suggest you go off all caffeine. Within a few days the pain and lumps should subside.

Thyroid

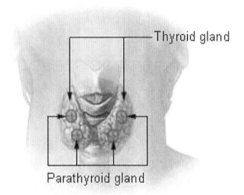

Symptoms of hypothyroidism or low thyroid function include cold hands and feet, low body temperature, a feeling of always being chilled, headaches, pale skin color, puffy tongue body with tooth marks along the edge and a white, sticky tongue coating. Thyroid imbalances create insomnia, dry skin, puffy eyes, hair loss, brittle nails, joint aches, constipation, mental dullness, fatigue, frequent infections, hoarse voice, ringing in the ears, dizziness, loss of libido, painful irregular periods, and weight gain.

Here's a thyroid test to see if your thyroid is functioning properly.

It is more accurate than a blood test in telling you how hungry your thyroid is for iodine! Put a drop of iodine on your skin over your thyroid. Do this right before bed. If the iodine is still there in the morning, your body has enough iodine. If it's gone, keep putting it on every night until the iodine remains there the next morning.

There are a number of foods known as goitrogens that block iodine. Two goitrogens are quite prevalent in the American diet-peanuts/peanut butter and soybeans used most often in prepared foods as textured vegetable protein (a refined soy food) and soybean oil. I believe that GMO'd soy and peanuts are contributing to the misalignment of the thyroid. It is one of the reasons I suggest we be very careful with these products and understand they are both hard starches and move very slowly through the digestive system and can turn toxic quickly.

Environmental stress such as chemical pollutants, pesticides, mercury, radiation, and fluoride are also tough on the thyroid. A growing body of evidence suggests that fluoride, which is prevalent in toothpaste and water treatment, may inhibit the functioning of the thyroid gland. Additionally, mercury may diminish thyroid function because it displaces the trace mineral selenium, and selenium is involved in conversion of thyroid hormones T4 to T3. A little about radiation here due to Japan's worldwide lesson. First Angel, remember your vibration is higher than radiation's vibration when you are in a loving feeling and energy. Love is the power you use to be safe. Drink lots of water with blessings and eat lots of greens including some kelp which is high in iodine. Fear will lower your immune system and your vibration!

Unsaturated oils block thyroid hormone secretion, its movement in the circulatory system, and the response of tissues to the hormone. When the thyroid hormone is deficient, the body is generally exposed to increased levels of estrogen. The thyroid hormone is essential for making the 'protective hormones' progesterone and pregnenolone, so these hormones are lowered when anything interferes with the function of the thyroid. The thyroid hormone is required for eliminating cholesterol, so cholesterol is likely to be raised by anything which blocks the thyroid function. Cinnamon is very useful for treating the symptoms of hypothyroidism.

71

A good recipe for hypothyroidism: Add pepper, 3 g; ginger, 20 g; and tangerine peel, 10 g to about half a pound of fresh white fish. Cook with an appropriate amount of water, and simmer for one hour over a low flame. Eat three servings a week.

Soy Wisdom

There is a growing body of research concerning soy's detrimental effect on the thyroid gland. Much of this research centers on the phyto-estrogen's ("phyto" means plant) that are found in soy. In the 1960's when soy was introduced into infant formulas, it was shown that soy was causing goiters in babies. When iodine was supplemented, the incidence of goiter was reduced dramatically.

There is other important information about soy you should know besides the fact that it is a very hard starch to digest and can turn toxic because it moves so slowly through the digestive system. It can interfere with protein digestion and may cause pancreatic disorders. It disrupts endocrine function and has the potential to cause infertility and promote breast cancer in adult women. It is a potent anti-thyroid agent that may cause thyroid cancer. In infants, it has been linked to autoimmune thyroid disease. Vitamin B12 is not absorbed and it actually increases the body's requirements for B-12 and vitamin D. It results in the formation of highly toxic carcinogens and contains high levels of aluminum which is hard on the nervous system and the kidneys. MSG, a potent neurotoxin, is formed during soy food processing, and high levels of phytic acid in soy reduces assimilation of calcium, magnesium, copper, iron, and zinc. It is also one of the most GMO'd products on the market! Be careful with soy and only allow 10% or less into your diet.

Coconut oil is saturated and very stable (unrefined coconut oil has a shelf life of about three to five years at room temperature). Coconut oil does not require the enzyme stress that vegetable oils do, preventing T4 to T3 hormone conversion, not only because it is a stable oil, but also because it is processed differently in the body and does not need to be broken down by enzyme dependent processes. Since the liver is where much of the conversion of T4 to T3 takes place, eliminating long chain fatty acids from the diet and replacing them with medium chain fatty acids found in coconut oil can, in time, help rebuild cell membranes and increase enzyme production that will assist in promoting the health of the thyroid.

Diaphragm

The diaphragm is a shelf muscle extending across the bottom of the ribcage. The diaphragm separates the thoracic cavity from the abdominal cavity. In its relaxed state, the diaphragm is shaped like a dome. The diaphragm also helps to expel vomit as well as urine from the body by increasing intro-abdominal pressure. If the diaphragm is struck, or otherwise spasms, breathing will become difficult. This is called having the wind knocked out of you. I have found that the ancient Greeks called the phrenos/diaphragm a work of art. I was inspired as I studied the diaphragm and found out what an amazing organ it is.

Diaphragm

In ancient Greece the diaphragm was Phrenos-Unifying all possibilities of body, mind and breath. Fill your body with

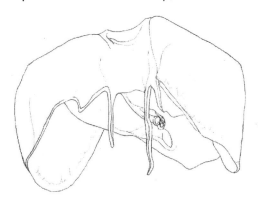

your breath. This relaxes the nervous system. Feel the Peace. Follow the breath paying attention only to the breath. Your Precious Diaphragm profoundly affects your posture, digestion, elimination, and respiration Your Life! Your breath, feel the connection. Your diaphragm is attached to your spine. Your heart rests over it. Your liver and spleen lie below it. As it moves it touches and loves your abdominal organs, lungs, and spine with gentleness and compassion. Yummy! It is said to be a work of art! It is the mediator of all rhythms, both physical & emotional, ebbing and flowing, all in one movement. At one in body, mind, and Spirit with what you feel, what you say, what you breathe. Phrenos-The unity of all possibilities of human expression. Feel your internal(ness) with love!

Be thankful for your precious diaphram and give a nice belly breath as you get to know yourself through your breath.

I believe as Dr. Siegel believes that 'All disease is ultimately related to conditional love or a lack of love.' If you learn how to love yourself, your body will respond automatically. I have seen disease disappear the very moment the Angel remembers forgiveness and loves instead. Staci lost 2 inches on the first day of the Cleanse. For the first time in her life she forgave herself! 2 inches is a lot to let go of in one day!!!

Unconditional love toward ourselves and others keeps us in health, peace, and happiness. Think of your day by day activities and interactions and how much time you spend defending various positions that make you feel right, worthy, okay, etc. When you no longer feel a need to defend yourself, that is, when you accept yourself, the body can naturally relax. I learned in Huna teachings that when things are not working out like we want them to, we EWOP it! We remind ourselves that Everything is Working Out Perfectly! It really is.

Loving others as they are, and seeing them perfect as they are created, allows them to grow and unfold at their own rate. When you do not see the situations in your life as being perfect, there is no energy for anything to change, you actually create more of what you don't want by focusing on it; whether it be in yourself, your friends, your family or the world. Be an instrument of peace and transformation: see everyone and everything as whole.

It helps to love our illnesses because love heals and allows wellness to take place. While it is true that illness is a result of imbalance, it does no one any good to beat themselves up for health problems or to resist (fight) their illness. Trying to change things without first accepting them is like trying to get handcuffs off through resistance and struggle. The key is to relax and let the energy flow. Remember what we fear we draw and what we resist, will persist.

Joy is preceded by gratitude.

The Pancreas

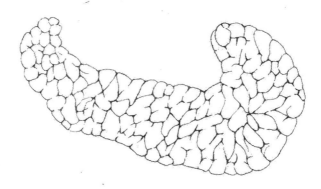

The pancreas is a narrow, flat, glandular organ about seven inches long and looks like a sea cucumber in the shape of a smile. The pancreas secretes digestive enzymes and hormones. The pancreas produces 325 different enzymes. What does that say about raw food and no body enzymes? When Angels come and they have been on a raw food diet with the premise that we do not get enzymes from our food when it is cooked, then you do not understand your pancreas. Please, Angel, understand how the body works and you will live freely without judgment. The enzymes are designed to digest foods and break down starches. The pancreas also helps neutralize chyme and helps break down proteins, fats and starch. Chyme is a thick, semi-fluid mass of partly digested food that is passed from the stomach to the duodenum.

The pancreas lies beneath the stomach and is connected to the small intestine at the duodenum. It contains enzyme producing cells that secrete two hormones. The two hormones are insulin and glucagon. Insulin and glucagon are secreted directly into the bloodstream, and together, they regulate the level of glucose in the blood. Insulin regulates the blood sugar level and increases the amount of glycogen (stored carbohydrate) in the liver. Glucagon slowly increases the blood sugar level if it falls too low. If the insulin secreting cells do not work properly, diabetes occurs. The bile duct and the pancreatic duct join just before entering the duodenum and so have a common opening into the small intestine.

Insulin is manufactured by a small clump of pancreatic cells called the 'islets of Langerhans'. High blood sugar levels prompt the release of insulin from the islets of Langerhans, so that the sugars can pass into cells. Just a note here to realize, Angels is that the pancreas is not the only one responsible for blood sugar imbalance. Your liver is involved also because the pancreas and the liver work together!

The pancreas adds its own digestive juices and enzymes to the food, via a small duct attached to the duodenum. This process is said to belong to the 'exocrine pancreas'. The pancreas also produces the hormone insulin, which helps control the amount of sugar in the blood. The pancreas also helps digest food, particularly protein. Pancreatic juices contain enzymes that only become activated once they reach the duodenum. This is to prevent the protein-digesting enzyme trypsin from 'eating' the protein-based pancreas or its duct. This protects us from having holes eaten through us! Other enzymes produced by the pancreas include amylase (to break down carbohydrates) and lipase (to break down fats). The pancreas also makes sodium bicarbonate, which helps to neutralize the stomach acids.

The connection to inflammatory issues and the pancreas is amazing. The pancreas produces the enzyme amylase which is then released in the mouth behind the second molar. This is designed to break down carbohydrates in the body. Only Carbs! If you are having inflammation problems stop eating carbohydrates and rest your pancreas so it can help your inflammation. You need one carbohydrate a day to be healthy or your pancreas would not produce amylase. Those of you with immune system affunctions should be aware of reducing carbohydrates under an attack or illness to speed up healing. Did you know the average person produces a quart of saliva a day or 10,000 gallons in a lifetime designed to break down carbs?

Pancreatic insufficiency is the inability of the pancreas to produce and/or transport enough digestive enzymes to break down food in the intestine and allow its absorption. The pancreas is your center of joy. If you are having pancreas problems including diabetes this is the time to understand your pancreas. It is the smile in your body. If you are not happy you are turning your pancreas upside down and dumping all your happiness out. Picture a pancreas losing "its smile" Is it worth it, Beloved Angel, to rely on others to make you happy or sacrifice your happiness for others? When you are happy who is? When you are not happy who is?

Diabetes

I have witnessed many who no longer live with diabetes through the Cleanse. It begins with understanding what your body needs and how it works and finding your joy. It is written- you are created to have great joy. It does not say great sorrow, struggle, manipulation, and control. It says great JOY! Your pancreas is waiting for your smile!

I had an Angel come and do the Cleanse with Type 1 diabetes. She was diagnosed at age 13 and she was 26 when she came to Hawaii to Angel Farms. After learning about her pancreas and her immune system and letting go of things that made her sad she shifted on the 4th day of the Cleanse. I knew it! I told her not to take her evening medicine because her pancreas was working. She did not trust and out of habit she took the pill. Her blood sugar dropped to 38 and she had to eat sugar. The next day she said, " I need to take my insulin," and I said, "Why?" She said her blood sugar felt low so I had her test both our blood sugars. We were one point off. Then we ate the same amount of delicious soup and then 20 minutes later we took our blood sugar again. We were again only one point off! She was never taught what was normal or how it felt! Do you know what is normal? By the way she does not have diabetes anymore!

Tonsil

Thymus Gland

Spleen

Lymph Nodes

Lymphatic Vessels

The Lymphatic System

The lymphatic system is a complex extensive drainage network of lymphoid organs, nodes, lymph ducts, and lymph vessels that produce and transport lymph fluid throughout the body from tissues to the circulatory system.. Lymph fluid is a clear, watery fluid that contains protein molecules, salts, glucose, urea, and other substances. This helps keep bodily fluid levels in balance and defends the body against infections.The lymphatic system is a network of very small tubes (or vessels) that drain lymph fluid from all over the body. The major parts of the lymph tissue are located in the bone

77

marrow, spleen, thymus gland, lymph nodes, and the tonsils. The heart, lungs, intestines, liver, and skin also contain lymphatic tissue. The lymphatic system is a major component of the immune system.

Two of the major lymphatic vessels are the left thoracic duct, which begins near the lower part of the spine and collects lymphatic fluid from the pelvis, abdomen, and lower chest. The thoracic duct runs up through the chest and empties into the blood through a large vein near the left side of the neck, and the right thoracic duct is the other major lymphatic vessel and collects lymphatic fluid from the right side of the neck, chest, and arm, and empties into a large vein near the right side of the neck.

Lymph nodes are round or kidney-shaped, and can be up to 1 inch in diameter. Most of the lymph nodes are found in clusters in the belly, neck, armpit, and groin area. Nodes are also located along the lymphatic pathways in the chest, abdomen, and pelvis, where they filter the blood. Inside the lymph nodes, lymphocytes called T-cells and B-cells help the body fight infection.

The lymphatic system has three interrelated functions: removal of excess fluids from body tissues, absorption of fatty acids and subsequent transport of fat and chyle to the circulatory system. Lymph originates as blood plasma that leaks from the capillaries of circulatory system, becoming interstitial fluid, and filling the spaces between individual cells of tissue. The excess interstitial fluid is collected by the lymphatic system and is processed by lymph nodes prior to being returned to the circulatory system. Lymph vessels are present in the lining of the gastrointestinal tract. Most other nutrients absorbed by the small intestine are passed on to the portal venous system to drain fats which are then passed on to the lymphatic system, to be transported to the blood. The enriched lymphatic fluid originating in the lymphatics of the small intestine is called chyle.

When micro-organisms invade the body or the body encounters other antigens such as pollen, the antigens are transported from the tissue to the lymph. Did you know that sometimes the body's immune system reacts to things that are harmless? That is what causes allergies.

Antigens are germs which can be toxins, bacteria, viruses or other foreign substances that can cause infections in the body. Each white blood cell makes just one special kind of antibody. When an antibody meets an antigen, it grabs onto it. Then it kills the antigen and takes it out of the body. Each antibody fights off a different antigen. When an antibody discovers an antigen, it begins producing more and more antibodies. These rush to where the germ or other foreign object is, like soldiers to battle.

The lymphatic system sits right under the skin tissue and responds well to gentleness. It moves 45 pints per day of lymphatic fluid as it exchanges potassium and sodium between red blood cells and lymphocytes. Your thigh muscles are your lymphatic pumps! You must bounce, walk, or swim to move your lymphatics. Your bras and shirts should leave little or no marks on your skin.

If you wear tight elastic or wires in your bra, you will stop the flow of lymphatic fluid and develop problems with your breasts because you are unable to move the lymphatic fluid and it can turn toxic. Go to a professional and get help getting fitted for a proper high quality bra. Your breasts deserve good health and so do you. The same thing happens with men that wear their belts or pants too tight. It puts pressure on the lymphatic system, and the prostate is a lymphatic gland. You need to have a free flow, so if you have to, it is better to use suspenders and not a belt. If you stop the flow of anything, you have problems. If you stop the flow of your breath, you will pass out. If you stop the flow of your love, you will die. If you stop the flow of anything, it hurts.

One of the lymphatic system's major jobs is to collect extra lymph fluid from body tissues and return it to the blood. This process is crucial because water, proteins, and other substances are continuously leaking out of tiny blood capillaries into the surrounding body tissues. If the lymphatic system didn't drain the excess fluid from the tissues, the lymph fluid would build up in the body's tissues, and they would swell.

The lymphatic system also helps defend the body against germs like viruses, bacteria, and fungi that can cause illnesses. These germs are filtered out in the lymph nodes, small masses of tissue located along the network of lymph vessels. The nodes house lymphocytes, a type of white blood cell.

Lymph fluid drains into lymph capillaries, which are tiny vessels. The fluid is then pushed along when a person breathes or the muscles contract. The lymph capillaries are very thin, and they have many tiny openings that allow gases, water, and nutrients to pass through to the surrounding cells, nourishing them and taking away waste products. When lymph fluid leaks through in this way it is called interstitial fluid.

What causes the lymph system to get out of balance other than tight clothes? Self doubt and stop and go behaviors, and difficulty in finishing things. Not going with the flow and unable to flex and bend continually. The Lymphatic system drains the head and neck of excess interstitial fluid via lymph vessels or capillaries, equally into the right lymphatic duct and the thoracic duct. Lymph nodes line the cervical spine and neck regions as well as along the face and jaw. The tonsils also are lymphatic tissue and help catch the ingestion of pathogens. Lymph nodes are bean-shaped and range in size from a few millimeters to about 1-2cm in their normal state. They may become enlarged due to a tumor or infection. In some cases, they may feel enlarged due to past infections; although one may be perfectly healthy, one may still feel enlarged. Great food for the lymph system are grapes and cilantro. Yum!

Happiness is a choice. Choose well!

Pregnancy Myths

Did you know that your body grew faster before birth? If a person grew as fast after birth as before, he or she would be over a mile tall by age one! True! Your immune system is suppressed during pregnancy in order to protect your fetus (an outsider) from being rejected by your body. Therefore, pregnant women should be wary around public places, especially around children for the chance of catching a bug. Absolutely False!

The immune system is very strong due to the mother's body making immune cells extra for the baby. Pregnancy is the most natural thing a woman's body does. Pregnancy cannot be detected in the iris because it is natural. The body remains whole during pregnancy. Does it make any sense to say that something that is natural to the body could be "rejected"? I don't think so! Let's change this perception to the correct one. Pregnancy is not a "condition" that has to be treated.

Once we realize this, the gift of life will be seen as the natural thing it has always been. Your immune system's job is to hunt down and destroy invading organisms. So why does it leave your fetus (which, genetically speaking, is half foreign) unharmed? Because the placenta -- the organ that delivers oxygen and nutrients to your growing baby -- cranks out an enzyme that stops the "natural killer" cells circulating in your blood and lymphatic system from attacking. Does this downshifting of the immune system mean that expectant moms are more prone to colds and flus? Paradoxically, the opposite may be true: Pregnant women seem to be less likely to catch them. "We're not sure how this happens, but immunity to viruses revs up in pregnancy," says Roberta Ness, M.D., an epidemiologist at the University of Pittsburgh School of Public Health.

In order to boost your immune system and reduce nausea, I suggest having protein at every meal. Vegetables and fruit will give you immune-boosting carotenoids and flavenoids. Minimize sugar and refined flours: studies found that consuming about two sodas' worth of sugar knocked down the effectiveness of white blood cells by roughly 50% within one hour, with residual effects lasting for several more hours. Finally, a low-fat diet with minimal caffeine has also been shown to improve immune function.

"A diet rich in whole foods will support your immunity," says Latham Thomas, a certified holistic health counselor who specializes in maternal and child wellness. "Eat lots of fresh garlic, green leafy vegetables, fresh citrus, and lots of water. Fruits and vegetables as carotenoids will increase your immune-fighting ability while still protecting the fetus. You cannot consume enough protein." "Essential fatty acids are important, too," adds Thomas, "so load up on flax seed oil, nuts and seeds."

Many tests performed during pregnancy are not accurate and the false positives are used to scare the mom and family instead of empowering them. For something as natural as pregnancy, why have we decided it is such a condition to be feared instead of a miracle to embrace? I want you to understand that the medical world has so much fear in it over the "condition" of pregnancy. Please be strong and trust in yourself when working with any practitioner and make sure you have full knowledge and do your own research on the different tests and procedures. Make sure that everything you do during your pregnancy is done with full awareness and trust. This will create the best outcome, a very healthy mother and baby and family!

Iridology

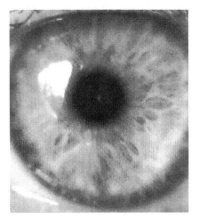

I have used iridology for over 20 years now and I truly love and admire every eye I see as the eye of God! Iridology is the scientific practice which involves correlating the markings and patterns of the iris to reflex manifestations and bodily malfunctions among the many organs of the body. By studying the eye, Iridologists can reveal a client's overall degree of health, as well as weaknesses. The eye is perceived as the gateway to the body whereby its condition reflects the overall condition of the client.

The word "iris" is Greek and means "rainbow" or "halo." The iris is the colorful portion of the eye that surrounds the pupil. When we think of the eye, the most distinctive feature we visualize vividly is none other than the iris. This science has some aspects of an art because of the brilliant array of colors that the irides (plural for iris) offer. Surprisingly, Iridology is one of the oldest forms of alternative medicine. The idea of Iridology, if not its practice, is more than 2,000 years old. The idea is found discreetly in the Bible in Luke Chapter 11:34. Luke was a physician. "The eye is the lamp of your body; when your eye is clear, your whole body also is full of light; but when it is bad, your body also is full of darkness".

Iridology was "rediscovered" by two European men in the 19th century. Together, these two share the title of "Father of Iridology." These men were Hungarian Ignatz von Peczely and Swedish clergyman Nils Liljequist. Legend has it that in 1837, Von Peczely captured an owl in the family garden. In an effort to escape, the owl fractured its leg. Ignatz soon noticed a streak or line begin to develop in the owl's eye after it had been injured. According to the traditional story, this line became a black spot at the 6:00 (six o'clock) position of the owl's iris. When Von Peczely examined a man with a similar marking in his iris, Von Peczely suddenly recollected his encounter with the owl. Fascinated by his findings, he began research and investigation into what is now called modern Iridology. Thus, a man's strange encounter with an owl directly led to the onset of the formation of the science of Iridology. Later, Von

82

Peczely and Liljequist made separate but strikingly similar iris charts that matched eye markings with specific body parts. Iridology represents a holistic approach to health care because it analyzes and diagnoses weaknesses in the tissues of the body. The eye is seen merely as an instrument unlocking the many symptoms of the body. Just like a throat culture, thermometer, or a blood pressure instrument that helps reveal the body's overall condition and can give clues as to what specific organs are hindered, so does the iris of the human eye. On the iris chart, the brain areas are represented at the top while the feet are at the bottom, and the bowel area is on the inside while the skin is on the outside.

An Iridologist analyzes the iris, rather than making a diagnosis. There are no iris markings or colors that are uniquely associated with a particular dis-ease state. By definition, iris analysis is: To discern by observation of the irides the various stages of tissue inflammation-acute, sub acute, chronic, and degenerative-and where the inflammations are located. Iridology is in sync with Hering's Law of Cure, which was developed by Homeopaths. This law states that 'All cure starts from within out, from the head down, and in the reverse order as the symptoms appeared,' when treating chronic illnesses. Iridology uses iris analysis to determine how a client should go about enacting a reversal process which involves a remission of the troubles and illnesses which exist at the present in the patient's body and which have been experienced in the past.

The iris contains hundreds of nerve endings which are attached to the optic nerve, the base of the brain, and all of the tissues of the body. Therefore, the neural circuitry of the eye is able to express the continuity of the body, an integrated unit composed of various cells which all communicate with the irides about their overall wellness. Weaknesses in body tissues or organs often show up in the eye before they show up in medical tests.

Iridology is mainly a preventative tool. A potential illness will show up in an examination. A person's progress can also be charted by observing the iris. Cleansing and healing of the body are verified from changes in the iris. A client's irises look significantly different after analysis and treatment. Iridology diagnosis works well with colon therapy and other natural healing modalities. An Iridologist might suggest a colon cleanse such as the one at Angel Farms. I am a certified Iridologist. I have been reading eyes for over 20 years. I have witnessed lucunas (inherent weakness) closing in one treatment. A major iris landmark is the autonomic nerve wreath. There are several iris signs that can be visualized on the nerve wreath. They concern the heart, thymus gland, and solar plexus. Several more iris signs are found inside the nerve wreath. Once healing occurs, healing lines appear, dark areas lighten and lines recede to what is referred to as a normal manifestation. As an iridologist and a speaker at conventions, I really emphasize that every time you are looking into someones eyes you are looking at God! What an honor! Please do not teach with fear. That is what caused the problem in the first place. Teach only love and it will teach you! If you go to an iridologist and they recommend a lot of supplements and scare you, simply walk away. You have nothing to fear. Seek healers who are clear already by their actions and words of acceptance and love.

Chlorine

Now let me talk about Chlorine. Chlorine is a natural substance and is NOT a chemical that builds up in the body. That is one of the reasons they can use it in the municipal water system. All they do is hydrate it and put it in bleach bottles and it becomes chlorine. Chlorine kills 99.99% of viruses bacteria and fungi. We have to honor that it is here for us. Remember, it is one of the elements on the chemistry chart so it is already part of us.

With all the different contaminants on the planet right now, it saves our lives. If you have hesitations over using bleach, please research bleach right now and then you can make your own informed decision about this! I want this to ring true to you! Chlorine processes through our bodies thanks to our wonderful kidneys! That's why we don't have a buildup of chlorine in our systems. It does "bleach" your hair color, and can in larger amounts cause an irritated stomach. It is not meant to drink anyway! Drinking a couple of glasses of water will help. Make sure bleach/chlorine is used in awareness- in a well ventilated space and wear gloves for possible skin irritation/absorption. I trustbleach and all the research behind it to keep us safe and clean.

Chapter 3

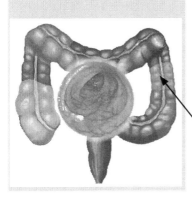

The Heart & Lung

Do You Know You Can Heal Your Heart and Know Your Purpose?

I am important. I am wanted.

3rd Day
Heart

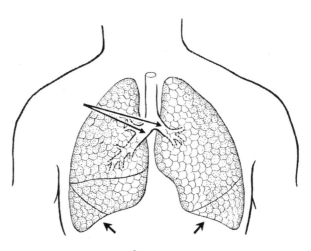

Lungs

Now let's talk about your miraculous lungs! The lungs combined are one of your largest organs. The trachea connects with each lung. The lungs are 2 sizes; the left lung is smaller than the right to allow room for the heart. The lungs are protected by the rib cage. The functions they do for your body are inspiration: diaphragm contracts (moves down rib cage expand lungs- volume increases) and expiration: diaphragm relaxes (moves up rib cage retracts, lung volume decreases). Look how Inspired you are (In Spirit) every time you BREATHE! Did you know Precious One, that on average, you breathe 23,000 times a day. You take about 600 million breaths during your lifetime! The lungs are about purpose: your "inspiration" in life. Your purpose is your inspiration!

How do you understand what your purpose is? First you understand who you are. You are a seed of God walking on earth. You were created in the likeness and image of God, and God is love and so are you. Just understanding this helps you out of depression. If you have depression, it's because you are questioning your purpose.

Many of you have come to Angel Farms feeling invisible and non-existent. The belief that you are non-existent or invisible was created before you even took your first breath of life! Have you ever felt like you don't exist on earth? Have you ever felt invisible? Have you ever felt others were more important than you? Maybe you decided, "If it's going to be this hard, I'm not going to do it." Depression is a check out or escape tool. You heard yourself say: 'I am here, I am here,' and your brain says 'no you are not.' You crash, hard, and then have to drag yourself up again sooner or later, only to crash again! Depression disappears when we remember it is written: Mankind is created to have great joy! It doesn't say great sorrow, struggle, manipulation, and control. It says great JOY! Why not! Try it, you might like it! Joy and happiness are a choice. Did you know that? You are here to master your love. You are here to awaken your Christed self and to love. Jesus the Christ, was a master teacher of love. He walked Christed. So can you! You are here to be a lover like God! You are on purpose, you always have been on purpose and if not you then who and if not now then when? Beloved Angel, you are the one we have been waiting for.

My first realization about this was when I was around 9, in the Mormon Church; I learned that God loves us bigger than words can speak in any language. I went home after church and on the back of one of my master teachers, Sunshine, my horse, my heart woke up! We walked by a meadow lark that just kept on singing. I said to her, God loves that meadow lark bigger than words can speak. WOW, so do I!' We passed a willow tree that we could hide in and no one knew we were there. I said to her, 'God loves this willow tree bigger than words can speak. WOW, so do I!' I told Sunshine 'God loves you bigger than words can speak. WOW so do I! ' I then said to her, 'Someday I will be a lover like God.' I felt my heart literally expand! That has been my goal ever since then.

Some people spend thousands of dollars and many days in the hope of finding out who they really are, and what they really need, which-when it comes right down to it, everyone makes their purpose so hard...it's not hard at all, and it's the same for everyone...to love, and to drink water!!! That's it! You can never love enough, so if you love all you can and drink a gallon of water a day, you are living your purpose!

Your loving purpose is about where you can take all your life experiences including the trauma-drama that you drew into

88

your life. How will you take these experiences and use them in the highest service of another? How will you help them and be a master teacher, because of your journey and not despite it? BE the cause of it. If you really look at how purpose works, you wake up and are tickled in your heart. The surface space in the lungs is as large as a tennis court! That's a lot of tickles!

I can only remind you, if you really know who you are, you'd be full of giggles and there would be no room for sadness. People tell me they understand why we are all grinning at Angel Farms. At Angel Farms we teach you not to give a "shit", literally, what people think about you. I quote Mother Theresa often, "It has never been between you and them; it has always only been between you and God!"

 **Get your tool box out! I would now like to give you another tool to stay in present time: practice deep belly breathing.**

Remember what a newborn baby looks like while it breathes. The belly goes up and down with its breath. Not its lungs, just its belly. Put your hand on your belly. Raise your belly with your breath. Inhale, your belly and hand goes up, exhale, your belly and hand goes down. Inhale: up-- exhale: down. Practice 15 breaths when you wake up, through-out the day, and 15 breaths before bed, raising and lowering your belly and hand with your breath. Put sticky notes around your house to remind you to put your hand on your belly and BREATHE into your belly, until you are breathing this way all the time. When we breathe this way, you relax the diaphragm, which relaxes the nervous system. Feel the peace.

We often forget to breathe this way when we are young because someone scared us. When this happens, we take a deep inhale in our upper lungs in fear and continue this breath throughout our lives. You may think this shallow breath is normal, but I assure you it is not. With this shallow kind of breath, it only allows half the lung capacity, and creates a low oxygen content in our bodies; setting us up for dis-eases such as cancer, yeast, and Candida conditions.

Now pay attention to what you see right now, what you smell right now, what you taste in your mouth right now, what you hear right now, feel the clothing on your skin, or not, and now repeat this mantra. Where I am God Is, and Where God is I am. How does that feel? Now look in a mirror and say that 3 times. Now see yourself 5 years ago, was it true then? What about 10 years ago? 20 years ago? 50 years ago?

Yes! It has always been true. You were just not aware of it. Remember you pulled the veil up to forget who you are so you could have a journey of who you are not. I know how hard it has been and how separate and alone you feel. Consider how awesome you are when you notice that even when you didn't know or you didn't remember, yet still you loved!!! You did it anyway!!! You are an Angel!!!!

Even Tagore said, "I too have been covered with thorns". The best way to get free is to forgive yourself for judging your journey too harshly. Someone gave you expectations and they are the beginning of the unconsciousness. You were born to love!! Cause no harm and raise your frequency to a higher joy. May you go to bed peaceful and unafraid.

My grandmother told me often, put more gratitude in your attitude and it will change your life. It is important to be in gratitude, and stay centered. There is always plenty to be grateful for. Be grateful you are alive. Be grateful you are breathing! When you go to bed, make a list of what you are grateful for, even if it is in your mind. I have fallen asleep with a list so long I can never reach the end. How big is your list?

Your turn, Angel, to make your gratitude list.

Some ideas to get you started to be thankful for-body, mind, loving, partners, pets, beautiful scenery, etc. Relax your breathing and bring yourself into a peaceful center. Send the people, places, and events around you uncondi-tional love and gratitude. See them responding only in a loving way. KnowAS YOU SEND THIS LOVE, YOU ARRAISING YOUR VIBRATION and the vibration of your world. Thank you for fulfilling your purpose!

Listen to the language of your soul, your feelings. Remember, Angel, you will not heal from outside yourself. Healing comes from within through understanding, gratitude and love. Now, put your hand on your belly and Breathe. Expand your entire lung cavity and relax your diaphragm, therefore relaxing your entire nervous system, which brings you in to a whole new state of peace. If you do not go within, you go without.

Do you see now how your misperceptions caused you pain? Choose Now to OWN your journey, and then you can change it. You are not a powerless victim. You are only Love. You are POWERFUL BEYOND MEASURE.

Nelson Mandela's speech in 1994 after being imprisoned for almost 30 years. Quote taken from A Return to Love by Marianne Williamson, whom I love!!

Our deepest fear is not that we are inadequate,
Our deepest fear is that
We are powerful beyond measure.
It is our light, not our darkness
That most frightens us.
We ask ourselves,
Who am I to be brilliant, gorgeous,
talented and fabulous?
Actually, who are you not to be?
You are a Child of God.
Your playing small does not save the world.
There is nothing enlightened about
Shrinking so that other people
Won't feel insecure around you.
We were born to make manifest
The Glory of God that is within us.
It is not just in some of us; It is in everyone.
And as we let our light shine
We unconsciously give other people
Permission to do the same.
As we are liberated from our fear,
Our presence automatically liberates others.

Isn't it amazing how so many have shown us with their life experience, how to love no matter what. It is the key to health, happiness, and the transformation of the world. What is your legacy, Beloved, Angel? Are you loving enough?

The foods that feed your lungs are onions, leeks, and garlic because they are high in sulfur. The one ingredient that changes your carbon dioxide into oxygen in your lungs is sulfur. We feed the tree and the tree feeds us.

Onions Are Amazing!

They attract and catch dis-ease. There are stories of onions preventing the plague. Once you are done with an onion that you are chopping up, either decide to use the whole thing or compost the rest of it. Don't put it into a baggie or container to use later. RAW onions will absorb whatever viruses and dis-ease is around, so like the lungs, great filters that they are, they just keep working. Many people tend to avoid onions, leeks, and garlic, but when people are sick or have lung issues or sulfur imbalances, these high sulphur foods really help.

To find your purpose, let go of your past, follow your heart and your heart will lead you, and use those experiences to love and be of service. Make your work your worship. Those of us who are not having fun with what we are doing; we are not following our path of joy.

Smoking is especially bad for your respiratory system. When you smoke a cigarette, you inhale the smoke into your lungs. This means that your lungs are directly exposed to the 4,000 toxic substances that are in over-the-counter cigarette brands. Most smokers smoke to have a break from emotional overwhelm. Did you know, Angel, that smoking is a subconscious death wish? Are you sure you want to make that choice? TAKE time to breathe and exhale. Take time for yourself. See how to break a habit in chapter 9.

Now I want to share some information for any of you that partake in marijuana or cigarette smoking. If you hold on to anything, it hurts. If you hold on to smoke, it blows your blood vessels. The capillaries are so small the blood discs have to go single file through them. The lungs are in a regeneration cycle between 9 am to 1 pm and 9 pm to 1 am. If you smoke during these times the lungs will shut down their regeneration to protect themselves. How long can your lungs go without regeneration? Please be aware of these important facts about your precious lungs and tell your friends, they will thank you in 2 days!

I have had many Angels come in and during their Cleanse they threw up black toxic junk from their lungs because they were taught to hold smoke as long as possible. Please teach yourself and others those things that cause your precious lungs to hurt and choose better health practices for yourself. You are worth it! Let go.

Money and Worth

Health and Money seem to be related and often presented together! When someone continually worries about money they develop lower back pain! Do you find your lower back hurting? Angel, you are supported and loved. Tune in and Know! Miracles happen when you express more gratitude. Negative thoughts are a luxury none of us can afford. Gratitude is the key. Give thanks that Everything is Working Out Perfectly.

Angel, I am going to talk to you about the Bible now and don't kid yourself that there is no truth in the Bible...get over that too. There is truth in all the holy books and there is silliness in it too. If it's not teaching love, it's not teaching truth. In the Bible, it says in the first chapter God created heaven and earth, and 31 lines down, it says, all that God created is good. That would be YOU and everything else! Rumi says, "All is done in heaven and earth, already" If you are created in the likeness and image of God/Love, which you are, there's no reason not to know you're absolute goodness and worth. I had a beautiful Angel Isaiah who was raised Jehovah Witness. He would go around and teach only the good, uplifting and inspiring parts of the Bible. He already intuitively knew to weed out the great and good(God) parts and teach only love! Just like I had felt from Mormon teachings when I was 9! If we teach our children to trust their own hearts through inspiration we can find truth in all religions.

If you don't know your worth, you have a hard time drawing money. This is often the biggest obstacle for people to come and do The Cleanse. I always tell them to just say "Thank you I am worth it" and then watch what happens. Spirit is going to say, 'oh yes you are, I agree, and here you are, and money is just a part of your worth. You are of infinite worth, infinite goodness, infinite amazement, of course, the more you have money, the more you can help the planet. Being in poverty consciousness is so not it in this day and age.

MONEY to me means "My Own Natural Energy Yield."

Yield means to put forth. What are we here to put forth? LOVE OF COURSE! Every piece of money created by the United States of America has the same four words on it. "In God we trust." John is the only writer in the Bible to define God, and he uses only three words to define the indefinable which is "God is Love." If you change the word "God" into "Love," you have "In love we trust" and "we" is a plural translation of "I", so all money says "In love I trust!" Do you trust in love? Yes. Everybody says yes!

All money is the free flow of God's love that moves through you, out to others, then back again in the form of money, and how do you limit love? You don't. As you pay for things, (you don't have to say this out loud to the cashier, but you can say it in your mind) "just say, in love I trust, in love I trust" and when you receive money be sure and say "thank you for the love, thank you for the love," and it changes your whole concept about money. When someone pays you for products and services you want, how does that make you feel inside? Good! All feelings come from one of two sources, love or fear. So again you are feeling or experiencing the energy of love.

Now say these words out loud: I am a mighty money magnet. Waves of money engulf me. I am wonderfully rich in consciousness.

And bountifully supplied with money therefore wave after wave of visible love, in the form of money, flows to me now. I use this money for the highest good with love!

When you are open to love, you are unlimited. When you are moving God's love around in the form of money, you are sharing that unlimited love with others. Be grateful for the love you have to share with others for goods and services. It will attract more love to you!! Can you limit love? NO way. It is unlimited the amount of love you can receive and spread around the world, even if it is in the form of money.

94

Practice these Mantras in an exhale and inhale breath each night when you go to bed.

I am worthy and I am abundant-These two are very true about you but your awareness needs reminding.

The next issue that affects the human being/body is questioning your infinite worth. Worth is the number 2 cause of dis-ease on an emotional level. If you don't know your worth, you have a hard time drawing money. At Angel Farms we see the biggest issue that keeps people from receiving a miracle Cleanse. is money, so if you have a question about worth, you can't draw enough money to get yourself better and over your struggle, right?

I always tell them just say "Thank you I am worth it" and then watch what happens. Spirit is going to say, oh yes you are, I agree, and here you are, and money is just a part of your worth. You are of infinite worth, infinite goodness, and infinite amazement, the more you have money, the more you can help the planet, so being in poverty consciousness is so not it!

Bones

The human skeleton is made of individual or joined bones (such as the skull), supported and supplemented by a structure of ligaments, tendons, muscles, cartilage and other organs. The skeleton changes composition over a lifespan. Early in gestation, a fetus has no hard skeleton; bones form gradually during nine months in the womb. At birth, all bones will have formed, but a newborn baby has more bones than an adult. On average, an adult human has 206 bones, but a baby is born with approximately 350 bones! The difference comes from a number of small bones that fuse together during growth, such as the sacrum and coccyx. An infant is born with pockets of cartilage between particular bones to allow further growth. The sacrum (the bone at the base of the spine) consists of five bones which are separated at birth but fuse together into a solid structure in later years. Growing is usually completed between ages 13 and 18, at which point the bones have no pockets of cartilage left to allow for more growth. I believe that is how we survive childhood when we fall down and bump into everything and we bend and not break!

Not all bones are interconnected directly. There are 6 bones, the auditory ossicles (three on each side), in the middle ear that articulate only with each other. Another bone, the hyoid bone in the neck, does not touch any other bones in the body, and is supported by muscles and ligaments; it serves as the point of attachment for the tongue. Some of the ribs called floating ribs only hang by muscle and are not attached to the spine. The longest and heaviest bone in the body is the femur and the smallest is the stapes bone in the middle ear. In an adult, the skeleton comprises around 20% of the total body weight. More than half the bones in the human body are in the hands and feet. The human thighbones are stronger than concrete.

Angel, when you take calcium, find a blend of calcium and magnesium with double magnesium to calcium. It is the only ratio the body can absorb. I have found in my work, that Coral Calcium is very difficult for the body to absorb at all! It lines my tanks daily until the accumulation of calcium is released. It is very harmful on the coral reefs of our beautiful planet also! Look for a plant based calcium supplements.

I have found many Angels with great regret of their past. Many people are crushing themselves because of a bad marriage, family squabbles, failed businesses, bad investments, cranky neighbors, and missed opportunities. Your skeletal system is your body's' structure. Your regrets and past judgments are like taking a two by four, or a six by six and whamming your structure. Some of you are harder on yourselves than others! If you do not want to develop osteoporosis, then forgive yourself and others and stay in the present moment. None of those things are happening right now in this moment as you read these words. Right? This is the time to let it go and stop letting it affect your structure of your life and body! Great foods to feed your bones are celery, artichokes, and lots of greens, and all foods high in silica and msm.

Shoulders and Neck

Hey Angel, are you carrying too much responsibility? Are you being inflexible and stubborn? You never do that, do you? Do you ever feel tight in your lungs? Do you find yourself questioning your purpose in life? Who doesn't? Are you allowing love to surround you? Relax your shoulders and release tension in your neck. Be aware of when you tighten your shoulders, let Go and let God.

I have a practice that I do and often share with people doing the Cleanse who have a lot of tension in their shoulders and neck. Imagine that your hands are big clawing earth movers. Get a hold of all this stuff you are carrying around on your shoulders: your partner, your family, your job, etc with these big claws. As you pull it up up up with the claws, give it to God with a big deep breath release and pull the tension and responsibility off your shoulders. Instantly, you feel a big relief!

Toolbox to relieve shoulder tension:

Are you blocking (not allowing) love to surround you? Relax your shoulders and release the tension in your neck today. Be aware of when you tighten your shoulders, let Go and let God. Practice deep belly breathing Remember what an infant looks like as it breathes into the belly. Feel your breath enter your lower lungs. Raise your belly with your breath. You relax the diaphragm, which relaxes the nervous system. Feel the peace. Listen to the language of your soul, your feelings.

Heart

The heart has been mentioned as the seat of Consciousness. The heart is an amazing organ that continuously pumps oxygen and

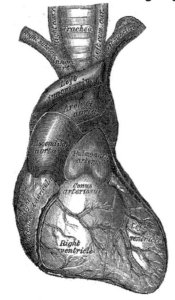

nutrient-rich blood throughout your body to sustain life. This fist-sized powerhouse expands and contracts 100,000 times per day, pumping five or six quarts of blood each minute, or about 2,000 gallons per day.

The right side pumps blood into the lungs that is received from the body. The left side does the opposite; it receives blood from the lungs and pumps it out to the body. There are two chambers on top of the heart, on the right and left side, called the atria that fill with blood returning to the heart from the body and lungs. The two chambers on the bottom of the heart are called ventricles-left ventricle and right ventricle. They squirt blood out to the lungs and body. The septum is a muscle wall that separates the left and right side. There are blood vessels that carry blood away from the heart and veins that carry blood back to the heart. Arteries and veins together are called blood vessels. The ventricles then squeeze and pump blood out of the heart. Four valves control the direction and flow of blood.

The heart has four chambers like a tomato. Tomatoes are heart food. It takes lessthan 60 seconds to pump blood to every cell in the body at an amazing speed of 48 miles per hour. The blood supplies oxygen to the cells. When the cells use oxygen, they make carbon dioxide that gets carried away by the blood and expelled by the lungs.

As the heart beats, it pumps blood through a system of blood vessels, called the circulatory system. Your heart beats about 100,000 times in one day and

98

about 40,000,000 times a year. It beats about 3 billion times in the average person's lifetime. In one hour the heart works hard enough to produce enough energy to raise almost one ton of weight one yard from the ground. The vessels are elastic tubes that carry blood to every part of the body. In addition to carrying fresh oxygen from the lungs and nutrients to your body's tissues, it also takes the body's water products, including dioxide, away from the tissues. This is necessary to sustain life and promote the health of all the body's tissues. The heart includes a vast system of blood vessels-arteries, veins and capillaries-and is over 60,000 miles long. That's long enough to go around the world more than twice! Blood flows continuously through your body's blood vessels. Your heart is the pump that makes it all possible.

How does the Heart beat? The atria and ventricles work together, alternately contracting and relaxing to pump blood through your heart. The electrical system of your heart is the power source that makes this possible. Your heartbeat is triggered by electrical impulses that travel down a special pathway through your heart. The heart is a seven layer crystalline oscillator that moves life force through us. Honor it! At rest, a normal heart beats around 50 to 99 times a minute. Exercise, emotions, fever and some medications can cause your heart to beat faster, sometimes to well over 100 beats per minute.

In Ayurveda, the heart is concerned not only through its physical value, but mental and spiritual also, thus the care of heart is most important. According to ancient Indian philosophy and Ayurveda, heart takes higher position not only anatomically and physiologically, but also by its mental and spiritual value. The heart has a major role in our body system.

Deepak Chopra says in his book, Magical Beginnings, Enchanted Lives, according to Ayurveda, an ember of consciousness is present in every living cell. This flame of awareness becomes brighter as the level of biological sophistication rises. These elemental energies fuel one's brilliance, vitality, and love.

Have you ever seen your blood on a dark field micro scope? Every cell glows! Every cell has infinite intelligence!

Over many years of working with Angels I have found heart disease to be more common than is even diagnosed. There is so much deep seeded grief in the world it is hard not to get caught up in it. Grief! How do we let it go? What is it anyway? Grief comes from someone we have loved that has crossed over. Did they know how much we loved them? Did they know what we needed them to hear? It is the things unsaid. Have you had someone you loved cross over? Are you sad and missing them? Heart carries grief, loss of a loved one, words unspoken (how much I loved them) or a feeling of betrayal, being wronged somewhere along the way or re-grets from the past. (Oh, I didn't get to do that because of ....)

Sweet Angel, here is a wonderful way to remember and recognize what a beautiful body you have created.

Did you know you are the creator of your body? When you were in your mother's womb, (and you chose her for gifts she will awaken in you); you drew from the elements of the earth and put your own body together. Remember the chemistry chart we all saw in Biology class. That is us!! Every element! Mostly Water! That is one reason the Native Americans call the earth the Mother Earth. We are the exact same elements. That is why we can continue to regenerate and not be hooked up to an umbilical cord, which would be a WHOLE different experience, wouldn't it?

So, every time you take a bath or a shower, love your hands, and fingers, and joints. Love your elbows, knees, and toes. Love your butt, and your hips, and your belly, and your chest. Love your colon, and your spleen, and your heart, and your throat, and your face, eyes, and nose. Love your ears, hair, tongue, and every cell in your beautiful body. Send your body so much gratitude for the awesome job it does every day to carry a Spirit of God (Love), to bless everything and everyone in its path. If you cannot love every part of your sacred temple then who will?

Diseases that affect the Heart
and Cardiovascular system:

Heart disease includes a number of conditions affecting the structures or function of the heart. Cardiovascular disease was just surpassed by obesity as the leading cause of death for both men and women in the United States. The number one time of death is at 9:00 am on Monday morning! How can this happen? Sweet Angel, are you walking around with grief and sadness? You were created to have great joy. If you are

100

not, you will find a way to return to joy. Sometimes that means dying. My dad Paul, one of two dads I chose, had a massive heart attack at 53. He always had so much sadness that began in his childhood that never got healed. He was a very precious gift to me in my life and part of his gifts carry on in me to help others.

The term "heart failure" means the heart does not pump as well as it should. It does not mean the heart has "failed" or stopped working. Heart failure is a major health problem in the United States, affecting nearly 5 million Americans. It is the leading cause of hospitalization in people over 65.

Approximately 80% of all patients with diabetes die of cardiovascular disease. Research indicates that insulin resistance is associated with heart disease and type 2 diabetes. Insulin resistance occurs when the body does not respond properly to its own natural insulin, a substance critical for blood sugar to enter the body's cells and be converted into energy. High Blood Pressure is often a precursor to heart problems. Hypertension is an extremely common form of cardiovascular disease usually resulting from a decrease in the elasticity or interior diameter of arteries. This is caused by plaque build-up in the vessels, which means your filtration system needs help.

Miracle Story

I had a beautiful Angel, Larry come through the Cleanse with a new diagnosis of heart disease.

He was only 45 years old. Coming back from the hospital his wife stopped by Angel Farms. She asked if The Cleanse could help, and I said of course! They wanted to do open heart surgery. He did the Cleanse and we found out he was grieving for past loved ones and yet his biggest grief was for his relationship with his wife. They were headed for a divorce. After his Cleanse he was completely well. Larry got over his heart dis-ease. He went to his Dr. and they were amazed; his blood pressure regulated and his heart had de-swelled. The Doctor said maybe he didn't have to have heart surgery.

His wife was on the next Cleanse. I then sat with the two of them and asked them when they had last made love. They looked at each other for a few minutes and came up blank. They figured not since their 7 year old daughter was born. WHAT??! She was still sleeping in their bed! She did not have a bed of her own. We sent a bed home with them that day and I told Larry to put a lock on the door and explain to the children that mommy and daddy needed some time together. She bought The Gift of Love by Deepak and Friends and candles and they seduced each other. They had a remarriage ceremony 2 weeks later and have been happy and healthy ever since.

How are you supposed to have an intimate relationship with a partner if you are not connecting on that level? How two people come together on that level is when they touch the true essence of God in physical form and it's pretty awesome. So if you are not making love or connecting on a deep level, you are either finished with the relationship or you need to fix the problem. Most of the time, it's fixable. Love works. If you love each other, there is still hope. I was going to put their 7 year old daughter on the next Cleanse. A few days later Elle called me and said Clara's digestive problems and all of her issues were gone. She is so peaceful and happy we don't know what to do with her. She is like a whole new kid. I had already taken her off the Cleanse list! When we heal, our children no longer have to be our master teachers.

The heart always deals with issues of trusting, opening and reaching new levels of acceptance and understanding others. Life itself will bring you many opportunities to keep an open heart and mind no matter what. Remember, Gratitude is the Key!

I tell my Angels to see your loved one in your mind's eye and tell them what you need them to know.

Angel's Toolbox

See them. Hear them. Smell them. Visualize them fully with you. Tell them your frustrations and not being able to say goodbye, or how much they touched your life. Do they hear you dear One? Of course they do! Do you think they want you to have heart dis-ease over their living, loving, and things "unsaid"? Of course they don't! Then, ask yourself, what do they really want for me? Happiness of course!

They do not want you to die because of your love for them. They want you to live and be happy! It does not matter the circumstances of their crossing whatsoever. There are contracts we all hold for each other about our lives and our deaths. So, Angel, stop judging your loved one's crossing, whether it be age, illness, accident, war, or murder, all things are in divine perfection.

Trust the process. Souls communicate without words. No feeling ever goes unheard.

Thank them for blessing your life with their love and presence. Be thankful you had a soul connection with them, that they would so love you and so bless you that you just had to tell them thank you. If you will not do this for yourself, will you do it for them? Honor them for the lessons they have taught you. Honor yourself for bringing more love and light to the most difficult moments of your life. Love transforms everything, even heart dis-ease! Nothing can hide from love!

Deepak Chopra defines death as when we have imagined ourselves into another space and time. Know now that we are all eternal Beings. We have been, we are now, and we will always be. We just are. There is no end to God and therefore no end to us. Let your loved ones go with gratitude of how they did touch your life and just be happy. It is your birthright. I have seen heart disease disappear every time that love and gratitude replaces grief and sadness.

Changing this perception of loss, grief, and sadness, will allow your heart to return to a state of wholeness and love. We cannot see the wholeness in the world when we are sad. Angel, only love and happiness can set your heart free. Let love fill your blessed heart, completely and fully, and know that your loved ones only want this for you. Everything in every situation, including death, is perfect. There is a reason for everything.

The heart always deals with issues of trusting, opening and reaching new levels of acceptance and understanding others. Life itself will bring you many opportunities to keep an open heart and mind no matter what. Please trust in yourself and the Universe that you can transform all your fears to love. Remember, Angel, YOU don't have to hurt anymore!

Bring yourself into a peaceful center, and relax your breathing.

Focus on your partner or someone dear to you. As you send the person love, your heart becomes open to receive. Let them go. You did enough. You loved! That was your only job. Just know: AS YOU SEND THIS LOVE, YOU ARE RAISING YOUR VIBRATION to heal your beautiful heart.

It is important to remember that you really need to love and feed your bodies well. If you have trouble really integrating your mind and body, thus accepting and recognizing your body's needs over your mind's driving enthusiasm, I recommend quieting the mind, drinking more water, feeding your spirit, eating more vegetables, loving and blessing even more, and getting back into this moment! It is a delicious one!

On Crossing Over
A Dog's Purpose (from a 6-year-old).

A veterinarian had been called to examine a ten-year-old Irish wolfhound named Belker. The dog's owners, Ron, his wife Lisa, and their little boy Shane, were all very attached to Belker, and they were hoping for a miracle.

He examined Belker and found he was dying of cancer. He told the family we couldn't do anything for Belker, and offered to perform the euthanasia procedure for the old dog in their home. As we made arrangements, Ron and Lisa told me they thought it would be good for six-year-old Shane to observe the procedure. They felt as though Shane might learn something from the experience.

The next day, he felt the familiar catch in his throat as Belker 's family surrounded him. Shane seemed so calm, petting the old dog for the last time, that he wondered if he understood what was going on. Within a few minutes, Belker slipped peacefully away.

The little boy seemed to accept Belker's transition without any difficulty or confusion. We sat together for a while after Belker's Death, wondering aloud about the sad fact that animal lives are shorter than human lives. Shane, who had been listening quietly, piped up, 'I know why.' Startled, we all turned to him. What came out of his mouth next stunned the veterinarian. He had never heard a more comforting explanation.

The little boy said, 'People are born so that they can learn how to live a good Life -- like loving everybody all the time and

104

being nice, right?' The Six-year-old continued, 'Well, dogs already know how to do that, so they don't have to stay as long.'

Ways to Heal the Heart

Let go of all your grief and sadness. Reducing your emotional stress directly affects the blood flow from the brain to the heart. Meditation is another great tool because it reduces systolic and diastolic blood pressure. Stop smoking. Reduce your alcohol consumption to extreme moderation. Reduce intake of fat and cholesterol, and bless what amounts you do eat. Reduce your amount of salt intake to under 3 grams daily. Do not eat food within three hours of bedtime. Increase your fibrous foods such as salad, grains, vegetables, etc. Increasing garlic lowers the cholesterol level and increasing ginger breaks down blood clots. Increasing cayenne assists in circulation. Do a walk 1-3 miles daily, 3 times per week or more. Get some fresh air! Start a yoga program and your heart will rejoice! Other Heart Healthy Foods are; tomatoes, onions, apples, and leeks. The best way, Live in Love. Breathe in Love. Talk Love. Accept Love. Go with the flow, in Love.

Remember, if a dog was the teacher you would learn things like:

When loved ones come home, always run to greet them.
Allow the experience of fresh air and the wind in your face to be pure Ecstasy.
Take naps.
Stretch before rising.
Run, romp, and play daily.
Thrive on attention and let people touch you.
Avoid biting when a simple growl will do.
On warm days, stop to lie on your back on the grass.
On hot days, drink lots of water and lie under a shady tree.
When you're happy, dance around and wag your entire body.
Delight in the simple joy of a long walk.
Be loyal.
Never pretend to be something you're not.
If what you want lies buried, dig until you find it.
When someone is having a bad day, be silent, sit close by, and nuzzle them gently.

Miracle Story

ENJOY EVERY MOMENT OF EVERY DAY!

A young man named "Hedeki" came for the Cleanse at 19. He was so sick he would get in bed with his parents, because he didn't know if he was going to live until morning. When he came, he would cover himself up in a blanket and shake and break out into a sweat and soak everything. He'd be cold and hot, over and over again. He had been sick most of his life, and his parents took him to do everything they could think of to do, and nothing had worked. They finally brought him to the Cleanse. The first two days he passed nothing at all. The third day he stood up and bumped his head on the ceiling. He had gotten taller that day. I personally did his session on the third day, that's when he shifted. He went back to when he was 16, in the hospital and he died. He said he felt this presence come over him that was so ecstatic...an enlightened moment. He walked out of the hospital the very next day. He had a miracle. He became sick again because he lost that connected spiritual feeling. In his session with me, he repeated over and over, "I remember, I remember." He is living and loving and healed in the now!

Heart disease could very well be over in our world as soon as enough of us see ourselves as eternal and never ending and live from love and not from loss!

Chapter 4

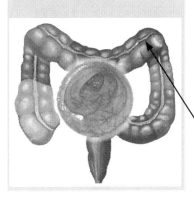

Digestion

Your Amazing Digestive
System And How To Keep
It Healthy.

I am worthy. I am abundant.

4th Day
Digestive System

Here we go!! The human body is a phenomenal event! I have witnessed for years the miracles that happen when this system gets clear. The absolute enjoyment of our bodies requires a deep understanding and respect of how nature has gifted us. The earth has given of herself so we could have this experience. We are the same elements of a chemistry chart except a lot more energy and information. The average human body contains enough sulfur to kill all the fleas on an average dog, enough carbon to make 900 pencils, enough potassium to fire a toy cannon, enough fat to make 7 bars of soap, enough phosphorus to make 2,300 match heads, and enough water to fill a ten gallon tank! According to Ayurveda, the traditional Indian science of health, most diseases originate as an imbalance in the digestive system. Everything possible should be done to avoid digestion problems for good health and I have found this begins with education.

We all know that good digestion to build strong cells is essential for great health. Poor digestion is a major factor for disease, because without good digestion the cells are not strong.

Do you know that your digestive system is the first organ that is created in utero, in the umbilical cord? It first connects your mouth to your anus and then buds are formed to create your internal organs. These organs are nourished along this same system all of your life! An average sized man eats about 33 tons of food in his lifetime. Every time we eat it takes 85% of our energy to digest our food. That is why we are not supposed to swim after we eat. How important is your digestive system? Organs that make up the digestive tract are the mouth, esophagus/pharynx, stomach(four parts), small intestine (3 parts), liver, pancreas, spleen, gall bladder, large intestine, also called the colon, rectum, and anus. Throughout the digestive system is a lining called the mucosa. Run your tongue over the inside of your cheek. Feel the soft gentle tissue. This is the same tissue that is all through your digestive tract.

What's the first step in digesting food? Believe it or not, the digestive process starts even before you put food in your mouth. Just by smelling that homemade apple pie or thinking about how delicious that coconut soup is going to taste, you begin to salivate and the digestive process kicks in, preparing for that first scrumptious bite. The digestive system begins inthe brain. Your body is being renewed and replaced every moment of your life.   98% of the atoms in your body were not there a year ago!

When you eat foods such as bread, meat, and vegetables they are not in a form that the body can use as nourishment. Every morsel of food we eat has to be broken down into nutrients that can be absorbed by the body, which is why it takes 20 hours to fully digest food. In humans, protein must be broken down into amino acids, starches into simple sugars, and fats into fatty acids and glycerol. The water is also absorbed into the bloodstream to provide the body with the fluid it needs.

During the process of absorption, nutrients that come from the food (including carbohydrates, proteins, fats, vitamins, and minerals) pass through channels in the

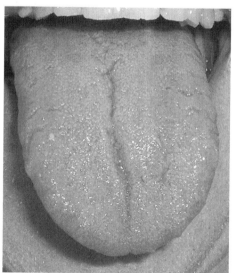

intestinal wall and into the bloodstream. The blood works to distribute these nutrients to the rest of the body. The waste parts of food that the body can't use are passed out of the body as feces.   Food is the body's fuel source.   Digestion involves mixing food with digestive juices, moving it through the digestive tract, and breaking down large molecules of food into smaller molecules.

In response to the sensory stimulation of food about to enter the body, the brain sends impulses through the nerves that control the salivary glands telling them to prepare for a meal. As the food enters your mouth, the taste buds on your tongue begin to be stimulated. This then turns on communication in the body, readying the organs to receive what they need. Did you know that you have brand new taste buds every 10 days? Amazing!

The taste buds register sweet, sour, salty, pungent, bitter, and astringent. Try to include all 6 tastes in your diet every day. Your body and organs will appreciate you even more. Here are some examples:

Sweet—sugar, honey rice, pasta, milk, cream, butter

Sour—lemons, cheese, yogurt, plums, vinegar.

Salty—any salty food, pungent-chili peppers, cayenne, ginger any hot spice

Bitter—greens such as endive spinach romaine lettuce.

Astringent—beans, lentils, pomegranates, apples, pears.

Do you know that sweet is digested first? It is wise according to Ayurveda to eat your dessert first and then eat foods in the same order as listed above.

A digestive enzyme called amylase, which is found in saliva, starts to break down the carbohydrates (starches and sugars) in the food even before they leave the mouth. When we see, smell, taste, or even imagine a tasty snack, our salivary glands, which are located under the tongue and near the lower jaw behind your second molar, begin producing saliva/amylase. This is a great time to send a wonderful blessing to your meal! Our bodies make about one liter of saliva per day and if saliva cannot dissolve something, you cannot taste it! The organ that produces saliva is the pancreas. We need at least one carbohydrate a day to be healthy. Those no carbohydrate diets are dangerous, Angel. If you have inflammatory issues, be careful to only have one carbohydrate a day. Do not overwork your pancreas which is working for you to break down inflammation!

It is a very big point to know that carbohydrates and sugars are digested in the mouth. I have so many of my Angels come in with such confusion of what to eat and how to eat it. Some books have stated to not mix carbohydrates and proteins. This is ridiculous because people are not educated about the digestive system. Proteins are digested in the stomach, not in the mouth! This can also be extremely time-consuming to always be concerned about what combinations of food to eat together.

The digestible carbohydrates, starch and sugar, are broken into simpler molecules by enzymes in the saliva, in juice produced by the pancreas, and in the lining of the small intestine. Starch is digested in two steps. First, an enzyme in the saliva and pancreatic juice breaks the starch into molecules called maltose. Then an enzyme in the lining of the small intestine splits the maltose into glucose molecules that can be absorbed into the blood. Glucose is carried through the bloodstream to the liver, where it is stored or used to provide energy for the work of the body. The Dietary Guidelines for Americans in 2005 recommended that 45 to 65 percent of total daily calories be from carbohydrates. Carbohydrate foods include anything that grows like a grass such as wheat, barley, oats, bananas, millet, and corn. Many of these foods contain both starch and fiber.

Then the teeth tear and chop the food, saliva moistens it for easy swallowing. If you don't chew your food to the consistency of liquid DO NOT SWALLOW IT! It does your body no good. My daughter says that if you aren't chewing your food to this consistency, you might as well be eating fast food for the nutrients you absorb! You only have teeth in your mouth, not in your stomach or intestines. One thing the Graduates of Angel Farms tell me is they definitely chew their food. I tell them on the first day of the Cleanse is if you don't chew your food we will catch you! And we do!

When I was 16 I met a beautiful man in his late 90's out walking briskly in Sun Valley, Idaho. I asked him what his words of advice for long health were. He told me to chew my food to liquid. I am the last one done at every meal and I am proud of it! You can be too!

Swallowing, which is accomplished by muscle movements in the tongue and mouth, moves the food into the throat, or pharynx. The pharynx, a passageway for food and air, is about 5 inches long. A flexible flap of tissue called the epiglottis reflexively closes over the windpipe when we swallow to prevent choking. From the throat, food travels down a muscular tube in the chest called the esophagus. At the end of the esophagus, a muscular ring called a sphincter allows food to enter the stomach and then squeezes shut to keep food or fluid from flowing back up into the esophagus. Waves of muscle contractions called peristalsis force food down through the esophagus to the stomach. Although you are able to start swallowing by choice, once the swallow begins, it becomes involuntary and proceeds under the control of the nerves. Food will get to your stomach in 7 seconds even if you are standing on your head! A person normally isn't aware of the movements of the esophagus, stomach, and intestines that take place as food passes through their digestive tract. Why is that? Because you have no nerve endings after the food leaves your mouth until it gets to your anus. It is the alpha and the omega, the beginning and the end, the first and the last. Your body does it automatically!

Nerve Regulators

Two types of nerves help control the action of the digestive system. Extrinsic, or outside, nerves come to the digestive organs from the brain or the spinal cord. They release two chemicals, acetylcholine and adrenaline. Acetylcholine causes the muscle layer of the digestive organs to squeeze with more force and increase the "push" of food and juice through the digestive tract. It also causes the stomach and pancreas to produce more digestive juices. Adrenaline has the opposite effect. It relaxes the muscles of the stomach and intestine and decreases the flow of blood to these organs, slowing or stopping digestion. What happens to your digestive system when you are stressed and are not in present time?

The intrinsic, or inside, nerves make up a very dense network embedded in the walls of the esophagus, stomach, small intestine, and colon. The intrinsic nerves are triggered to act when the walls of the hollow organs are stretched by food. They release many different substances that speed up or delay the movement of food and the production of juices by the digestive organs. Together, nerves, hormones, the blood, and the organs of the digestive system conduct the complex tasks of digesting and absorbing nutrients from the foods and liquids you consume each day.

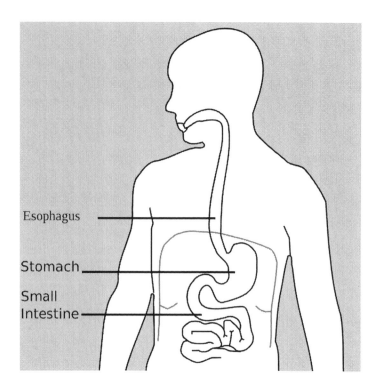

Esophagus

Stomach

Small
Intestine

Movement of Food Through the System

The large, hollow organs of the digestive tract contain a layer of muscle that enables their walls to move. The movement of organ walls can propel food and liquid through the system and can also mix the contents within each organ. Food moves from one organ to the next through muscle action called peristalsis. Peristalsis looks like an ocean wave traveling through the muscle, like a snake swallowing an egg, or like milking a cow. The muscle of the organ contracts to create a narrowing and then propels the narrowed portion slowly down the length of the organ. These waves of narrowing push the food and fluid in front of them through each hollow organ.

The Stomach

The stomach has three mechanical tasks. First, it stores the swallowed food and liquid. The second job is to mix up the food, liquid, and digestive juice (hydrochloric acid) produced by the stomach. The stomach muscles churn and mix the food with acids and enzymes, breaking it into much smaller, more digestible pieces. An acidic environment is needed for the digestion that takes place

112

in the stomach. The stomach's main job is to break down proteins! Glands in the stomach lining produce about 3 quarts of this hydrochloric acid each day. One great way to eat with conscious-ness is to listen to your body and to stop eating when your stomach is 80% full and has room to move. Most people have no idea what this feels like. I have seen a live x-ray of the stomach in action. It moves like a washing machine. If you overload your washing machine how clean do your clothes get? Remember not to overfill the machine!

The third task of the stomach is to empty its contents slowly into the small intestine. When it's empty, an adult's stomach has a volume of one fifth of a cup, but it can expand to hold more than 8 cups of food after a large meal. Does that include Thanksgiving? On Holiday meals, remember your digestive enzymes! You only need them when you over-eat! Hold your hands together like a cup. Imagine your hands cupping over your hands. This is how to measure what your stomach can easily process and not overload.

Production of Digestive Juices

The next set of digestive glands is in the stomach lining. Your stomach lining glands produce mucus, pepsin, and HCI to a PH of 100,000 times the acidity of your bloodstream. These glands produce stomach acid and an enzyme that digests protein. A thick mucus layer coats the mucosa and helps keep the acidic digestive juice from dissolving the tissue of the stomach itself. This is why you have a new stomach lining every 5 to 7 days. In most people, the stomach mucosa is able to resist the juice, although food and other tissues of the body cannot. Other enzymes that are active in the process come from glands in the wall of the intestine.

By the time food is ready to leave the stomach, it has been processed into a thick liquid called chyme. A walnut-sized muscular tube at the outlet of the stomach called the pylorus keeps chyme in the stomach until it reaches the right consistency to pass into the small intestine. Chyme is then squirted down into the small intestine, where digestion of food continues so the body can absorb the nutrients into the bloodstream. Most substances in the food we eat need further digestion and must travel into the small intestine. Carbohydrates, for example, spend the least amount of time in the stomach (because the mouth did the job) , while protein stays in the stomach longer, and fats the longest.

The mucosa of the small intestine contains many folds that are covered with tiny finger like projections called villi. In turn, the villi are covered with microscopic projections called microvilli. These structures create a vast surface area through which nutrients can be absorbed. Sugars are digested in one step. An enzyme in the lining of the small intestine digests sucrose, also known as table sugar, into glucose and fructose, which are absorbed through the intestine into the blood. Milk contains another type of sugar, lactose, which is changed into absorb-able molecules by another enzyme in the intestinal lining. Specialized cells allow absorbed materials to cross the mucosa into the blood, where they are carried off in the bloodstream to other parts of the body for storage or further chemical change. The small intestine is made up of three parts: the duodenum, the jejunum, and the ileum. The small intestine then uses enzymatic and bacterial breakdown to make smaller and smaller particles for absorption.The small intestine is approximately 23 feet long!

Fiber is indigestible and moves through the digestive tract without being broken down by enzymes. Many foods contain both soluble and insoluble fiber. Soluble fiber dissolves easily in water and takes on a soft, gel-like texture in the intestines. Insoluble fiber, on the other hand, passes essentially unchanged through the intestines. Foods such as meat, eggs, and beans consist of giant molecules of protein that must be digested by enzymes before they can be used to build and repair body tissues. An enzyme in the juice of the stomach starts the digestion of swallowed protein. Then in the small intestine, several enzymes from the pancreatic juice and the lining of the intestine complete the breakdown of huge protein molecules into small molecules called amino acids. These small molecules can be absorbed through the small intestine into the blood and then be carried to all parts of the body to build the walls and other parts of cells.

Caffeine Wisdom

Let's talk about caffeine and the protein relationship you must know for good health. Caffeine has tanic acid in it. We use tanic acid to tan leather, right? When you drink caffeine on an empty stomach, which is what most people do, the tanic acid mixes with the hydrochloric acid and creates a hardening effect on your stomach lining, preventing your body from properly breaking down proteins. Uh oh!! We are protein producing machines. Our muscles, skin, hair, and major components of our bodies are protein. It also kills your bowel flora which is vitally important for bacterial breakdown into smaller particles for absorption. By the way, never take flora when you are on an antibiotic. It gives the antibiotic something else to kill other than your illness or infection. Wait until after the antibiotic is gone, to take flora and then pound it!

Caffeine can be consumed without harm by eating protein first and then taking a bowel flora at night to replace the flora it killed. Caffeine should be used in extreme moderation and with wisdom. Do not let it take the place of your water!

Enzymes and hormones regulate the body's water balance and maintain proper pH. They also assist in the exchange of nutrients between inter-cellular fluids, tissues and lymph. Proteins form the structural basis of chromosomes passed from parent to child. Proteins are chains of amino acids linked together by peptide bonds. Dietary protein is broken down into amino acids which the body then uses to build the specific proteins it needs.

Amino Acids are the carriers of the chemicals that carry information from one nerve cell to another (neurotransmitters) and can pass through the blood brain barrier. This is a kind of defensive shield to protect the brain from toxins. Additionally, Amino Acids enable vitamins and minerals to properly do their jobs. Various symptoms mean low levels of amino acids. By the way, if you need an amino acid and you take the right one, you will have an immediate chemical shift in your mood and body within 15 minutes. This response will last several hours.

Once the balance is found again and maintained for a few months, the body takes over and does the job itself. We have to maintain healthy diets that support this chemical change and those who are using various supplements to achieve well-being rather than adjusting their diet and re-balancing their body chemistry, are still on a search to find a healthy balance. Another

115

vital part of food that is absorbed through the small intestine are vitamins. The two types of vitamins are classified by the fluid in which they can be dissolved: water-soluble vitamins (all the B vitamins and vitamin C) and fat-soluble vitamins (vitamins A, D, E, and K). Fat-soluble vitamins are stored in the liver and fatty tissue of the body, whereas water-soluble vitamins are not easily stored and excess amounts are flushed out in the urine. This is why your urine turns yellow when you are on B vitamins. Most of the material absorbed through the small intestine is water in which salt is dissolved. The salt and water come from the food and liquid you swallow and the juices secreted by the many digestive glands.

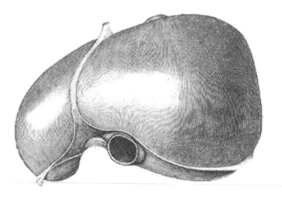

The Liver

The liver, produces yet another digestive enzyme—bile. Bile is stored between meals in the gallbladder. No worries, Angel, if you do not have a gallbladder your liver still produces bile. You just have to be moderate in your healthy fat intake and eat it slowly. At mealtime, it is squeezed out of the gallbladder, through the bile ducts, and into the intestine to mix with the fat in food. The bile acids dissolve fat into the watery contents of the intestine, much like detergents that dissolve grease from a frying pan. After fat is dissolved, it is digested by enzymes from the pancreas and the lining of the intestine.

Fat molecules are a rich source of energy for the body. The first step in digestion of a fat such as butter is to dissolve it into the watery content of the intestine. The bile acids produced by the liver dissolve fat into tiny droplets and allow pancreatic and intestinal enzymes to break the large fat molecules into smaller

116

ones. Some of these small molecules are fatty acids and cholesterol. The bile acids combine with the fatty acids and cholesterol and help these molecules move into the cells of the mucosa. In these cells the small molecules are formed back into large ones, most of which pass into vessels called lymphatics near the intestine. These small vessels carry the reformed fat to the veins of the chest, and the blood carries the fat to storage depots in different parts of the body.

The liver, the gallbladder, and the pancreas are not part of the alimentary canal, but these organs are still important for healthy digestion. The pancreas produces enzymes that help digest proteins, fats, and carbohydrates. It also makes a substance that neutralizes stomach acid. Good thing because the stomach acid would eat holes in you. The liver produces bile, which helps the body absorb fat. Bile is stored in the gallbladder until it is needed. These enzymes and bile travel through special ducts directly into the small intestine, where they help to break down food.

It is important to make healthy food choices such as organic, etc. The liver also plays a major role in the handling and processing of nutrients. These nutrients are carried to the liver in the blood from the small and large intestines. The major hormones that control the functions of the digestive system are produced and released by cells in the mucosa of the stomach and small intestine. These hormones are released into the blood of the digestive tract, travel back to the heart and through the arteries, and return to the digestive system where they stimulate digestive juices and cause organ movement.

The main hormones that control digestion are gastrin, secretin, and cholecystokinin (CCK). Gastrin causes the stomach to produce an acid for dissolving and digesting some foods. Gastrin is also necessary for normal cell growth in the lining of the stomach, small intestine, and colon. Secretin causes the pancreas to send out a digestive juice that is rich in bicarbonate. The bicarbonate helps neutralize the acidic stomach contents as they enter the small intestine. Secretin also stimulates the stomach to produce pepsin, an enzyme that digests protein, and stimulates the liver to produce bile. CCK causes the pancreas to produce the enzymes of pancreatic juice, and causes the gallbladder to empty. It also promotes normal cell growth of the pancreas. Additional hormones in the digestive system regulate appetite. Ghrelin is produced in the stomach and upper intestine in the absence of food in the digestive system and stimulates appetite. Peptide is produced in the digestive tract in response to a meal in the system and inhibits appetite. Both of these hormones work on the brain to help regulate the intake of food for energy. From the small intestine, food that has been digested (and some water) travels to the large intestine through a valve that prevents food from returning to the small intestine.

Most medical professionals are under the illusion that the colon is not so important. They teach that the only purpose of the large intestine is for evacuation purposes. Eastern medicine teachings are much different, and over 1000 year old! They teach that the large intestine is the gateway to health. They believe, live and teach to clean the bowels first before healing can happen. Many indigenous people worldwide also know the absolute value of cleaning the system before healing is possible. What I have discovered in working with colons for over 20 years is that the colon is the MAIN absorber of our nutrients. It is the most important not the least. The colon is 5 to 6 feet long!

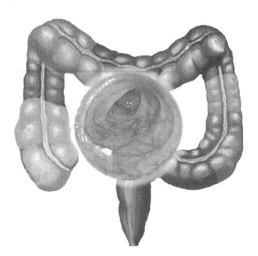

Ayurveda Medicine

I want to give you a brief overview of the 3 Doshas in Ayurveda medicine. Ayurveda medicine is over 1000 years old. It has helped me to understand myself and my digestive system and many other things about myself. I recommend you check out Deepak Chopra or other great teachers of this ancient and profound information. The three Doshas are Vata, Pitta, and Kapha. Pitta is responsible for metabolism and digestion. Kapha

118

governs the structure of the body and Vata controls all movement.

Vata types have a light thin build. They like to walk and do things quickly, to be hungry at any time, and love fun and excitement. They have a tendency to worry, have sleep issues and constipation.

Pitta types are enterprising and intense. They are warm and loving and can be ravenously hungry if dinner is 5 minutes late. I am like that. Pittas rarely like spicy food because they have a lot of heat in the digestion.

Kapha type are relaxed and naturally strong. They are peaceful and happy and great to have in an emergency. I call them the energizer bunnies. They have great stamina and tend to be athletic. They usually carry extra weight when out of balance. I think they make the best cooks because they do not have such a fire in their bellies. They like spicy food that helps speed up the digestion.

Toxic Overload

It is essential that our diet and digestion are optimal, and toxins are removed from the body the way they are supposed to. If the diet is not proper or the digestion is poor, it results in the accumulation of partially digested food in the body. This partially digested food, in association with bile from the gall bladder and the bowel bacteria, results in the formation of what Ayurvedic medicine calls 'ama' or 'toxins.' These toxic materials are absorbed in the body, and, over time, block the body's ability to absorb essential nutrients, sometimes known as auto-intoxication.

Auto intoxication is when every cell of the body is affected by poisoning. When the toxins accumulate in the nervous system, one becomes depressed and irritable. When one feels weak, it indicates toxins have backed up into the heart. If one is bloated and has foul breath, toxins have reached the stomach and intestines. If poisons try to escape through the skin, other systems are overloaded. Our skin is the last place where toxins show up: blotchy rashes develop or one looks pale and the skin appears to be much older than their actual age.

Toxic overload is caused by exposure to air pollutants, cigarettes, alcohol, and junk food and of course, toxic thoughts. Anything we intake or breathe that is negative for our bodies, coupled with parasites can cause toxic overload. We can become allergic to life. The four cleansing systems of the body are the lungs, kidneys, skin and bowel. With toxic bowel syndrome, which is a side effect of toxic overload, the excess of toxins absorbed from a clogged bowel goes to the liver. The liver is then over-burdened, eventually unable to cope with the toxic load and toxins start to spill into the blood stream.

Chemically sensitive people can't deal with the smell of life. People have come to Angel Farms and complained about the shampoos or candles people use that have smells in them. I too make decisions on whether this candle is going to be a chemically perfumed candle or if it comes from a natural scent. I love candles. I don't move the candle anymore; I used to. Chemically sensitive people just see the candle, without even smelling it and turn and run! They feel they can't be in there because of the candle, because you color your hair, because you wear lavender essential oil, oh no! People lose their sense of smell, because of their rejection of it. Be aware of how powerful the mind is. You will eventually lose your sense of taste. If you can't smell something before you take it into your mouth, you are not using some of your taste buds in the way your body can activate the specific enzymes and electrolytes effecting the digestion. If you have chemical sensitivities are you free or are you in prison? You can still have your choice of what you put on yourself but that doesn't mean you have to judge what others put in their space or on their body.

What can we do to correct this misperception so you can move back into life instead of stepping out of it? I recommend that you start seeing everything as God and keep it a secret. Become like a mocking bird with this song resting sweetly on its tongue. — Hafiz.

 **One guy, Cory from Oregon—**
Miracle Story   drove 22 hours to see me in LA.
10 years before he did the Cleanse he had been pummeled in his face, beaten up to a point where his cheekbone was broken and his eyeball literally fell back into the socket— in the sinus cavity. That is what actually saved his eye; there was lots of blood in there and it kept the eyeball moist. They wrapped him up, sent him to the hospital and he had multiple reconstructive surgeries. The irony is that the guy beat up the wrong person; as if

there are accidents!? Cory didn't hold anything against him that was judgmental or hateful or critical—that is why he healed so well- literally why. When somebody does those things to you—bless them- bless them- bless them-bless them anyway. Otherwise, it's difficult for the body to heal—you are carrying issues about it. Instead think, wow this happened to me and how can I heal—how do I let it go? How do I not go into resistance because of what somebody did to me? On the 5th day of his cleanse his tongue started going completely numb—he could hardly swallow water—and he couldn't eat at all. It also smelled like someone had dropped a big quart bottle of anesthesia on the floor---and it permeated the whole room. What was coming out of him was the anesthesia from all the surgeries! He hadn't even accessed that he couldn't smell or taste until they came back 100%. He was like a little kid—oh can you taste this? Can you taste this? WOW! 10 years later.

Miracle Story

Sally is a sweet Angel who had an amazing story.

She had such chemical sensitivities that she had not left her house for nine years! If she would smell someone's shampoo, it would put her into a seizure. She pulled all the carpets out of the house. Her twin daughters did not appreciate their mother very much either because they had to live her life and buy her underwear, toothpaste, food, and everything! Kids really don't want to live the lives of their mothers or fathers because they have their own lives to live. She was sponsored to come and do the Cleanse by her friend of 20 years. Sally came with a face mask and was very unhappy. On the third day of the Cleanse after her session with me she SHIFTED! She became un-allergic to life! On the 5th day of the Cleanse she went out on Kahuna Road and hitch- hiked to the coconut market place. She wanted to get some painted coconuts that she could mail to her daughters. When she told me this I asked her how the car smelled. She said she didn't notice! Miracle one! She was then guided into an art gallery. Most people with chemical sensitivities would not go into an art gallery. Canvas and paint smells can be strong, and again she did not notice! Miracle two! She was then guided to a painting of a chair by a window. It had nice shadows and color but was still just a simple chair by a window. But then she started to see a light growing in the chair. She realized that the light was her and

121

she was now ready and able to get out of the chair and Live!! And guess what the name of the painting was...the name of it was "Sally's Chair." It took me 3 months to track down the artist and let him know that because he listened to his inspiration on what to name his painting; he was a part of Sally's miracle. Miracles happen. Sally had to come all the way from California to Kauai to find this miracle. She was able to go to her children's sport games with lots of people and even helped them to get full scholarships. She is now living life!

It is important that you really love and feed your bodies well. If you have trouble really integrating your mind and body, thus accepting and recognizing your body's needs over your mind's driving enthusiasm, I recommend quieting the mind, drinking more water, feeding your spirit, eating more vegetables, loving and blessing even more, and thereby getting back into the present moment! It is a delicious one! Here are some great facts about food and nutrition you may like.

Eating Organic!!

In awareness we choose organic. We choose naturally, locally grown fruits and vegetables. We buy dairy products and local meats that are growth hormone free. We chew our food. We have a lot of variety in our lives. We understand how the body works. We develop an awesome respect for the body temple we move around in and what exactly lives within us! We laugh and live a more innocent and childlike life. Every moment is precious and delicious. We may not always be able to eat organic foods, however; we make the best and most loving life giving choices each time we eat.

Of course adding your gratitude and blessings makes all the difference. Why go organic? We do so to protect the future generations, to prevent soil erosion, to protect water quality, to save energy, and to keep chemicals off our plates and out of our bodies. When we protect small farmers and their worker's health, support a true economy, and promote biodiversity- everything tastes better. I look forward to the day when all restaurants go organic. Do you ask? Are you insisting you have organic non-chemical laced food and drink for you and your loved ones? I do.

I remember growing up in Idaho when my dad reached his hand into the corn hopper to unplug it and his arm would come out purple. (Chemical lased corn.) He had a massive heart attack and died at only 53! Was it related to these chemicals? He was never told of the dangers of these chemicals. I believe many farmers still do not know how toxic these chemicals are to themselves and to the land.

Genetically Modified Organism (GMO)

A genetically modified organism (GMO) or genetically engineered organism (GEO) is an organism whose genetic material has been altered using genetic engineering techniques. These techniques use DNA molecules from different sources, which are combined into one molecule to create a new set of genes. This DNA is then transferred into an organism, giving it modified or novel genes. Transgenic organisms, a subset of GMOs, are organisms which have inserted DNA that originated in a different species. In other words, a Scientist takes a segment of a DNA chain and removes it and then takes a segment of salmonella, or botulism, or Roundup and they then put it in the missing link they just removed. Then the intelligence of the plant does not see the new addition as harmful. For instance, corn thinks roundup is a part of itself. It then allows the harmful stuff in. What does this do to our bodies? It makes our DNA chain then think salmonella and botulism and roundup are OK! I believe and feel they are not. Could this be setting the world up for an epidemic? Do your own research and be aware of this unnatural practice of manipulating nature. This practice also destroys the crops next door and can spread from there. Large storage of grains have been contaminated and burned! Even ancient seed! The largest share of the GMO crops planted globally are owned by the US firm Monsanto. I sure hope these people are doing their homework first! Are they hurting us and the earth or even hurting themselves and their families!

In 2007, Monsanto's trait technologies were planted on 246 million acres throughout the world, a growth of 13 percent from 2006. In the corn market, Monsanto's triple-stack corn—which combines Roundup Ready 2 weed control technology with YieldGard Corn Borer and YieldGard Rootworm insect control—is the market leader in the United States. U.S. corn farmers planted more than 32 million acres of triple-stack corn in 2008, and it is estimated the product could be planted on 56 million acres in 2014-2015. In the cotton market, Bollgard II with Roundup Ready Flex was planted on approximately 5 million acres of U.S. cotton in 2008. According to the International Service for the Acquisition of Agri-Biotech Applications (ISAAA), of the approximately 14

123

million farmers who grew biotech crops in 2009, some 90% were resource-poor farmers in developing countries. Monsanto gives everyone a good deal and promises to buy their crops. These include some 7 million farmers in the cotton-growing areas of China, an estimated 5.6 million small farmers in India, 250,000 in the Philippines, South Africa (biotech cotton, maize and soybeans often grown by subsistence women farmers) and the other twelve developing countries which grew biotech crops in 2009. 10 million more small and resource-poor farmers may have been secondary beneficiaries of BT cotton in China.

The global commercial value of biotech crops grown in 2008 was estimated to be US$130 billion. Do you think money and lack of integrity might be a part of this? The safety of GMOs in the food chain has been questioned by some environmental groups, with concerns such as the possibilities that GMOs could introduce new allergens into foods, or contribute to the spread of antibiotic resistance. All studies published to date have shown no adverse health effects resulting from humans eating genetically modified foods, however, environmental groups still discourage consumption in many countries, claiming that GMO foods are unnatural and therefore unsafe. Such concerns have led to the adoption of laws and regulations that require safety testing of any new organism produced for human consumption.

What is going on worldwide?

Several states of Australia had placed bans on planting GMO food crops, beginning in 2003. In 2005, a standing committee of the government of Prince Edward Island (PEI) in Canada assessed a proposal to ban the production of GMOs in the province. The ban was not passed. As of January 2008, the use of GMO was rapidly increasing. Mainland Canada is one of the world's largest producers of GMO canola.

Japan

As of 2009, Japan has no commercial farming of any kind of genetically modified food. Consumers have strongly resisted both imports and attempts to grow GMO in the country. Campaigns by consumer groups and environmental groups, such as

Consumers Union of Japan and Greenpeace Japan, as well as local campaigns, have been very successful. In Hokkaido, a special bylaw has made it virtually impossible to grow GMOs. GMO Campaigns collected over 200,000 signatures to oppose GMO farming. Way to go Japan. We can do this too! Cross-pollination has commonly occurred in Japan, as canola seed is imported from Canada. Around ports and the roads to major food oil companies, GMO canola has now been found growing wild. Imported canola seeds have been found to be GMO varieties, including the Roundup Ready and Liberty Link types not grown in Japan. Activists and local groups, as well as the No! GMO Campaign and others, are alarmed that imported GMOs may harm the biodiversity and cause irreversible damage.

Pakistan

Monsanto once tried to sell their hybrid seeds of important crops such as wheat and rice via the government. Even though yields would have increased, it would have made the Pakistani population dependent on the seeds of one company. The contract was never given.

New Zealand

In New Zealand, no genetically modified food is grown and no medicines containing live genetically-modified organisms have been approved for use. However, medicines manufactured using genetically modified organisms that do not contain live organisms have been approved for sale.

United States

In 2004, Mendocino County, California became the first county in the United States to ban the production of GMOs. The measure passed with a 57% majority. In California, Trinity and Marin counties have also imposed bans on GMO crops, while ordinances to do so were unsuccessful in Butte, Lake, San Luis Obispo, Humboldt, and Sonoma counties. Supervisors in the agriculturally-rich counties of Fresno, Kern, Kings, Solano, Sutter, and Tulare have passed resolutions supporting the practice.

Zambia

The Zambian government has launched a campaign to educate and increase awareness of the benefits of biotechnology, including genetically modified crops, in order to change negative public opinion. Could it be there is a lot of money behind Monsanto to manipulate public opinion by not educating people of the hazards?

Eastern and Southern Africa

In 2010, after nine years of talks, the Common Market for Eastern and Southern Africa (COMESA) produced a draft policy on GMO technology. This proposed policy was sent to all 19 national governments for consultation in September 2010. Under the policy, a member country which wants to grow a new GMO crop would inform COMESA who would have sufficient scientific expertise to make the decision as to whether the crop was safe for the environment and for humans. At the moment, few countries have the resources to make their own decisions. Once COMESA had made their decision, permission would be granted for the crop to be grown in all 19 member countries. Member countries would retain the power not to grow the crop in their own country if they wanted.

France

The cultivation of Monsanto's corn was forbidden in France on February 9, of 2008. It was the only GMO authorized in France. The safeguard measure is taken as far as side effects on human health will be known. In 2010 Marion Guillou, president of the National Institute for Agronomical Research and one of France's top farm researchers, said she can no longer work on developing new GMOs due to widespread distrust and even hostility by European consumers.

Germany

Germany placed a ban on the cultivation and sale of GMO maize in April 2009.

Where is the proof they are not harmful? Why is Mansanto so secret? Listen to your heart on this and not potential propaganda from the food companies. If we stop buying the products-ncluding the seeds- things will change. Research both sides of the story always! Make your own informed choices on how you want your world to be and you become the change! It starts with one!

Angel Graduate Ray with tugofwarseeds.com can get non-GMO seeds.

Food Awareness
Get ready for an Enlightened moment.

Eating becomes your meditation. Imagine you are inside an organic peach coming to blossom. Listen to the bees huming. Notice the rain and sunshine. See the farmers and helpers. As the peaches grow, see the farmer and the workers smiling as you ripen. The first one ripens, they squish it to see how juicy it is. Now it is picked and goes to the market. Where you can choose it. Break it open as you sit in your porch chair. Smell and Taste the nectar of the peach. Gratefully celebrate all the sunshine, the bees, the rain and the wind. Remember the hands that brought it to you. Remember the earth that gave of herself for you. All of this becomes part of you. You are one with the elements.

Why do you think the Creator of the Universe put more veggies than any other form of food on the planet? Second is fruit, third is protein and forth is grain. Eat from the variety of the abundance in nature. That is the way the earth is designed and because you are a part of the earth, follow what is the most abundant for your best health. Ayurveda defines healing as a process of extracting intelligence from food and then processing it to support the intelligence inherent in the entire body and returning the body to its own natural functions.

I have been taught by my Native American teachers to eat from a radius of 500 miles from where you are. This keeps you connected to your living environment. Eat in abundance of the season and have a lot a variety. Enjoy your food! Support the local organic farmers. Shop with consciousness. You have total control of what nutrients your body gets, so choose well. Enjoy the honey from the bees that buzz in your community. Start by gradually modifying your existing diet to incorporate as many of the local foods as possible. Many small adjustments can collectively have a measurable impact on your health. If you are ill it is best to return to the foods you grew up on. For example, if you grew up in Idaho, eat Idaho grown potatoes. The molecular structure of the potatoes have the necessary nutrients to help your body heal. The elements that you pulled from the earth to create your body in utero are what your body recognizes to speed up the healing process.

We owe our very existence to the plant kingdom. Even the air we breathe is a gift from the plant world. We breathe in

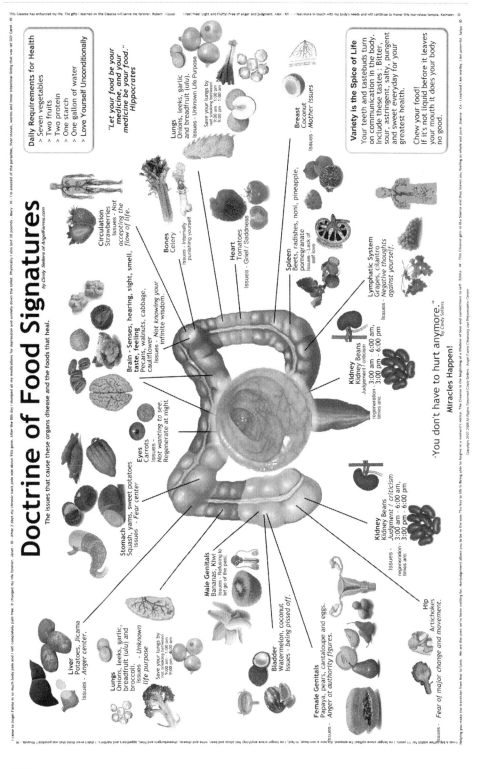

oxygen from them and breathe out carbon dioxide for them. They breathe in carbon dioxide from us and release oxygen for us. What a relationship with our earth we have! Every health need of the human body is found in plants. Plants obtain food from the Earth for us and turn it into a form that we can use. Throughout history, man has sought a remedy for his ailments in the fields and woods

The Doctrine of Food Signatures —Chart by Cindy Sellers

The Doctrine of Food Signatures has been an idea of herbalists for centuries, but it did not become part of the medical thinking until the middle of the seventeenth century. In simple terms, the "Doctrine of Signatures" is the idea that God has marked everything He created with a sign (signature). The Doctrine states that, by observation, one can determine from the color of the flowers or roots, the shape of the leaves, the place of growing, or other signatures, what the plant's purpose was in God's plan and how that feeds and nourishes the body.

In the 1500s, a master physician and herbalist named Paracelsus originated the Doctrine of Signatures. He and many others of the time believed that the shape, color, taste, smell and other properties of a plant gave hints of its use in healing. For instance, he observed that the leaf of an herb used to treat the liver was in fact shaped like the liver. Red and bitter indicated that a plant was good for the blood and the heart, yellow and sweet were good for the spleen and as a treatment for jaundice, and black and salty were good for the lungs. You are what you eat, so eat well. What has been found in the past is now being confirmed by today's scientists. It proves that every whole food has a pattern that resembles a body organ and that this pattern acts as a sign as to which specific organ they may benefit.

My chart on the Doctrine of Food Signatures shows that every living thing is marked with a specific food signature that gives an indication for its intended use. For example, a carrot is full of beta carotene that feeds our wonderful eyes and when cut, resembles the iris of an eye! Science shows that carrots greatly enhance blood flow and function of the eyes.

Amazing! Here is just a short list of some other of Food Signatures.

A Tomato has four chambers and is red. The heart is red and has four chambers. All of the research shows tomatoes are indeed pure heart and blood food.

Grapes hang in a cluster and look like your lymph system. . Each grape looks like a blood cell and all of the research today shows that grapes are also a lymph and blood vitalizing food.

A Walnut looks like a little brain, a left and right hemisphere, upper cerebrums and lower cerebellums. Even the wrinkles or folds are on the nut just like the neo-cortex. We now know that walnuts help develop over 3 dozen neuron-transmitters for brain function.

Kidney Beans actually heal and help maintain kidney function and yes, they look exactly like the human kidneys.

Celery, Bokchoy, and Rhubarb look just like bones. These foods specifically target bone strength. Bones are 23% sodium and these foods are 23% sodium. If you don't have enough sodium in your diet the body pulls it from the bones, making them weak. These foods replenish the skeletal needs of the body. They are also high in silica which is necessary for cartilage regeneration between the bones.

Eggplant, avocados, papayas and pears target the health and function of the womb and cervix of the female, they look just like these organs. Today's research shows that when a woman eats 1 avocado a week, it balances hormones, sheds unwanted birth weight and prevents cervical cancers. And how profound is this? It takes exactly 9 months to grow an avocado from blossom to ripened fruit.

There are over 14,000 photolytic chemical constituents of nutrition in each one of these foods (modern science has only studied and named about 141 of them). Figs are full of seeds and hang in twos when they grow. Figs increase the mobility of male sperm and increase the numbers of sperm as well, to over-come male sterility. Sweet Potatoes look like the pancreas and actually balance the glycemic index of diabetics. Olives assist the health and function of the ovaries. Coconuts look just like the breasts of the female and actually assist the health of the breasts and the movement of lymph in and out of the breasts. Onions, leeks and garlic look like lungs! When we have lung illnesses we crave onions and garlic to help the lungs heal. Today's research shows that onions help clear waste materials from all of the body cells. They even produce tears which wash the epithelial layers of the eyes.

Eggs and Amino Acids!

Eggs contain all nine essential amino acids used for our growth and development, making them an excellent source of easily digestible protein. One large egg contains 6 grams of high quality protein. Scientists use eggs as the standard for measuring the protein quality of other foods. At 93.7%, eggs score higher than any other food. The protein is almost equally split between the egg white and the egg yolk. Egg Whites are an excellent source of biologically valued protein because they provide the only protein, which is instantly absorbed by the body.

Other high protein foods such as beef, fish, chicken, and turkey must first be broken down before your body can absorb the available protein. Even then, not everyone can metabolize meat protein properly. The same goes for protein powders and other meal replacements. It should also be noted that egg whites have no fat, and no cholesterol. The amino acid content of a raw or cooked egg is basically the same.

Free Range Eggs

If you choose to be vegan, eat non fertilized free range eggs. Eggs raised without roosters can never hatch. Gandhi even saved his daughter-in-law because she was protein deficient and starving to death. He told his son to feed her non- fertilized eggs (no rooster) and she lived! When eggs are produced commercially (where the chickens are put into tiny pens with artificial lights) an egg drops about every 24 hours and goes down a conveyor belt. Someone cleans it and stamps it, puts it in a carton and it goes off to your store! These eggs are low in lecithin, which makes your cholesterol go UP! And now there are many instances of salmonella coming from the unconscious egg farmers. If your eggs come from aware chicken farmers that care about their chickens, you will never have a carton of eggs in your fridge that have to be recalled. If you have a free range chicken that gets to run around and scratch in the dirt, and she gets natural sunlight, then the eggs become very high in lecithin which lowers cholesterol and they taste much better too! Happy chickens doing what happy chickens love. Fertilized or not doesn't matter to lecithin level, only dirt, love, and sunshine! The epidemic of higher cholesterol in the US started when farmers caged chickens in tiny pens to make more money. This is when people were told to restrict how many eggs they could eat per week. Do you know that right now we have egg producers in America that do not care about your health or the health of the chicken? Be Aware Angel. Know your food and know your meat. And remember, moderation in all things except loving and drinking water. Besides, what a wonderful gift you can give back to the chicken by supporting their happiness!

Protein is essential to maintain lean muscle mass. Lean mass optimizes your metabolic rate and an increase in muscle mass leads to an increase in calories burnt at rest. On average people require between 1.5-3 grams of protein per kilo of lean mass to maintain health and efficiency. Eggs are a great resource and you can grow your own!!!! Another great source of protein is whey, the clear liquid drained off milk during the making of cheese or ghee. It contains protein and all 8 essential amino acids, but not in sufficient quantity to be a sole source of protein unless you plan to eat over 2 cups or 133 grams per day. None the less, whey (acid or sweet) is a complete protein. Amino acid pills vary a lot and it depends on the source and structure of the protein. Gelatin and corn contain protein, but are incomplete sources because they don't contain all 8 essential amino acids. Amino Acids are the chemical building blocks that make up proteins. Proteins are essential to life and provide the structure for all living things. Proteins are necessary for every living cell and next to water proteins make up the greatest portion of our body weight. Your body uses protein to build and repair tissue. Some cells in your body are replaced rather frequently and need protein in their structure.

Goat Milk

Goat milk, another great protein is used for human consumption. In fact, more people in the world drink goat's milk than cow's milk, although in the US the opposite is true. Goat milk protein forms a softer curd (the term given to the protein clumps that are formed by the action of your stomach acid on the protein), because it contains smaller fat globules which make the protein more easily and rapidly digestible, which gives an advantage to lactose-intolerant persons. Moving rapidly through the stomach could be an advantage to infants and children who regurgitate cow's milk easily. Goat's milk may also have advantages when it comes to allergies. Goat's milk contains only trace amounts of an allergenic casein protein, alpha-S1, found in cow's milk. Goat's milk casein is more similar to human milk. Goat's milk contains slightly lower levels of lactose (4.1 percent versus 4.7 percent in cow's milk). Although the mineral content of goat's milk and cow's milk is generally similar, goat's milk contains 13 percent more calcium, 25 percent more vitamin B-6, 47 percent more vitamin A, 134 percent more potassium, and three times more niacin. It is also four times higher in copper. Goat's milk also contains 27 percent more of the antioxidant selenium than cow's milk. Cow's milk contains five times as much vitamin B-12 as goat's milk and ten times as much folic acid (12 mcg. in cow's milk versus 1 mcg. for goat's milk per eight ounces with an RDA of 75-100 mcg. for children). The fact that goat's milk contains less than ten percent of the amount of folic acid contained in cow's milk means that it must be supplemented with folic acid in order to be adequate as a formula or milk substitute for infants and toddlers, and popular brands of goat's milk may advertise "supplemented with folic acid" on the carton. I hope this information will help tender bellies.

.

Eating Before Bed

It is best to not eat after 10 pm. The liver collapses and rests at night. When people get up and eat in the middle of the night, they activate the liver which is supposed to be collapsed and resting. Most of the body is in resting mode, not in a working mode, and when you eat, you are turning on the digestive system, the metabolism, the electrolytes, and the body no longer has the chance to rest. When people eat in the middle of the night, they also don't wake up really rested. The liver is not able to do its functions properly because of the activation.

Many people ask how I have so much information about the human body. I receive research studies from Stanford University, the University of Washington, the Dallas/Fort Worth Medical Journal and the New England Journal of Medicine. I regularly receive and read the research studies on various topics such as why women crave chocolate before their menstrual cycle. A study done by the University of Washington with over 200 participants did a study on why women crave chocolate before their cycles. They found that cocoa had the highest source of bioflavinoids of any food, the particular kind that strengthens blood vessels. Cocoa also had a specific relaxant for nerve endings. Who knew? Our intuition is so amazing, even worldwide.

Now Angel, let's talk about becoming more body conscious; learning the language of your body. Your body is talking to you. We often put a Band-Aid over what our body is trying to tell us instead of figuring out the message. Here are some examples. Don't feel good, take a pain pill. Don't feel good, drink something. Don't feel good, smoke something, emotionally over run have a cigarette.

This is the way our whole culture handles everything, which is to slap a band aid on it and keep working. In our society you are valued by what you do and not how you are, which justifies your existence. Walking as a god or goddess as the divine instead of walking as a slave to society is a great gift to all of us. Just walking in peace and love is enough. Remember, Angel, you are a seed of God/Love, not the seed of man! Do what you en-joy. You are free; you needn't be a slave to this culture's social consciousness or your pocket books or your family, culture or religion. Sometimes we feel safer inside the cage, because it is what we have known all our lives. The cage door is open. Are you ready to spread your wings and fly?

Remember that most headaches are caused by dehydration so drink some water! We think we are hungry, and we may just be thirsty. If you constantly crave sugar, and if you are kinda 'itchy' around the full moon, maybe you have parasites. If you hurt in your knees, you may be inflexible and stubborn, if you hurt in your lower back, you are worrying about money, if you hurt in your eyes you don't want to see something, if you hurt in your liver you are angry! Every time you hurt you are asked to look at something you are not loving. Love is the healer!

Do you have a friend that says things like I don't want to eat here because it is not organic, not vegan, or its not vegetarian? This limits a person's ability to see God every where. Just send the vibration of gratitude that if you ask, you will be fed. If someone makes you a cheesecake with love eat it with gratitude. Notice the main ingredient is love. There will be something wonderful for you, if you go in and bless it and be thankful, your gratitude as the Seed of God, it puts more energy of wholeness into the food than you can even imagine. I have read studies of Masters eating poison and transmuting it. It's all God anyway. Be aware of the Macro diet, micro diet, vegan diet, raw food diet, or fruitarian diet, or the 'can't have' diets. These only confuse the human experience. Instead, remember to love yourself enough to feed your body good food, and goodwater, and good love and watch what the food does in your body.Easy to eat 7 different vegetables, 2 fruits, 2 proteins, 1 carb/starch, 1 gallon of water every day for full health. Keep it simple and fresh and fun. Allow yourself 10% grace in all things, it keeps you out of judgment. Is this doable? Even teachable? Of course!

Parasites

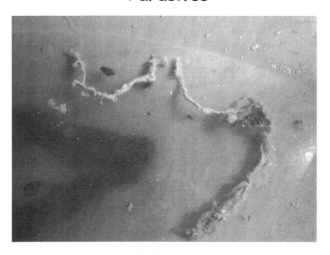

I am going to talk to you now about an uncomfortable subject to most people. I have seen more parasites than probably most people on the planet. No Kidding! Parasite literally means "one who eats off the table of another." Parasites exist in every country of the world. At least 85-95% of the American Population has parasites, (worms). I have never met anyone who did not have some worms, until they don't anymore! The Cleanse clears their homes and then they have no place to live.

There are over 120 different kinds of parasites that we can see with a naked eye. Medical tests are available on 40-50 types. This explains why many who come and do the Cleanse have had tests done and found nothing. During the Cleanse, we actually see parasites and worms coming out of their bodies. Many feel it is important to know where they came from. I let them know, it does not matter. Parasites are associated with parasitical thoughts and behaviors of fear, eating you up. Some of the most common varieties are: fish parasites, tapeworm, roundworms, pin worms, flukes, whip worms, hookworms, single-celled protozoa, and trichinae.

Large and small parasites emit secretions, which are poisonous in our bodies and must be neutralized. These poisons can be debilitating. At lower levels, the toxins stress the immune system to the point where a variety of health challenges may develop. Parasites live within our bodies, feeding off our energy, our cells, our blood, and the food and supplements we use. Some people feed them very well. Larger parasites are usually located in the digestive tract where they can reside for decades. The biggest ones I have found are on the right side of the body. They get all the good food coming in from the small intestine. I have seen them 6 feet long!

Hookworms will migrate down the digestive track and attach themselves to the intestinal walls, then proceed to ingest their host's nutrient rich blood. Tapeworms also live in the intestines and absorb nutrition through their skin. People with a weakened immune system tend to frequently feel tired, often diagnosed as Chronic Fatigue Syndrome, really have parasites eating their food and life-force. Fear not, Beloved Angel. parasites are associated with parasitical thoughts and behaviors of fear. How much fear are you willing to release to be free from these life forms?

I had a beautiful Angel, Lynn come to do the Cleanse. She was on SSI and had been diagnosed with chronic fatigue syndrome for 17 years. She slept over 15 hours a day. On the 6th day of the Cleanse she passed a 3 foot tapeworm that was just lying in her transverse colon and she could not get nutrients to her brain properly. The next day she WAS BACK!!! She is now teaching and editing and living again. We still survive because the body robs other areas for survival. It sacrifices itself to live.

We live in a mobile and social environment. Exposure to parasites is unavoidable. Parasites can be contracted through fruits, vegetables, grains, seeds, nuts and ANY raw or undercooked animal flesh, and through your feet and hands.

Pinworm is the most common of the roundworm type found in the USA. Pin worms are passed in crowded areas such as schools, day cares, hospitals and anywhere groups of people gather. Transmission is easy and re-infection rate is high. This is similar to lice infestation. It takes diligence and is worth the effort to be free of these little irritations. I have found many people report having pin-worms when young and were too embarrassed to tell anyone. This does not mean they have disappeared. We see them all the time at Angel Farms. An easy natural method to help with pin-worms is to get some zinc oxide and put it around the anus before bed around full moon. They come out to lay the eggs and the zinc oxide kills them. It is easy to do for children and causes no harm. If you have anal itching and irritations around full moon you might have pin worms.

Some common symptoms of parasites can be remaining hungry after meals, having constant gas and bloating, unusual intestinal movement, like the "butterfly" feeling during pregnancy, grinding teeth while asleep and anal itching especially around the full moon. Parasites are more active around the full moon! If one transforms the environment of the body, the parasites will have to leave or die.

Parasite Wisdom

Wash your hands often! Wear gloves whenever you clean the litter box and disinfect naturally with essential oils. Limit all animal flesh consumption and eat organic, grass fed, and free range, (know your meat); wash hands and cutting boards after cutting animal flesh; cook your meat until it is done, and avoid pork always, avoid drinking untested water supplies. Boil camping water for tooth brushing and cleaning. Always remember to thoroughly wash your produce.

Be sure to wash your feet, especially if you live in a place where you don't wear shoes and socks every day. Even if you do wear shoes, wash your feet every night before you go to bed, as a kind of a gratitude that you are washing the Master of loves, feet! Yours! Be conscious of it! I have a box of wet wipes by my bed and every night I wash my feet. If Larry doesn't do his, I wash his too. It let's him understand that I honor the Master in him too, even if he's too tired and can't wash his own, which is usually the case. It is nice to connect that way. And it keeps parasites out of MY bed.

Remember that parasites are part of this world we live in. Breathing, eating, and walking allow parasites to"visit" our temple.

Do not fear them for they are a part of you just like the trees and flowers and animals! My daughter says that when people have completed the Cleanse, their bodies are like a hotel, and not a house, for parasites. If they come in, they have to check out by 10:30 a.m. the next day!

Rat Lung Disease

Have you heard about this parasitic disease? What is it? A rat poops and pees and a snail comes along slowly gliding over this feces and urine. A parasite living in the rat waste gets in the snail (or slug's) body and transforms into a rat lung parasite. Then the snail carries it to our organic vegetable gardens. When people eat their organic vegetables without washing them thoroughly, they can get a parasite in their body known as Rat Lung Disease. Within 24 to 48 hours of exposure to this parasite, it gets into the human spine then into the brain and then starts to immediately die off. The die off causes all the damage as it affects the central nervous system. Angel Farms is getting known on the Big Island for being the place that can help people heal from Rat Lung Disease. It is not contagious. As humans we have much to look at about rats, cleanliness and disease. Cleanliness is close to Godliness!

De-Worming Yourself, Your Kids
and Your Animal Friends

Parasite herbs have several important ingredients. Here's what they are and what they do: Wormwood KILLS THE PARASITES; Fresh ground black walnut hulls KILL THE LARVAE and fresh ground organic cloves KILL THE EGGS. Remember how our grandmothers put cloves on ham? It was not only for the taste. Clove kills eggs! Who knew?!

Be aware that if you are doing a parasite cleanse always listen to your body. If you notice flu like systems or pain in your joints then back off or stop the program. You are having some die-off and there are some blockages that are not allowing the body to get rid of the dead or dying parasites. Also, make sure you are drinking your gallon of water daily.

The key to all this Angels is to not have fear of them or we give them power over us. Parasites are associated with

138

parasitical thoughts and behaviors of FEAR. When you walk without fear, you walk without parasites. (No resonance.)

Many of our Angels have incredible friends called pets. I have them too. Shilo and Orion have been my therapy assistants for over 12 years. Many of you know them well. I have seen so many of our clients coming in with massive parasites because they sleep with their animals. Animals do not bath as much as we do and they have certain behaviors we do not have. Such as, licking their butts and others too, and rolling in you know what! Many varieties of parasites do their egg cycle at night. They can crawl off our furry friends and host in us. Do you know fleas carry tape worms? We recommend you get your friend a bed of their own and let them sleep next to you in their own beds. Better for you and for them. Be patient- all animals are trainable.

Stanford University did a study on pork parasites. They took 3 pork roasts the size we cooked for Sunday dinner. They left one raw, one cooked as usual, and the other one they burnt. Then they checked for parasites. They found the one cooked for dinner still had over 50 % of the parasites still alive. They found the one they burnt still had over 30% of the parasites still alive! Even burning it did not kill the parasites! Do you think, Angel, that maybe our ancestors knew this and told us to not eat pork? It is in the Bible, the Koran, and many more Ancient texts, over a thousand years old and on at least 3 continents. I see many pork parasites coming out of people and many have symptoms of anemia, exhaustion, and low beta carotene's.

You can see what kind of heart someone truly has and it is demonstrated by the way their pets respond to them and to others. I have heard animals talking to me since I was a young girl. Are you quiet enough to listen to the animals around you? Can you hear them tell you they are hungry, need water, or just a hug? I hardly ever have to use flea and tick medicine; my animals never get ticks. The health of the animals, primarily dogs and cats, comes from peaceful cohabitation and being with them on a daily basis. One of the things I constantly do with my animals is that when I pet them, I internally say, "Thank you for your wholeness; thank you for your clarity; thank you for your love and I release you from all fleas and ticks and parasitical things because I am the creator of them, not you. Thank you for choosing to walk with me and love me unconditionally". I also send this vibratory message out to all the animals in the world. We have been given dominion over the plants and animals of the earth, which means I am the caretaker of you and I see you clear. Shilo, my twelve year old Jack Russel Terrier, always understands me.

I keep clear within myself and so when I am taking care of my animals, I can say with authority, 'I bless you to be free of ticks; I bless you to be free of parasites and I bless you to be free of fleas!' Fleas are such an irritation to our beautiful beloved animals. Why should they have to suffer because of our unconsciousness? That is exactly what creates parasites in our space in the first place: our little irritations that we are sending out all over the place instead of our gentle love.

Dwight's dog got cancer.

Miracle Story She showed him how to survive cancer. This dog showed him how to handle it with effortless ease. Then, Dwight got cancer. He had a 10 inch fast growing GIST tumor in his belly. He constantly referred back to his loyal dog's example. She didn't think about it. She just was totally in the moment. She didn't 'try to do anything'. She had no regrets because as a dog she didn't have that consciousness. She was just in the moment and really all any of us ever has, is just this moment. What a great teacher this dog was! Way to allow her to teach you Dwight. The Cleanse and her example helped him heal, it helped him live. He is still a miracle to his doctors; they hadn't seen someone totally and completely release such a large tumor in the belly with no surgery!

Lyme Disease is caused by a tick. It is a small spirochete or parasite that lives in the blood. Using fire to remove them is very dangerous. They regurgitate what is in their bodies into yours, with heat. It is best to use an essential oil to remove them or just twist them off and be sure and get their head. Use a people pack to pull any toxins out asap. See chapter 8. Everyone with Lyme Disease that has come to Angel Farms is over it! We treat parasites and yeast, as well as parasitical thoughts and behaviors, aggressively in our Cleanse.

Practice receiving anything and everything with gratitude.

See everything and everyone that comes your way as your gift and opportunity to love. In Ancient Greek, giving and receiving mean the same thing. Own your journey and then you can change it!

Chapter 5

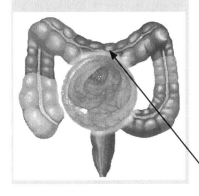

The Brain

Your Amazing Brain and The 100% Wisdom Within

I am Wisdom. I am Knowledge. I am Experience. I choose to Now Remember.

5th Day
The Brain

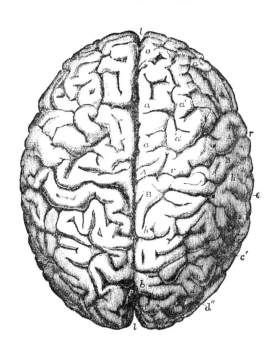

Typically, we are taught that we use only 1/10 of our brains. When I first heard this in school I was shocked. I didn't believe it then either. I wondered what we were doing with the other 90%! Our brain is more complex than the most powerful computer and has over 100 billion nerve cells! Except for your brain cells, 50,000,000 of the cells in your body will have died and been replaced with others, all while you have been reading this sentence. Imagine when everyone awakens their ability to utilize their full 100%!

What would the world be like if everyone awakened the God wisdom within?

An adult brain weighs about 3 pounds. When dehydrated it weighs 8 ounces! It is made up of 93% water. In the first year after birth, a baby's brain triples in size and becomes three-quarters of its adult size. Neurons, or nerve cells, form the connections called 'synapses' and produce chemicals that are released at the synapse. There are about 1 quadrillion synapses in the brain.

Miracle Story

Tammy's grandmother came through the Cleanse.

I have before and after pictures that just blow your socks off. Her skin changed. Her brain was so dehydrated. All she drank were pots of coffee for years and years and years and she never drank water. When she hydrated her brai and kept it hydrated, her brain came back! Even her hair changed color! Its never too late to regenerate! Thank you Lucille!

These neurons are the electrically charged units that, as they communicate with each other, organize electrical energy to make the brain work through a network of connections and interrelated parts. It actually looks like lightning in the brain! While distinct areas of the brain are associated with distinct functions, when injury or surgery silences one area, other parts may compensate by taking over its tasks. This also explains why, when someone does not hear or see or smell, their other senses get much sharper to compensate.

Persons with a tendency to have psychotic experiences seem to show increased activation in the right hemisphere of the brain. This increased level of right hemisphere activation has also been found in healthy people who have high levels of paranormal beliefs and in people who report mystical experiences. It also seems to be the case that people who are more creative are also more likely to show a similar pattern of brain activation with some being viewed as crazy, while others are lauded as prophets or visionaries. Ram Das used to say, "If you think we are all God, you can walk the streets. If you think only you are God, you will get locked up." Ram Das and Timothy Leary were the Harvard Professors who experimented with LSD. The brain in a cat scan from the top down looks like four leaves of a plant. Metals will start forming around

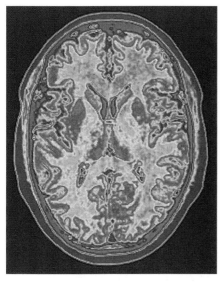

the four lobes, creating lack of information going from one lobe to another. As we age, we tend to not think so clearly. This is caused by metals depositing and interfering with information moving from one lobe to another. The number one cause of this is lack of water in the brain. When the transverse colon which feeds the brain gets congested, and most people's are, even the brain goes hungry and starves. Feeling thirsty yet? Remember your brain in 93% water!

Around the fifth day of the Cleanse, many Angels notice what I call brain drain symptoms such as a metal taste in the mouth, dizziness, temporarily forgetting simple things, such as your best friends' name, and ringing in the ears, due to toxins releasing in the brain. These symptoms are temporary! The most exciting changes happen from the metals moving out of the brain. We notice a dramatic increase in everyone's ability to smell, taste delicious food, to see better because colors become more vivid, sleep more soundly, to have a greater sense of balance, greater ease of movement in limbs and joints, and to have an elevated sense of touch and hearing! Remember, Beloved, that one of the great reasons you incarnated into human experience is BECAUSE of your senses. When they are clearer you have a much richer life experience! Yum it up! By cleaning house you get more food and oxygen to the brain and become more aware of the 100% of who you really are. Rejoice!

When we eat junk foods, we strip ourselves of vital nutrients needed to make and operate the brain's neurotransmitters. White bread, pasta, sugar laden cereals and snacks, fried and hydrogenated fats, caffeine and aspartame actually interfere with the brain's efforts to create good moods.

No Soft Spot.

Miracle Story   One of our Angels had no soft spot when she was born. So they cut her head open and put a piece of plastic in that area so her brain could grow without crushing itself. As it grew, her forehead got bigger. This caused the other children to tease her. When were we taught to look upon each other as different and then judge these differences-even to the point of causing harm to another by words or deeds? We ought to also remember here, that this is the journey she chose, so she gained great things out of it. There are many things people are never able to access unless they choose a more difficult or enlightened journey. Trauma brings us to our intent! When this angel was 19, she really disliked how her forehead looked and she began having symptoms of not being able to think clearly. She thought this was because she was too obsessed with her forehead. She saved as much money as she could for an operation so she'd look more normal. When they went in for the surgery they found a tumor the size of a baseball. They were able to remove it completely. Otherwise, she would have died. She lives today and promotes community and a healthy lifestyle and continues to touch lives without judgment, because she no longer feels judged and is a great teacher of non judgment! She loves who she is and it shows. Way to go Victoria!

Another thing that affects the brain area is trying to make everybody else happy. Being a people pleaser is a very dysfunctional way to live. Understand that if you are not happy, no-body around you will be happy, and if you are, they will be too. In the Bible it says that "Mankind is created to have great joy," If you are not having great joy, you will find a way out so you can return to joy. Do it while you are living, otherwise you will literally "die" for joy.

Jet Lag

If you are traveling you may be susceptible to jet lag because of time line changes. The key is to get up with the sunrise and go down with the sunset, this will automatically set your clock for wherever you are. The sun is the key to rebalance as fast as possible. Do not look at a clock or focus on your previous timeline. Be where you are now with the time and your body will adjust to it, but if you are saying it's 6 at home, and it's 9 here, your body will be confused.

Here are ways to heal your brain: Drink more water. Remember the first glass of water is called brain food. It bypasses the entire system and directly feeds your brain. Good brain foods include broccoli, cauliflower, cabbage, pecans, walnuts, small amounts of fish, and green leafy vegetables. Get out of the brain and into the heart though meditation and silence. Most importantly, if you never want to look at Alzheimer's, dementia, or senility then never, ever, let your brain get dehydrated!!

Miracle Story

I had a gal who had such trauma, drama in her past, and I thought for a moment her story was indeed the only one of its kind.

Any time anybody hurt her or caused her harm, she put them in a box in her mind, and then locked the box. This became her tumor. After her inner child session I asked her to go and open the box, and she said no way! I said, "You have to...remember that you are the Goddess-you chose them to show you who you are not. Honor them, what a contract that must have been. Take the box into the hallway and carry it through the two huge doors on the right hand side, and God can open it. God can see them for their contracts, what they did and didn't do, where they loved or didn't love. God would never judge them, and if you really want to get over this, you must stop judging them as well. Love does not judge!

This was the reason for her brain tumor. She put it all in a box and held onto it, not wanting to look in the box. If you look at this on a physical level; the self-destructive thought finds places that are weak that it can use as a storage container. It continues to get larger because the body finds a way to empty toxins into that area, whether they are toxic thoughts, emotions, or food.

147

A polyp, boil, tumor, or a cyst can also store toxins, releasing those toxins through the skin, or whatever it is that tends to keep growing until we stop adding fuel to it. By the way, her tumor disappeared and she is well! Way to go, Angel!

In the beginning, God/Love created Heaven and Earth... Count 31 lines down...and all that God/Love created is Good. In Hebrew, the definition for giving and receiving are the same.

Today, your assignment is to receive with gratitude.

See everything and everyone that comes your way as your gift and your assignment to love. Make every moment rich and full with your love!

Sweet Angels, I have found that the only way to remember who you are and to live it is to get out of the brain. Let your brain become in service to the heart and give up thinking it has to be in charge any more. You can trust your heart to guide you without thinking things to death! At Angel Farms the biggest issue I help others clear is to get out of the brain. The thinking about tomorrow and yesterday and trying to figure out what will happen tomorrow and what you will say in the meeting next week or what you did or didn't say to your friend or that lady at the bus stop. Get very serious in finding ways to quiet the mind. If you find yourself doing repetitive or habitual things, just stop. Do them at different times or different places. This is how the brain rewires to a more peaceful state. Let your new mantra be" Don't think, don't think, don't think, don't think, and don't think!!!! Your brain already does enough for us without trying to make it put matter together in yesterday or tomorrow that does not exist!! Stop wearing your brain out.

How To Increase Your Memory

One of the greatest ways to improve your memory on the planet is to write down your dreams before you get out of bed in the morning. Place a sheet of paper and pen by your bed and write down everything you remember before you move very much. It does not have to make sense. To increase your memory read your dream several times during the day. The brain will open doors for you that you do not access very often. Your memory will amaze you.

Chronic pain complaints comprise 70 percent of doctors' office visits. Back pain is the most common pain complaint. Recent brain scan studies show that chronic pain is associated with abnormalities in the frontal cortex. This area of the brain is involved in making interpretations and decisions about incoming sensations. Pain is highly influenced by emotion and interpretation. Mainstream medicine likes to treat back pain with surgery even though it has been demonstrated that it is usually not helpful in alleviating suffering long term.

Depression and Pain

Pain is a powerful indicator of growth, and it can be changed with love. Perhaps you needed the pain or discomfort in order to pay attention to Spirit or seek your truth. When you feel pain, it is an indication that some area of your life is not working. Some belief, thought, or emotion is crying out to be loved and healed. Do not make yourself or the things you see as wrong or think of yourself as a bad person. Pain is an area that is waiting for love. Instead know that those areas are being revealed to you so that you can bring the light of consciousness and the love of your heart to them.

Long term depression is often treated with talk therapy and drugs. Perhaps by now in reading along with me you have come to understand there is no benefit in revisiting the emotional past. Depressed people are anchored to a past trauma. They have difficulty letting go of people or events that have hurt. It is better to transform it and realize how brave you were and how the trauma has made you who you are. That's the importance of Inner Child Sessions during *The Cleanse* — to clear hurts at the source, which changes our perception. A miracle is just a change in perception. Depression has emotional roots stemming from

149

forgotten early childhood traumas and is kept in the subconscious body/mind. When chronic pain sufferers don't respond to classic pain medications, they are often given antidepressants that seem to be more effective, only because of the close relationship between pain and depression. Did you know that when a person is on an anti-depressant, they are neither happy nor sad? They are just going along in life: no highs and no lows. Doctors attempt to help their patients by blocking their emotional pain. They are blocking their joy also! Your doctor may not be aware that these medications block your feel good receptors, your ability to remain happy and healthy. Most people on antidepressants don't know what they feel. They can't. Joy is so awesome!! The more you taste of joy, the more joy you will choose to en-joy. Joy is in the NOW. Depression and too much stress can deplete the brain of feel good neurotransmitters and wear them out. Sadness and pain are all about the past. Choose Joy Angel! Let your past go! Be proud of yourself at how great you are to have come this far.

Rosemary's Story

Miracle Story　　　　Rosemary had a fall in the hospital in which she had cut her leg open from her knee down to her ankle. You could actually see the bone in the opening. She lived in the long term care center in Kauai. She was 76 years old. She also had Alzheimer's so badly she couldn't even remember her daughter's name. They were going to amputate her leg in 14 days because it hadn't healed. All the toxins were coming out of her leg because sometimes that's the only way the body can get toxic stuff out. Her daughter who had done the Cleanse, came to me to try to stop this. I went to the hospital to talk to the GI specialist and he said, "No, it's not going to help." I went back again, and again he refused claiming that to his understanding cleaning out the colon wasn't going to make any difference. I made one more attempt; three times is a charm, right? I was inspired to ask him "What will it be like for your staff if you have this lady with no leg and no memory!?" He then agreed it would be more difficult for his staff so he gave her a chance to participate in our amazing 10 day Cleanse. What is 10 days in order to have a chance to heal? She had 8 days left before they were going to amputate her leg and he rescheduled the operation.

　　　　We started her on the Cleanse and on the first day she wasn't' aware of anything. Second day-same thing- no awareness, just stuff coming out. On the third day she said, "I have been here before haven't I?" I said, "Yes you have." And she said, "What am I doing here?" I said, "We are cleaning out your colon so you won't have to lose your leg." She said, "I go poop everyday", and she held up her little finger and said," It's this big." I let her know that it should be $3\frac{1}{2}$ inches in diameter—which means you are leaving a lot of stuff in there and your body isn't working properly. As she went through the Cleanse her mind started coming back more and more- and she started telling us amazing stories like, she used to fly with Amelia Earhart! She used to call Amelia a sissy because she wore dresses all the time. She and her husband started the first airport this side of the Mississippi, in Dallas, Texas! She used to sell airplanes, fly them down to Mexico, collect $10,000, put it on her money belt and then hitchhike back to Texas! By the time the 10 day Cleanse was over, her leg was completely healed and she was thinking clearly and she could even take care of herself. Amazing! Again another one that blew the doctors away.

Her skin and hair were so youthful that the doctors and nurses could hardly believe it. Her brain function came back completely and she lived to the age of 93! What a miracle!

We picked her up almost daily from there. She went with us everywhere, we took her to Sufi dances; we took her to meetings, outings, the ocean, all over the place! Every Thursdays we took her to Auntie Angeline's place in Anahola for a temple lomi in the steam room. One time we took her to a GURU Swami something and he just kept falling asleep. Rosemary was so forward and in the now she said, "Would somebody put that little man to sleep and let's all go home!!!" Her mind and her strong courage came back. We love and cherish our Rosemary.

Nervous System and the Senses

The brain is the portion of the central nervous system that lies within the skull. The Central Nervous System relays, processes, analyzes, and compares information. The Central Nervous System serves as the control center of the body which consists of the brain and the spinal cord. Both the brain and the spinal cord are encased in bone. The Central Nervous system does not come in contact with the environment-that is left to the other major division of the nervous system called the Peripheral Nervous System. The brain is the main switching unit of the Central Nervous System where impulses flow from and originate. The spinal cord provides the link between the brain and the rest of the body. The nervous system is made up of the brain, spinal cord, and an enormous network of nerves that thread throughout the body. The central nervous system is the master system of all functions within your body. Subluxations (misalignments) of your spine, cranium and extremities, interfere with the flow of nerve impulse energy information within your body. The central nervous system is connected to every part of the body by 43 pairs of nerves. Twelve pairs go to and from the brain, with 31 pairs going from the spinal cord. There are nearly 45 miles of nerves running through our bodies! It's the control center. The brain uses information it receives from the nerves to coordinate all of the body's actions and reactions.

Messages travel along the nerves as electrical impulses at speeds up to 248 miles per hour! The nerves are the thin threads of nerve cells, called neurons that run throughout the body. Bundled together, they carry messages back and forth just the way that telephone wires do. Sensory nerves send messages to the brain and generally connect to the brain through the spinal cord inside the backbone. Motor nerves carry messages back from the brain to all the muscles and glands in the body.

Nerves pass along messages through the marvels of chemistry and a kind of electricity! Neurons are thin.

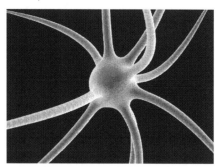

Some are very small, and some can be three feet long! All are shaped somewhat like flat stars which have, to varying degrees, been pulled at each end so that they have long fingers. The fingers of one neuron almost reach to the next neuron. When a neuron is stimulated by heat, cold, touch, sound vibrations or some other message it begins to actually generate a tiny electrical pulse. This electricity and chemical change travels the full

152

length of the neuron. But when it gets to the end of finger-like points at the end of the neuron, it needs help getting across to the next extended finger. That's where chemicals come in.

The electrical pulse in the cells triggers the release of chemicals that carry the pulse to the next cell. And so on and so on and so on; similar to a relay of dominoes in which one standing domino falls and trips the next and the next and the next. The Functioning Nervous System is an enormous network of "one-way streets".

In one square inch of skin there are four yards of nerve fibers, 600 pain sensors, 1300 nerve cells, 9000 nerve endings, 36 heat sensors, 75 pressure sensors, 100 sweat glands, 3 million cells, and 3 yards of blood vessels. The total length of your circulatory system stretches an amazing 60,000 miles. That is more than twice the distance around the Earth.

Amazing things that happen in your body because you have a central nervous system: Your heart beats, you breathe, you can taste, smell, see, hear, think, sleep, and dream! Running! Laughing! Singing! Painting! Writing! Feeling pain or pleasure!! Living!

This is a great time to stop and give gratitude for your brain and central nervous system. They are a work of art and so deserve your love and appreciation.

Eye Exercises

When you go outside, remember to do your eye exercises in the sun. Eye exercises are very easy. These come from Ayurvedic Medicine that is over 1000 years old. Without contacts or eye glasses look at the sun and then close your eyes. Begin to rotate your eyes up and down, side to side, make a figure eight a few times, hold the eyes up and count to 10 and down and count to 10. Do this for 5 minutes a day and you will be amazed. Eye exercises help stimulate the brain, strengthen the retina and keep your eyesight from weakening by not allowing the cornea to harden. They also stimulate your liver because it motivates Vitamin D production, and even make your bones stronger. Many people work inside for many years of their lives, and they don't get enough sun, so they are not producing enough vitamin D. Sunlight for at least 30 minutes a day keeps the brain, eyes, bone marrow, spleen and pancreas in alignment, because they all need a daily healthy dose. Do you know that your eyes can distinguish up to one million color surfaces and take in more information than the largest telescope known to man? Take care of your eyes.

X-rays

Whenever someone comes in with a disease, I ask them if they have seen the X rays of the area. If so, I tell them to cancel the whole picture that is in their mind, because their mind only sees that and continues to re-create it. I then have them look at a whole new picture from an anatomy book, a healthy picture of that same area. I even have them blow it up and stick it on the ceiling above their bed. This allows their mind to see the perfect picture. It's really important that those X rays get deleted from their brain and they no longer look upon them. Always give your brain a much better picture to create.

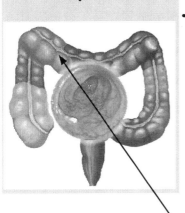

Chapter 6

How Does What You Think and Believe About Yourself Affect Your Health?

I am Intelligent
I am Eternal
I am Immortal

6th Day
The Brain

Karma

Karma in Indian religions is the concept of "action" or "deed", and is understood as that which causes the entire cycle of cause and effect, originating in ancient India, Hindu, Jain, Buddhist and Sikh philosophies. Karma is not fate, for humans act with free will creating their own destiny. According to the Vedas, if one sows goodness and love, one will reap goodness and love; if one sows negativity and fear, one will reap negativity and fear. I have found that even the most inflammatory comments help us learn something. What is this karma thing really? Karma is where we experience unloving behaviors and thought forms and have "regrets" about how we did not do something good enough. Then we beat ourselves up with 2 by 4's for the rest of our lives. We find the experience is again in front of us to choose differently the second time, or the third, or the fourth, etc. The Karmic Wheel is like a big paddle wheel. If you have issues still unhealed or un-awakened in you, it's going to keep coming up. Different faces and different places, but same theme to the story of your life. Dang-I did this before. Same content. Same kind of relation-ships, same kind of jobs, same kind of cars, etc. The karmic wheel occurs when you said, "I am going to create a situation where God and I are going to have an opportunity to love, and not judge." Many people believe they are here to process past life karma.

Don't kid yourself! We are eternal. In my experience I

have found belief this to be very harmful. It holds us in patterns that are often difficult to access. Why do you think we have little or no conscious memory of our past lives? It's because we have enough to heal and process in this lifetime. The creator must have known how hard we would be on ourselves for things we have done in the past. We would judge ourselves harshly. How can we love now when our focus is not in the NOW? The universe is going to keep giving you opportunities to love. Maybe this time you will do it. Karmic patterns show people who get raped repeatedly and others who haven't been raped at all, repeating relationship dramas, similar versions of the last ones, recurring health issues, to heal the stuff you didn't get in the first time around—that's that karmic wheel again. There is nothing any of us can do about the past. It is gone forever. It is important to realize that it is our choice whether things from our past will keep us in bondage, or if we can step into the NOW, opening the door to our freedom.

Miracle Story I had an amazing person come through the Cleanse in the beginning of my journey.

She did the Cleanse and then 3 months later she began having these recurrent dreams and they were happening concurrently. She was getting lost, and not able to care for herself or her family. We did dream analogy and other things to assist her and nothing helped. I then told her we should set an intent and I would take her back. I have always been resistant to past life stuff because my intuition tells me there is enough to deal with in this life. I stated my intent. (If you have brought something from your past life, I will help you clear it.) She said she just wanted to know what she did not want to forget. Bingo! We went in with that one.

In the session, we went through the Beloveds realm and back to a life were she was a little girl around 2 years old and her mother was washing clothes in a creek outside of her little cabin. Two Indians were coming across the prairie and the only thing I had her change in the whole story was to tell her mom she loved her and she would be OK.

The Indians scooped up the little girl and off they went and she never saw her mother or that family again. She was taken to a very large village and was raised with the Chief's family along with
156

a daughter of his own. I asked her if she felt alone or abandoned and she did not. In this lifetime she would have. She felt very loved and honored and was taught about healing herbs. When she was around 18 years old, white man struck! They hit the village hard and killed many and even burned the land around the village to run off the animal and food supply. After they left, the chief was leaning against her horse, while she was on it, and was ready to commit mass suicide. He could not understand why these people would do this for no reason and in his grief he was ready to have everyone go to the "happy hunting grounds". She began to point at all the ones who were still alive and said, what about that one and what about this one. He looked up at her and saw a light shining around her. We don't know if it was the sun or what, but he became present and knew, we must continue, we must carry on. That is how she saved her people. Could this be why she was taken in the first place?

The white people came again soon after and this time because she was the only white person in the village she was taken to another town and she never saw her people again. She spent the rest of her life in a little store and was very sad. She passed over around the age of 35. Crossing to the realm of the Beloved many were there that she had spent time with and loved. The love was so strong that it was very hard to describe. Do you know what the conversation was? They talked about where they loved and where they did not. Where they could have loved more and where they loved a little bit. They talked about how, if given the chance they would surely love more even in similar situations. Karma! There were no discussions about blame or judgment. Just love, of course. Love is all there is! We do not take anything with us but love.

Then they all asked, "Do you want to do it again?" They all felt great excitement and all but two said yes! One was the medicine man and one was the chief. They said, "We will walk with you the other way." I asked her to ask them, "What other way?" They said, "We have walked with you in this lifetime and you know our love and energy. You will feel us close to you whenever you need us and we will help you remember how to love in these difficult situations in which you want to shine love. You will feel us just outside your body." (In your ethereal field which is what holds your matter together in this body). "There is a multitude of us that walk with you which is your family. You are never alone."

As this Angel was leaving she asked God, "Can I take this strength that I developed in this last journey with me because I will need it in this one?" She heard very clearly, "Of Course Precious One, it is yours already." The dreams stopped and 3 months later she was in a very dangerous situation in which this very strength she remembered and accessed helped her survive. This experience really let me know that love is truly all there is and all we take with us when we die. It explains the times when I felt my "Family" with me so close I would undress under the covers because I was shy. We do have enough to deal with in this lifetime and putting our attention on things outside of the now keeps us in pain.

Rubber band theory: what you put out comes back. The more conscious you are, the faster the band comes back to smack you. Whenever you have unloving thoughts to yourself or others it will show up for you. That's Karma!

Cancer

According to the National Institutes of Health estimates, cancer is an epidemic around the world. Cancer is a class of disease or disorder characterized by the uncontrolled division of cells and the ability of these cells to invade other tissues, either by direct growth into adjacent tissue through invasion or by implantation into distant sites by metastasis in the bloodstream or lymphatic system. There are over 100 different types of cancer and while they have their unique symptoms and characteristics, I have found them all to look very similar.

When you look at a cancer cell under a microscope it looks 100 times bigger than regular red blood cells! It looks like it has small parasites wiggling on the outside of the cell as it literally eats surrounding cells!

The creation of cancer in the body starts with a good dose of hate. I have found that without hate you can never have cancer! Who you hate is a good indicator of where the cancer shows up. For example if you hate your mother you get breast cancer. I have even had many Angels come do the Cleanse who were wrongly diagnosed with cancer. As I talked to them, I knew that they had been misdiagnosed. They did not hate enough. For example, Leslie came in with this kind of a diagnosis in her lungs. The doctors had found a dark spot on her lungs and were preparing her for treatment. I recommend everyone consider Cleansing, because it helps the body heal faster after treatment, if the treatment is still even necessary. Leslie had been to India

158

and picked up a nasty cough. On the eighth day of the Cleanse she started to throw up really hard! Digging deep, her lungs expelled a crazy octopus shaped parasite out of her right lung. She wrote me a million dollar check which still hangs on my wall. She did not have cancer.

Remember Dr Emoto's work and the effect hate has on water by blowing it to pieces? You are mostly water! Through The Cleanse, many Angels have found the lesson they wanted to learn and moved on through the cancer. I consider cancer a master journey: a trauma that can bring you to your intent or send you onto your next adventure on another plane. You told yourself, I am going to get to this thing called love or I am going to kick my butt and cross over and get to this thing called love! Either way you will get to love! Cancer in your body indicates something is eating you up! While some choose surgery and some choose death, I have seen many who came through Angel Farms who chose to forgive themselves and others; with support and love they shifted it and it just disappeared! Doctor verified. Remember, you don't have to hurt anymore, grieve anymore, and be angry anymore. YOU can choose love in this moment and with that you are choosing life! "Whatever the problem, love is the answer. Whatever the fear, love is the answer. Love is all there is. Whatever the question, love is the answer." Dr. Gerald Jampol

Every time negative energy is used, it shuts down the receptors of light in the DNA and thus allows darkness and confusion to enter. This darkness totally covers the memory of perfection in the cell. The electrical system of the cell will eventually function in chaos with other cells throughout the body causing more malfunctioning. That is why it is so important to feel positive feelings, think positive thoughts, use positive words and eat the correct foods. The power plant of each cell must be stoked with appropriate energy in order for the cells to receive correct information and receive light. As you eliminate the negative feelings and blocks, you are healing the spiritual and emotional aspects of your life.

White sugar has been linked to several different types of cancer. In addition, white sugar decreases the number of disease-fighting immune cells. The average American consumes an astounding 2-3 pounds of sugar each week, which is not surprising considering that highly refined sugars in the forms of sucrose (table sugar), dextrose (corn sugar), and high-fructose corn syrup are being processed into so many of our foods. No wonder there is so much cancer eating us up! Cancer loves sugar!

Some important information about sugar. Did you know

that sugar can suppress your immune system and impair your defenses against infectious disease? It can cause premature aging and can lead to alcoholism. It can cause arthritis, asthma, and multiple sclerosis. It can assist in the uncontrolled growth of candida and yeast. It can cause drowsiness in children. It can damage your pancreas, liver, and kidneys and is the number one enemy of your bowel movements. It makes your tendons brittle and can cause headaches, including migraines. It can cause depression and inflammation and interferes with the absorption of protein. These are just a few issues sugar can have on your health.

Miracle Story

Jim came in with 4th stage prostate cancer.

As thCleanse progressed I discovered The was pissed off at his neighbor. It all came down to defamation of his character. I asked him how his relationship was with his neighbor now. Guess what, the neighbor didn't even live there anymore and hadn't for years! So, how long do humans hang onto stuff and not even express their feelings of frustration to the people they feel hurt or betrayed by? How much damage occurs inside of their bodies due to their unloving and unforgiving feelings toward others? Most of the time the other person doesn't even know we are angry at them, as what was true in Jim's story! As Jim learned what we teach at Angel Farms is to not give a shit (literally) about what others think of us because it is not between us and them it is always between us and God. Why are we killing ourselves over other people's unconscious behaviors? Jim called 2 weeks later and his cancer was gone.

Miracle Story

Stephanie also came in with three large tumors in her uterus, one already perforating the wall.

She had two children the youngest just 3 years old. As we progressed I found she hated her neighbor and had not spoken to him in 9 years. Why? She did not remember why except that he was just a jerk! I gave her an assignment for the next day. Take the neighbor some bananas and tell him Aloha.

She immediately refused. I told her, "Then die! That is still the same old patterns and look what they caused." She shifted and the next day went to see him. He was unaware she was still angry at him and he thought they were just really private people and did not bother him and his family. Her tumors disappeared that day!

Are you living a lifestyle that supports health? Are you eating lots of fresh vegetables, fruits and whole grains? Do you drink lots of water? Are you grateful; is your life full of love? You can enhance immunity by simple lifestyle changes, such as sleeping at the right time, reducing stress, emphasizing positive emotions, and especially feeding your Spirit every day. Detoxify your system using easy methods, adding herbal formulations when necessary.Bring harmony and peace into your life through meditation, that is, daily quiet time where you are not thinking and are receptive to the messages of your inner guidance.

Angel's
Toolbox

Say this truth very loudly as often as you need.

I AM powerful beyond measure! I will no longer allow hate and anger into my life. I choose forgiveness of myself and others, and I love myself enough to say, I am worthy of a shift and a change. I am worthy of loving more. I am worthy of receiving more love. I don't have to do this journey of unlove any more. If you wobble, pick yourself up, dust yourself off, pat yourself on the back, and love again. It all shifts. Even if you think you screwed up, grace works.

There are many therapies offered that suggest you express your anger and frustration such as screaming into your pillow to let go and vent. In my experience, this is not a healthy way to express your anger! Every time you get angry your body constricts within itself because anger comes from fear, fear is constricting, and love is expanding.You might want to know that every time you get angry it depletes your immune system for 5 hours! It takes 5 hours to recover! How much can you be exposed to in a 5 hour period because of your own anger and hatred? Anger comes from having expectations of what you think or feel people in your life either did, should, or didn't do. In other words, according to you, they did not get it right.   Many of us want to be clear in body, mind, and Spirit.   There are lots of programs out there. Always ask, does this program come from love or fear? Is this a struggle on my part, is it intense, does it hurt, is it painful and difficult? If the program causes the body to restrict in pain, which is what the body has been doing enough of already, there are other ways. Better choices might be temple lomi, feather-like lymph massage, yoga, energy work, gentle massage, acupuncture and soft, peaceful therapies and of course, the Cleanse at Angel Farms. You've hurt enough already Angel, you don't have to hurt anymore. So how do you live your life with no anger? You see everything in Divine perfection. So, your date didn't show up on time, or not at all. The cat is driving you crazy. That driver just cut you off. The dog just ate your steak dinner. Laugh! You are a divine being in a human experience. Did you think that it was going to be all flowers and sunshine? The flowers need rain to grow! The sunshine is most wonderful when it shines after a storm!

Remember to see the good in all things! It is there, just find it! Nothing is so "bad" that it can't be forgiven so you can be healthy.

Projection

I find many Angels can't forget the past, so they are projecting the past into the future. It's not even the same molecules! For instance, you have a new spine every three months, you have a new stomach lining every 5-7 days, a new liver every 6 weeks, a new entire body in 9 months, just like the time it took for you to develop in the womb. You created this body and you do it every 9 months. Congratulations-what a Master you are. Yes, you are still creating ulcers, cancers, because you haven't healed why you created it in your life in the first place. Time to get off the karmic paddle wheel once and for all!

In order to be accountable we must admit that perhaps we caused our own misery, illness and problems, thus admitting we have been wrong about many things over the years and especially about the way in which we viewed our problems. It's okay to make a mistake. We grew up in a culture that has programmed us to be right. The reason we or our clients may have a difficult time adjusting is due to our thinking mind-it always has to

162

be right or justified. Give yourself permission to be wrong. That's how we all learn. The Course in Miracles says would you rather be right or happy? Happiness is healthier! You are the one determining your happiness. When you accept yourself and accept what is, you can change it, you can make improvements. You need not wait for others to change. Your change will create an atmosphere for others to improve also. You are NOT responsible for changing anyone but yourself.

Shifting ourselves creates an environment of understanding and forgiveness of self and others. When understanding abounds in us, it is easier to let go of blame and judgment. We can honestly accept everyone, including ourselves, exactly where and how they are in this moment.

Inner Child Work-Womb

Be Beloved Angel, did you know every human has the experience of working out up to 8 issues in his/her lifetime? People pick up their issues in the womb, Did you know you are the creator of your body, not your mother? She gave you a safe place to pull the molecules and atoms of the earth together and God gave you the blueprints. When we are finished putting our bodies together, between the 7th and 9th month and just putting on weight, we pull up what is called "the veil" and we cause ourselves to forget who we really are, so we can have a journey of experiencing who we are not.

Whatever the mother is feeling at that time is transferred to us. This is part of the human journey; somehow God had to put itself to sleep so it could have a journey of who it wasn't through us. As young mothers we can feel unsafe, our first birth can be kind of a traumatic experience. We hear from other women what is going to happen (war stories like I was in labor for 18 hours) which create projection of another's experience onto our potential experience.The mother's feelings and behavior toward her unborn child or her body during her pregnancy are major. The mother and unborn child communicate largely via the hormones that flow through the umbilical cord. The second major influence is the father's attitude toward the pregnancy and his commitment/presence/absence to the relationship with the mother.

Consider what your parents were experiencing during your

gestation period. Consider your mother's attitude toward bearing you, what she endured during her pregnancy and how your birthing progressed. As babies we have feelings during the birthing process, without understanding the thought and reasons behind them. From the time of conception until we are adults, we are strongly influenced by the feelings, thoughts and attitudes supplied to us by others who love us, teach us, (including the media) and interact with us on a daily basis. When a thought is energized by an emotional response, positive or negative; we buy into it as though it is valid, actual truth. Sometimes this thought/feeling is further validation of our already established false belief. This is called implosion. If we felt the feelings in the womb, they now become real for us.

The importance of Inner Child work is that it begins to re-create a peaceful, loving birth (on a cellular level) with peaceful loving parents and a Spiritual guardian or Divine presence assisting from birth and walking through life with the child. The goal for the Inner Child session is to bring the child into this world with LOVE based feelings.

I take people back to before they where 8 years old when we believed in things like Santa Claus and the Easter Bunny. We believed what we were told because we just could not imagine those we loved were not telling us the truth. Have you ever felt any of these feelings in your life- not loved or not lovable, not wanted, not good enough(bad kid), stupid, alone, separate or abandoned, disconnected, numb, feeling non-existent, (manic depression which is easy to clear when you finally land here) questioning life purpose, not important, unsafe and powerless and unworthy? Who hasn't?

According to The Incredible Machine, published by National Geographic Society, an adult human is comprised of 100 trillion cells. Each cell has the Universal pattern of intelligence. The intelligence of the cell is called DNA and there are at least 6 billion steps of DNA in a single cell that record the life print of the individual. DNA is a blueprint that determines the makeup of every cell including the hereditary traits. Every thought, every feeling and every emotion we experience sends a message to each cell of the body. Some messages may be deeper or more intense than others, yet all affect the cells. We know that the mind is sending out impulses of intelligence and the DNA receives them.

I was in the grocery store with my 14 year old daughter, Shara, and we saw a beautiful little 3 year old boy with long curly hair. He had grabbed something off the shelf like little kids do and his mother called him stupid right then and there. I felt this as my hair raised on my neck and I kept on walking. Shara turned around and went over to the mother and said, "Hey Ma-am, do you know you just told your little boy that he is stupid and because he believes everything you say he is going to feel like he is stupid for the rest of his life- is that really what you want for him?" She said, "Oh my God, what have I done?" She didn't say you don't have any business saying that.

She heard Shara's heart even at 14 years old. The mom wonders what am I going to do now? Shara taught her, it takes 100 positive affirmations for you to cancel out the one negative you just said. If I were you, I would tell him how smart he is, because he is. The mother agreed, yes, he is! "Oh honey, mommy is so sorry." She must have said 100 times in the store how sorry she was. Shara was a good teacher for me that day, just like when White Eagle told me Spirit kicked my butt to get me over to where I needed to be. The present moment is the only one to correct a misperception into love. Do it now, not later!

The more conscious we are, the more responsible we are for every conversation Spirit brings us to participate in that day to raise it to a higher frequency. Don't think every conversation you are in everyday is not divinely guided. Every moment we have, we can make one of 2 choices; we can choose love or fear in all situations. Ask yourself often, does my thought come from fear or from love? If we are not in loving present awareness, Spirit kicks our butts! Believe me, love works better.

Feeling Alone

When somebody feels they are so alone in the world, this usually comes from being drugged in the womb. In the womb you felt unwanted and invisible and believed you were non-existent. You decide, if it's going to be this hard, I'm not going to do it. You felt alone, separate and disconnected. All of a sudden everything is gone and aloneness comes in. There is nothing here but me and that is really scary. This is the number one cause of Manic Depression; not knowing your purpose; feeling alone and disconnected. Sometimes this person is suicidal, with a history of on-going stays in mental institutions. I am here. The brain says, no you are not. This is a serious life long mind fight that causes the personality to crash hard. They have to dig themselves out of mental drama and self doubt constantly. If they feel they are alone, they are going to be making a lot of commotion in their lives to prove they are not separate. I am here, YOU see me? Ongoing drama: I don't know if I really see myself or really feel myself, if somebody else pays attention to me, I am seen and I am heard.

Angel's
Toolbox

See yourself in the womb.

See yourself now where a being of light comes in, takes you into its arms out of the womb. Now let the mother go to sleep and sleep off all fear and all medication, so when you return you will be clear and ready and this master being of light and love is going to now take you to this place through a lit hallway. Feel the joy it has for you for what you are about to know. See yourself going up through two huge doors usually on the right hand side, and go into the realm of the Beloved of God, of love— explore truth there—you are a true seed of God, not a seed of a flower or tomato or avocado— is it really possible you could be unlovable in any way? That's not possible because your definition of God and self is love. Is it true you could be unworthy in any way? When look what your love does to every person, place, or thing that it touches—it is worth every-thing. Is it possible that you could be unsafe, NO, because you are a seed of God. Is it possible you could be powerless, no because you are powerful beyond measure. Is it possible that you could be stu-pid, No, it's not possible because you carry the wisdom of God. All of it. 100%. Is it possible you could be "not good enough"? Or bad? Because our definition is good, we can trace our beginnings back to the bible where God says he created the Heaven and the Earth and 31 lines later he says and all he created is good. We need to keep that in our consciousness at all times that every particle is good.

If you actually see an orange, your brain fires one way. If you imagine the orange with your eyes closed the brain fires the same way. The mind doesn't know the difference between what it is real and what is imagined. This is proven by quantum physics. This is why it is so important to correct misperceptions you came in with and return to truth. We no longer need to carry these heavy weights of not being good enough or not being smart enough or not being loved enough, which of course have never been true!

We cannot know what feelings embraced others at birth and which have governed their life experiences. We don't have the same inner dialog nor were we disciplined in the same way. Our assignment here on earth is not to judge or blame but to FORGIVE. Remember most people do the best they can based on their perceptions.

When I am getting ready to bring them back into present time in a session I ask them, what are the good gifts of this mother? What are the reasons why you chose her? And sometimes there aren't any which means you chose her to show you who you were not, so thank her for that and all the gifts known and unknown. I am thankful for my mom because she showed me what I didn't want to do and what I didn't want to be. For instance, she would have us all line up in a row ask who took her hairbrush and I would wonder why was she acting like a 3 year old. I didn't go that route. I wanted my kids to understand when they went out of alignment of peace. If I was upset I would send them to their room so I could get re-centered and then I could handle the situation with more peace.

My sweet grandmother said a lot, "If you can't say something nice, don't say anything at all" and she carried it further. "If you can't think anything nice, don't think anything at all." Anyone, she says, can find the negative in others. It's more of a challenge to find the positive.

Joy is so awesome!! Joy is in the NOW. Sadness and pain are all about the past. Choose Joy Angel! Acknowledge how great you are to have come this far. Support your body in cleansing and regenerating. Come to the NOW body, mind, emotions and spirit! How we control others with unconscious behaviors. It is my belief as people begin to understand these truths, they will begin to stop the control that exists within all relationships. When we see our truth as God created us, we can begin to feel the infinite power that exists for us all. When we tap into this true source, we no longer need to control others to gain power. We will have an endless supply of power within, and the real beauty is that as we see our own light, we will be able to see another's light, and thus become an instrument for God in empowering others. Remember we all felt like victims of unconsciousness and abuse.

We need the opportunity to discover our own divinity. Focus on another's light, while not losing sight of your own. Everyone has a dominant way in which we control others, until we don't anymore. I prefer to let go and let God! We can and do use many creative ways of controlling others, depending on how the person we are relating to is trying to control us. When we are in conflict with another, can we stop and ask ourselves, "What is the control game I am playing here?" When we realize the game, then we have a choice to stop it by asking, "What does this person I am in conflict with really need?" Some of my thoughts on this are as follows: Remember you serve as a mirror for them. The negativity they see in you is merely a reflection of what they believe about themselves. Control becomes a survival issue for them because of these negative beliefs they hold about themselves.

How we control others with unconscious behaviors

"Bullying Behavior" is an obvious control method, such as abuse and verbal threats, a tendency to yell, call names and use body language to control others. These people are starved for personal power and they feel desperate need to have power over others.

What do they need? This person needs to know that you value him or her and that their opinion and feelings are important and matter to you. You don't need to buy into their bullying by accepting their opinion of you. You might say to them, "It's interesting you feel that way" or "I can understand why you feel that way." This indicates that you value them although you may not agree. I like the phrase, "I agree to disagree."

Some people gain power over others by being the victim. They control others with guilt trips; robbing others of their time and energy by never having enough; you can never do enough for a "victim" as they will then lose their control over you. Most victims are physically or emotionally ill so as to get another person's time and attention. They can be accident prone as well. Victim children usually get attention only when they are sick or hurt. Victims create bullies and unapproachable spouses, children, and occasionally another victim child.

Needs of the victim: As with the Bully, the Victim needs the opportunity to discover their light and truth. They need to learn how to nurture themselves. You might ask them what they could do to accomplish this nurturing of self. When a victim" learns how to do this, they can continually fill themselves with continuous nurturing, taking the burden off those they control with guilt and shame. Their bottom line belief is that they don't deserve to be nurtured, so as a result, they don't know how to nurture themselves. They are continuously setting others up to validate this negative belief through their method of control. No

168

one enjoys taking care of the endless needs of the victim. Consequently, abandonment eventually occurs, thus fulfilling their bottom line belief.

"Unapproachable" people control others through appearing to be emotionally not present or missing. They have power over others by ignoring them; making them guess their thoughts and feelings. These people appear to be shy and they think too much. "Unapproachables" are preoccupied with their own lives often giving the impression that they don't care. Spouses and children of "Unapproachables" become confrontational interrogators, always trying to get reassurance that they are important. "Unapproachables" create "confrontational interrogators" in their interpersonal relationships.

Needs of the Unapproachables: The "Unapproachable" person needs to be trusted. Remember they became "unapproachable" as a result of badgering either by an "confrontational interrogator", a "Bully" or an "Victim." This badgering resulted in a feeling of inferiority, making this person doubt themselves, focusing on their own faults. Becoming unapproachable is only natural; not wanting to risk someone else finding out their faults and validating their basic belief that they are incapable. When they feel trusted to make decisions or perform tasks, they will begin to open up and risk their feelings. "Unapproachable" people are generally dreamers who are desperately in need of sharing their dreams. Often, they are highly creative and imaginative with a great deal to offer society.

Confrontational Interrogators. Some people control others by asking questions. They must have an answer for everything. They never take NO for an answer. Constantly questioning, they look to find fault in another, then use that fault to feel superior, robbing others of their self esteem. "Confrontational Interrogators" create "Unapproachables" in their interpersonal relationships.

Needs of the Confrontational Interrogator: "Confrontational Interrogators" need to know they are worthy. Their basic belief is that they are not important. They are the "Confrontational Interrogators" because they are in relationships with "Unapproachables" who naturally validate this belief by not sharing with them. So, as you can see, they keep the power struggle going by badgering the "aloof" which pushes him or her even farther away. When a "confrontational interrogator" sees his/her truth, that he/she is a person of worth, he/she can release the need for constant validation from the

"Unapproachable" and begin to see the "Unapproachable's distance from him/her as insecurity, not as a covert attack.

How are you controlling others around you? Does it help to know we can change it?

Awareness it the only game in town.

"No man is free who is not master of himself."
—Epictetus

When you first learned to read words or were first learning and practicing a musical instrument, it took concentrated effort. You had to look at every symbol; you had to focus on every word. If you have ever been to a grammar school band recital, you know that some kids have quite a time learning to master their instruments. Years later, though, when you went to a high school band concert, you saw the same faces grown up and a great deal of mastery present in their playing. To become the master of your thoughts and feelings, instead of letting them master you, an intense desire is necessary. You must monitor, rule, manage, and govern your thoughts and feelings. Your prime responsibility is to tune into your internal dialog; to learn to recognize mindless chatter and self talk. You learn to focus on what you are saying to yourself-which shifts you into awareness.

Positive emotions create bodily sensations of openness and expansiveness; inviting the world in. The body is relaxed even though emotions such as joy are energizing. Developing body wisdom allows you to tap into what is really going on vibrationally. Positive feelings invite health while negative feelings cause discomfort Learn to listen to the language of your heart.

EGO-Edging God Out

Unconditional love toward ourselves and others keeps us out of the ego. Think of your day by day activities and nteractions, how much time do you spend defending various positions that make you feel right, worthy, okay, etc. When you no longer feel a need to defend yourself, that is, when you accept yourself, the body can naturally relax. Being tolerant and accepting of the experiences that challenge and teach us, allows our growth experiences to no longer be hard. Loving others as they are and seeing them perfect as they are allows them to grow and unfold at their own rate. When you do not see the situations in your life as being perfect, there is no energy for anything to change. I have found very few, if any, earth Angels who are not seeking God/Love.

Purpose of Emotions

The purpose of emotions is to help us feel and participate fully in our lives. To become aware of our inner guidance system, we must learn to trust our emotions.

**"IF YOU WANT TO BE ONE OF THE CHOSEN,
ALL YOU HAVE TO DO IS CHOOSE YOURSELF."**

Perhaps you deny that these old feelings exist, therebysuppressing them; they are still registered in the subconscious and in the DNA, and in the colon, the intelligence in every cell affecting the whole body's electrical system. Waves of energy slowed down into non movement solidify; that's matter. Thus positive energy is closer to the source and negative energy has wider frequencies, making them further from Source. The closer you are to your Source, the more peace you experience, the more joy you will feel, and the greater your capacity to love. Many people truly experience these characteristics.

#1 Meditation and Relaxation Technique

Every word has vibratory energy. Every word has power. Depending on the frequency of the word (positive or negative), every word you say has an effect for truth or for error. Develop the habit of listening to what you say. Whenever you say, "I am" it is extremely powerful. Make sure anything you say after "I am" you want to experience. Where I am God is: Where God is I am! So True!

Those areas where you are not certain, where you feel insecure, are often those you feel the most need to defend. Forgiveness is part of unconditional love. Forgive yourself throughout the day for all the moments when you are not loving and not wise. Forgive others for all the moments when they are not loving and wise. As you forgive, you make it easier to become those things you want to be. You also make it easier for others to become what they want to be.

#2 Nature

Nature is the best tool you can use to get yourself present. What do you see, smell, hear, taste, feel? When you are in a moment of not being present, then do your five sense test. It brings you back to where you ARE always.

#3 Relaxation Exercises

Take a deep breath. Imagine energy coming from the earth through the bottom of your feet. Bring the energy up through the top of your head. Send it up into the universe. Now imagine a clear light from the universe coming straight down from above into your head. Bring it down through your spine. Picture warmth spreading throughout your body. Run the energy out through your feet into the earth.

Feel light and free all over-remember; allow, visualize and feel

172

this. This gets your energy flowing and your channel fully open to the Source. Send out gratitude that you are you, alive and well and in a body. Send out love to the planet, to other people on the planet. Send out unconditional love to those you know, love, and serve.

#4 White Screen Your Mind

Picture a white screen in your mind. Every time a thought comes in just let it pass and see white again. Your image of the white screen will create the state of mind that you need and deep breathing will clear your emotions. Practice creating a state of relaxation until you can do it in a second.

#5 Whats Really In Your Eyes

Place a candle in front of a mirror in a dark room. Sit in front of the mirror and stare into your eyes. With out blinking, keep focusing on your eyes. You will notice thoughts come through when you lose focus. Just gently return to the focus in your eyes. Your eyes will tear, this is normal. Keep your focus. Eventually you will see both eyes become one and lift to your third eye. This meditation takes practice as they all do but it is definitely not boring! You are looking into the eyes of God. Aren't they beautiful?

In Fort Bragg, California there is a saying that it is the land of many illnesses. And in Mckensie Park here on the Big Island where many people have been killed, people feel uncomfortable going there. What happens when we carry the stories of ancient traumas is that we put focus back on them and re-create them! Do not be one to pass on unloving stories. Create the land of many healings.

Resisting something, a lot or a little, mentally or emotionally, ties you to it. If you want to move to a better place, start by loving where you are. Practice gratitude.

Look around and see what you can be grateful for about the person, place or situation. Tension or upset in your body magnetizes more problems to you. Worrying will bring you more of what you don't want.

Chakras

When I first became aware of who I am, I woke up, I knew nothing about chakras, crystals, stones, and color therapies. As I learned about them I noticed something so profound. We are the exact color of the rainbow even in the same order! Whenever you see a rainbow, stop and admire how absolutely beautiful you are! Chakras reflect various aspects of human experience and awareness. As you become centered in the NOW and come from a space of more gratitude for everything on a daily basis, you will be more aware of objects such as crystals that vibrate at a higher vibration. You will incorporate various healers' tools that make your work and life more fun.

Studying and working with the chakra system will help you become aware of the powerful life force energy that exists within your body, mind, and your environment. Your body is indeed your temple! Sometimes it can be to your advantage to specifically focus on how open or closed any particular chakra is. By getting in the NOW and remembering who you are and that we are all God having an adventurous journey here, you can choose to hold and experience wholeness. Your energy centers mirror your vibration. This is why it is important to clear yourself when issues come up.

Chakra Colors Used During Healing Work

RED   1st chakra: Root-Pelvic-Area-Life Force

ORANGE   2nd chakra: Lower-Belly-Creative Center

YELLOW   3rd Chakra: Stomach-Solar Plexis- Power Center

GREEN   4th Chakra: Heart-Love Center-Color

BLUE   5th Chakra: Throat Expression Center

PURPLE   6th Chakra: 3rd Eye-Intuition Center -Telepathy

WHITE   7th Chakra: Crown Connection to Source

Mix it up and you can see we are all full spectrum! Opalescent in our brilliance!

174

Religion

—Anonymous

"Let me explain the problem science has with religion." The atheist professor of philosophy pauses before his class and then asks one of his new students to stand.

"You're a Christian, aren't you, son?"

"Yes sir," the student says.

"So you believe in God?"

"Absolutely."

"Is God good?"

"Sure! God's good."

"Is God all-powerful? Can God do anything?"

"Yes"

"Are you good or evil?"

"The Bible says I'm evil."

The professor grins knowingly. "Aha! The Bible!" He considers for a moment. "Here's one for you. Let's say there's a sick person over here and you can cure him. You can do it. Would you help him? Would you try?"

"Yes sir, I would."

"So you're good...!"

"I wouldn't say that."

"But why not say that? You'd help a sick and maimed person if you could. Most of us would if we could. But God doesn't."

The student does not answer, so the professor continues. "He doesn't, does he? My brother was a Christian who died of cancer, even though he prayed to Jesus to heal him. How is this Jesus good? Hmmm? Can you answer that one?"

The student remains silent.

"No, you can't, can you?' the professor says. He takes a sip of water from a glass on his desk to give the student time to relax.

"Let's start again, young fella. Is God good?"

"Er..yes," the student says.

Prof. "Is Satan good?"

The student doesn't hesitate on this one. "No."

"Then where does Satan come from?"

The student falters. "From God"

"That's right.. God made Satan, didn't he? Tell me, son. Is there evil in this world?"

"Yes, sir."

175

"Evil's everywhere, isn't it? And God did make everything, correct?"

"Yes."

"So who created evil?" The professor continued, "If God created everything, then God created evil, since evil exists, and according to the principle that our works define who we are, then God is evil."

Again, the student has no answer.

"Is there sickness? Immorality? Hatred? Ugliness? All these terrible things, do they exist in this world?"

The student squirms on his feet. "Yes."

"So who created them?"

The student does not answer again, so the professor repeats his question. "Who created them?"

There is still no answer. Suddenly the lecturer breaks away to pace in front of the classroom. The class is mesmerized. "Tell me," he continues onto another student. "Do you believe in Jesus Christ, son?"

The student's voice betrays him and cracks. "Yes, professor, I do."

The old man stops pacing. "Science says you have five senses you use to identify and observe the world around you. Have you ever seen Jesus?"

"No sir. I've never seen Him."

"Then tell us if you've ever heard your Jesus?"

"No, sir, I have not."

"Have you ever felt your Jesus, tasted your Jesus or smelled your Jesus? Have you ever had any sensory perception of Jesus Christ, or God for that matter?"

"No, sir, I'm afraid I haven't."

"Yet you still believe in him?'

"Yes"

"According to the rules of empirical, testable, demonstrable protocol, science says your God doesn't exist. What do you say to that, son?"

"Nothing,' the student replies. "I only have my faith."

"Yes, faith," the professor repeats. "And that is the problem science has with God. There is no evidence, only faith."

The student stands quietly for a moment, before asking a question of his own. "Professor, is there such thing as heat?"

"Yes."

"And is there such a thing as cold?"

"Yes, son, there's cold too."

"No sir, there isn't."

The professor turns to face the student, obviously interested. The room suddenly becomes very quiet. The student begins to explain. "You can have lots of heat, even more heat, super-heat, mega-heat, unlimited heat, white heat, a little heat or no heat, but we don't have anything called "cold". We can get up to 458 degrees below zero, which is no heat, but we can't go any further after that. There is no such thing as cold; otherwise we would be able to go colder than the lowest -458 degrees."

"Everybody or object is susceptible to study when it has or trans- mits energy, and heat is what makes a body or matter have or transmit energy. Absolute zero (-458 F) is the total absence of heat. You see, sir, cold is only a word we use to describe the absence of heat. We cannot measure cold. Heat we can measure in thermal units because heat is energy. Cold is not the opposite of heat, sir, just the absence of it."

Silence across the room. A pen drops somewhere in the classroom, sounding like a hammer.

"What about darkness, professor. Is there such a thing as dark- ness?"

"Yes,' the professor replies without hesitation. "What is night if it isn't darkness?"

"You're wrong again, sir. Darkness is not something; it is the absence of something.. You can have low light, normal light, bright light, flashing light, but if you have no light constantly you have nothing and it's called darkness, isn't it? That's the meaning we use to define the word."

"In reality, darkness isn't. If it were, you would be able to make darkness darker, wouldn't you?"

The professor begins to smile at the student in front of him. This will be a good semester. "So what point are you making, young man?"

"Yes, professor. My point is, your philosophical premise is flawed to start with, and so your conclusion must also be flawed."

The professor's face cannot hide his surprise this time. "Flawed? Can you explain how?"

"You are working on the premise of duality," the student explains. "You argue that there is life and then there's death; a good God and a bad God. You are viewing the concept of God as something finite, something we can measure. Sir, science can't even explain a thought."

"It uses electricity and magnetism, but has never seen, much less fully understood either one. To view death as the opposite of life is to be ignorant of the fact that death cannot exist as a substantive thing. Death is not the opposite of life, just the absence of it."

"Now tell me, professor. Do you teach your students that they evolved from a monkey?"

"If you are referring to the natural evolutionary process, young man, yes, of course I do."

"Have you ever observed evolution with your own eyes, sir?" The professor begins to shake his head, still smiling, as he realizes where the argument is going. A very good semester, indeed..

"Since no one has ever observed the process of evolution at work and cannot even prove that this process is an on-going endeavor, are you not teaching your opinion, sir? Are you now not a scientist, but a preacher?"

The class is in uproar. The student remains silent until the commotion has subsided.

"To continue the point you were making earlier to the other student, let me give you an example of what I mean."

The student looks around the room. "Is there anyone in the class who has ever seen the professor's brain?" The class breaks out into laughter.

"Is there anyone here who has ever heard the professor's brain, felt the professor's brain, touched or smelled the professor's brain? No one appears to have done so. So, according to the established rules of empirical, stable, demonstrable protocol, science says that you have no brain, with all due respect, sir."

"So if science says you have no brain, how can we trust your lectures, sir?"

Now the room is silent. The professor just stares at the student, his face unreadable.

Finally, after what seems an eternity, the old man answers.

"I guess you'll have to take them on faith."

"Now, you accept that there is faith, and, in fact, faith exists with life," the student continues. "Now, sir, is there such a thing as evil?"

Now uncertain, the professor responds, "Of course, there is. We

see it everyday It is in the daily example of man's inhumanity to man. It is in the multitude of crime and violence everywhere in the world. These manifestations are nothing else but evil."
To this the student replied, "Evil does not exist sir, or at least it does not exist unto itself. Evil is simply the absence of God. It is just like darkness and cold, a word that man has created to describe the absence of God. God did not create evil. Evil is the result of what happens when man does not have God's love present in his heart. It's like the cold that comes when there is no heat or the darkness that comes when there is no light."
The professor sat down.

PS: The student was probably Albert Einstein

I AM

I read a book many years ago called The Autobiography of a Yogi by Parmahansa Yogananda. In his life journey he went around studying the different religions of the world. And guess what he found out? We are all praying to the same source! Who knew?! We might call Source by different names, such as God, Goddess, Source, Great Spirit, Divine Essence, Jehovah, Mohammad, Ra, etc and yet we found they are still all the same! I also discovered through this great book the true definition of Amen. Over the years of working with thousands of Angels I have discovered something interesting. After every prayer, in every language, in every religion, (whether we are in a tee pee, a synagogue, a church, or under a willow tree) on every continent all around the world we all say two words after every prayer! Feel the similarities in the words from many languages. Here are some of the many words we use after we pray, amen, aho, aleim, amenue, aheem, om, oymen, and many more! "Amen" means "I am". Isn't that Amazing! This knowledge changed my life. I knew that the world wasn't such a big place after all and that everybody really wants the same thing! We all want clean water, good organic food, clean air, healthy bodies, happy families, and a peaceful world. Can you believe we are having wars on this planet over religion and we are all saying the same thing. Silly kids!

The next day after I discovered this amazing truth, I was doing a session with a beautiful lady and I told her my new Aha! She jumped up off my couch and ran home and brought me this. It said, "I was regretting the past and fearing the future." (You never do that do you, Angel?) 'Suddenly my Lord was speaking. My name is I am! When you live in the past with its mistakes and regrets, it is hard. I am not there. My name is not I was! When you live in the future with problems and fears, it is hard. I am not there, either. My name is not, I will be! If you live in this moment, it is not hard. I am here! My name is I AM!"

The two most powerful words in the universe are "I am". They call forth creation, and they mean God. Every time you say something that is prefaced by "I am", such as "I am allergic" or "I am sick and tired," I am stupid, I am clumsy, I am ugly, you call it forth into your reality over and over again. By affirming your illness over and over with the powerful words "I am" or my diabetes, my cancer, my tumor, my bad knee, my bad ears, you continue to create dis-ease, and it's a nightmare in your life. Instead say, "Hey, wait a minute, I am the creator of my own universe, I am whole, I am complete, and I don't want to do or say anything negative to myself anymore!" All religions have truth and God/love in them! Find that there is truth in all religions--and silliness too—there is truth in the Bible, there is truth in the Koran—but it is not ALL about love. Only the love is true!

John 15:7 But if you stay joined to me and my words remain in you, (I AM), you may ask any request you like, and it will be granted!

One woman said "I am allergic to mosquitoes," "I'm allergic to shampoo," eventually she became allergic to life, which she really was not; she just forgot how to live in her life. I even had a beautiful One come in allergic to green! Can you believe it? One of her "healers" put her on a spectre-color machine and told her green aggravated her systems! How is nature supposed to help her if she believes it causes her harm? Be very careful "healers" that you teach only love and never fear! The Course in Miracles says-teach only love, and it teaches you. So True! When my kids were young I taught them about I Am. I taught them that if they said or heard others say "I am" followed by a negative to "Cancel that". I found that they soon taught all their friends to cancel that too! The kids helped their friends to speak in a more loving language with effortless ease. Now this has become a very common practice at Angel Farms. It is amazing how many of us are saying things that tell the universe how we see ourselves! How do you see your life? Sometimes I have Angels negatively joke about themselves and then laugh. (right Geno!?) Like it's supposed to be funny! Remember, Beloveds, there is only one of us here and it is called God!

 **Angel, keep a journal for one day and catch any time you use the words I am, followed by a negative or positive about yourself**

At the end of the day add up how many times you talked about yourself today. Put the good things on your gratitude list. Take your negative I Am's and turn them into positive I Am's about yourself. Cancel your negatives and then change them. For example, if you have "I am fat" you can change it to "I am beautiful in my own skin." "I am stupid" changes to "I am wise beyond measure" and "I am tired" to "I am energy!" Speaking of tired, the Course in Miracles reminds us that we are not capable of being tired but we are capable of wearing ourselves. What makes us the most tired is that we are telling ourselves, I am tired and then we are having that experience. Get It!

Prayer

A lot of people have confusions about prayer due to religions or family tradition. Prayer is not "please give me," it is rather, "thank you that I have received this already," and that is the proper way to do it. "Thank you for coming already," "thank you for being in my experience now," "thank you for creating this experience so I can have the joyful enfoldment of the thing I ask for." God never says no. God always says yes. Whatever you want, go for it! What you are asking for might hurt you, but God will never say no. Jesus said "ask and know that it shall be given unto you even as you have asked."

My first great teacher, my grandmother, says this about prayer. "Be Spiritual-pray for guidance in all that you do. If you ask God to give you happiness he may say I give you blessings-happiness is up to you. If prayer is properly understood and applied, it can be the most powerful instrument there is." (Refer to Poem in Chapter 7)

I grew up in the Mormon religion. I am thankful for this experience because I learned a great deal about where to seek God. When I was around 10 years old I learned in church that only Mormons were going to Heaven. I was devastated by this because by best friend was Catholic. I was with my grandmother and in tears I expressed how sad it was that my friend would not make it back to God. My grandmother said, "Not everything you hear in church is true." I said, "It isn't?" She said, "Of course it isn't. But you will know in your heart when it is." This gave me permission to question everything! And I did!

One day I learned that God loves us bigger than words can speak in any language. WOW! That is pretty big. I went home and got on by horse, Sunshine. We walked past a meadow lark on a fence post that did not stop singing as we passed. I realized that God loved that meadow lark bigger than words can speak. I felt my heart expand. "Sunshine, I love that meadow lark bigger than words can speak." We came to our favorite willow tree we could hide under and no one knew we were there. "Sunshine, God loves this willow tree bigger than words can speak." I felt my heart expand. "So do I!" "Sunshine, God loves you bigger than words can speak. Wow, so do I! Some day I will be a lover like God! Some day I will love bigger than words can speak." It has been my goal every since.

Then I learned that God gives us the most precious gift of freedom of choice. With my great friend, Sunshine, we came to a stop sign. I told Sunshine that we can go forward, or left, or right, or turn around and go back again and still we have the opportunity to love. In every direction we are loved and there is no wrong choice. How cool is that!!

Then I learned about the 10 commandments. I was taught that if you do not follow these commandments you will not get back to Heaven. While discussing this with my horse, (doesn't everyone talk with their animal friends?), she did not get it either. Why would God give us freedom of choice and then give us commandments and if we didn't follow them we could never get back to God? Where is the freedom of choice? In Mormonism, when we have these questions we take them to the Bishop. When I was 11 years old, I asked him how we could have this gift of freedom of choice and also the commandments that take our choice away. He simply said that I have to have faith that what we tell

182

you is true. I said, "No I don't! My grandma says if it is not true in my heart then it is not true." I just knew that this was not true.

Then I learned about the Devil! The story in Christianity is that Jesus said I will go and show them the way, and the glory be Thine. Satan/Lucifer said I will go and show them the way and the glory be mine. Then, God, who Loves us bigger than words could speak had a war, and lost the war, as in 1/3 Host of Heaven were cast out of Heaven. Did Love really stop loving Its own creation in the likeness and image of Itself? How can this be? God could not stop loving a particle of Itself/Love. Love cannot not Love. It just is.

In my young heart, and my horse's heart too, this did not make sense. So I went to the Bishop. "Bishop, I think someone made up the Devil to scare us. Why would God, who is only Love, even care about Glory in the first place? God and Love are Glory," I told him. He told me that if I choose to not believe in the Devil he will sneak up and get me. I told him, I hope he does because I have some questions for him. The bishop literally shook in his chair. He said, "I am going to call your parents." I told him again that if it is not true in my heart then it is not true. I was right. I have learned to listen to my heart in all things and it has never been wrong. Thanks Grandma!

By the way the teacher that told me only Mormons were going to Heaven was wrong too. The Articles of Faith which are the founding principles of the religion say this:# 11 We claim the privilege of worshiping Almighty God according to the dictates of our own conscience, and allow all men the same privilege, let them worship how, where, or what they may. And another of my favorites is: #13 We believe in being honest, true, chaste, benevolent, virtuous, and in doing good to all men; indeed, we may say that we follow the admonition of Paul—We believe all things, we hope all things, we have endured many things, and hope to be able to endure all things. If there is anything virtuous, lovely, or of good report or praiseworthy, we seek after these things.

I have been a graduate of Mormonism since I was in my early 20's. Religions serve a great and powerful purpose on the planet. They help us turn within and seek God, athough they are only meant to be what I call elementary. Where at first in church we learn about the Sabbath which is where we set aside one day a week to remember God/Love/You. Until every day is a Sabbath, every day is holy with God/Love/You. After you understand this, you can choose to stay in the religions as the teachers of Love or take it out wherever you go.

We are not meant to be in religions forever but they are here to help. They are good for our community and can help many not feel so alone. Remember, Angel, that what you seek is inside you and when you realize this, you are able to radiate your light unto the world. Do not judge religion as bad either. It will still hurt your kidney's. Ask Questions and never, ever let anyone tell you, you have to work hard to be worthy to be in God's presence. You already are in God's presence just Being. If you ever feel unworthy in a church, try another.

Many things are changing, even in old religions. In March the Vatican updated the traditional seven deadly sins with seven new social sins, to bring the list into line with the temptations of the modern world. The additions: bio-ethical sins, morally dubious experiments that harm human embryos, drug abuse, polluting, social injustice, accumulating excessive wealth and creating poverty. The Catholic church is finally ready to help all those that have been abused in its care. Remember, it is not the church that does these things, only people who do not know who they are. Forgive them and get on with your loving.

I have a lot of people come and do the Cleanse and call themselves Christians. I find when they come in sick, they have been holding onto mistakes from their past. I say to them, "Oh, you are still beating yourself up over that and you call yourself a Christian?" They say, "Well I am a Christian!" I remind them that they are not following their faith. People do not realize that holding on to the past is a "sin" when you have been forgiven of them already! Jesus knew our innate good-ness and knew how hard we are on ourselves when we don't do it exactly right according to what we think or are taught.

What if I tell you to give it all to me? What if I go to earth and carry all your sins/fears so you can get on with your loving? Give it all up Christians, and Get ON with your loving! That is what the true meaning of the crucifixion was. You can't keep love up if you are struggling with things you did in your past and judged yourself too harshly.

Many people ask me what the most difficult thing is that people come to heal during the Cleanse. They expect cancer or depression or something like an illness. I tell them it is being a Jehovah witnesses. In the Jehovah religion there are no oth-er names for God, only Jehovah. I asked them, "What is your

184

definition of Jehovah?" They always get to the definition of Jehovah as love. I tell them my definition of God is in agreement of John. John 15:12 (God is Love) If Jehovah is love and God is love, don't you think that really we are just talking about Love, just in a different language or spelled differently? I just let them know that any time they hear the word God on the tapes they are listening to in the Cleansing room or from me talking, they can just translate it in their mind knowing that we are talking about the same thing. Then when we're all on the same page, everyone gets a chance for a miracle.

God never says NO. Yes, I give you freedom of choice. I am going to witness what you are going through and be with you and love you no matter what, and it's still up to you what you want to experience and what your desires are and I will always say yes. Even if your desire is that you have that drug down at end of the street and what is that going to be like, or you are going to have sex with the prostitute on the street and what is going to be the consequence of that? I won't interfere in your choices, but I will love you no matter what, whatever direction you go. You can still have the journey and I will always love you.

We can't let religion be our only guiding force; we have to understand that religions are designed to help us find our way inside our hearts so we can find our connection back to God and then we are free. Let the truth set you free. The truth being that you were created in the likeness and image of God, you are loved beyond words and beyond measure. Jesus said if you knew how many walked with you, you would never be afraid. There is a multitude that walk with each of us. They all love and honor and cherish each and every one of us for our courage to come in and pull the veil up and forget who we are and become unaware we are god/goddess. Unaware that we are the love of the universe made manifest in physical form here to taste it and see it and feel it and smell it and hear it and live it and experience it. God couldn't do this journey without us, that's how important we are.

We are either in heaven/love, hell/fear, or limbo/in between right here right now! Where are you? Are you living by man's standards or God's standards? Do you think God created a particle of you that isn't really, really, good? Every particle, every cell, every molecule in you, in the TV, in the couch, in the floor, in computer, in the dog is absolute good! Why do we have to earn our worth and our good? When

185

it's already there! We just have to wake it up, it went to sleep, that's all. What does it feel like to not be good enough? What does it feel like in our experience to not feel worthy enough? What does it feel like in our journey to be so far away from feeling loved and lovable? What does it feel like to be so unwanted or feel so stupid? Why are we not accessing God's truth within us? Because we are dragging around our past! We cannot fully expand into our future or our consciousness until we let go of everything in our past, and dwell upon it no longer. When we understand the goodness that we already are, we can rise to that goodness. We can start being more joyful, more peaceful, more healthy.

Guru Story

So many people are going through life looking for the master who is going to help them to their enlightenment. Then they find the 'GURU'. Some gurus want your dedication and your money and your everything so that they can be the one. The true master or guru is the one teaching you that you are the master. If they can't say the real meaning of "GURU" is "Gee you are you", or if they can't say "You are the master and you are the one you are waiting for," in my opinion, they are not a master. You are the divinely orchestrated particle of God, that can't get it wrong. A true guru is the one who teaches you, you are the one you seek. There are many great and profound teachers in this world so find the ones that teach only love and that you are a master of it.

An Angel told me that her master is Parmahansa Yogananda. He comes to assist in many of the Inner Child sessions I do with each person. He comes because she recognizes him as having unconditional love and then becomes a Bridge to carry her and others to Source. When we got back from our Inner Child Journey, she said again..."he is my master." I explained to her that Parmahansa didn't teach "worship me" nor did he teach "I'm the only one." He said "What I can do, you can do." "What I am, you are, and you will do greater works than I, just like Jesus and all the other great ones." Over many years of doing this work, I find many people who are following a specific guru. Many "masters" really like this. They like to be followed. This is precisely how you will know they are not a master at all.

Corinne followed a guru. Her guru was caught abusing the children and of course it crushed the group! She asked herself, "How could I be so stupid and not see it?" She had pledged her intent and her power to someone else who was supposed to be more enlightened. He ended up going to jail. Corinne developed migraines after this and couldn't handle light or sound. She lived for months in a dark room. With migraines many can only handle low sensory perception such as, dark rooms, bland tastes, and low sounds. The eyes are weak and touch gets out of whack. Everything overwhelms the senses or the sensory location in the brain is overly aggressive. Pain creates an escape. Corinne decided she was not going into a dark room to die anymore. She was going to live! We introduced light scented citrus oils, daily sunshine, and of course she found forgiveness for the guru because he didn't know who he was. She forgave herself for thinking she did it wrong. Migraines are a 6 X 6! You might have feelings like you don't deserve to live, and perhaps want to back out of life and go into a womb so you can recreate yourself and come out and live again. You can't welcome yourself back into the world with health and wealth when you are hiding all the time. Please understand Dear One that finding a Master Teacher is a wonderful thing! I am so thankful for my Master teachers that saw in me what I did not know was there. Find teachers that teach only love. There are so many!

It's not just a select few who are chosen, but all of us. Lao Tzu in the Dao Te Ching says, "The master goes into town, and the town is improved. The master leaves, and the townspeople say, "Look what we did, all by ourselves." A "master" with an EGO is "Edging God Out" and is not a master. Many come to Angel Farms and feel like they live in ego. I still have yet to meet even one of you Angels who edges God out. Somewhere in all of us we seek our source. It is a built in code. If you tune in you will find you have always been seeking God. Sometimes God has felt so very far away that we search and search and still feel lost and alone. I want to assure each and every one who is reading these words that the one you seek is already within you!

What are our choices? Do we choose fear or do we choose love? Do we choose what's happening in the news, and what's happening with that parasite over there, what about that food, and what about the GMO's, what about the dolphins and the whales, what about this big trash pile the size of the state of Texas that is floating out in the middle of the ocean somewhere? How do we understand that God created every particle of it? Love it all and it will transmute.

Genesis 1:26: Dominion Over the Earth Gives Us Hope

Then God said, "Let us make human beings in our image, in our likeness, so that they may rule over the fish in the sea and the birds in the sky, over the livestock and all the wild animals, and over all the creatures that move along the ground." It gives us hope for the whole wide world. When we wake up, and recognize the powerful force of God that is within us, then the earth will shift all by itself. It only takes one in 144,000! Are you the one we have been waiting for? We don't have to give all our energies to the things outside ourselves and the FIGHT! Like what about when they took the Hawaiian Nation illegally, what did they do to the Native Americans, what are they doing to the Samoans or the Africans, instead of how to do we LOVE even more here? THE FIGHT HASN'T WORKED FOR MILLENNIUM! WHAT IF I/WE LOVE, WOKE IT UP AND SHIFTED IT? WHAT IF THAT'S ALL WE HAVE LEFT IS TO WAKE UP AND LOVE? And then the dominion over the plants and animals of the earth helps them shift into a higher frequency of love also? I always saw great hope in that passage.

How do we allow others to have freedom, but keep the integrity of the job, and hold space for everyone around you that they are in their wholeness. Ask yourself what would Jesus do here? What would God do here? What would love do with this situation or person? Fake it until you make it. Pretend that you are God until you know that it is true!

What is the definition of FEAR?
Fantasized Emotion Appearing Real

Fear is the opposite of Love. Stay in love and all is well. Are you afraid of anything? WHY? There is only love. All else is illusion. How does it feel to be free of judgment? You no longer need to try to fit yourself into someone else's box of expectations or fit them into yours. All you need is love!

"Dear companions,
we have been in love with God
for so very, very long.
What can we now do but Forever Dance!"
—Hafiz

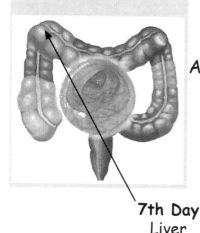

Chapter 7

7th Day
Liver

The Liver

What Kind of Records
Are You Holding In Your Liver?

Where I am God Is!
Where God Is I am!

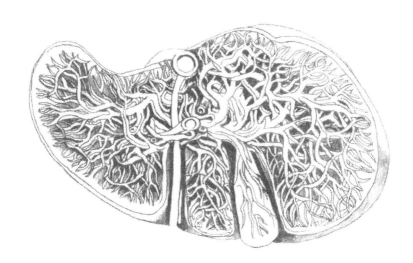

Angel, let's talk about your wonderful, amazing liver. According to Chinese Medicine, your liver performs over 535 functions. It is the largest internal organ that weighs up to 5 pounds and is the largest gland in the body! (The largest organ is the skin!) Notice your gallbladder in the middle. Isn't it beautiful? The liver is a soft, pinkish-brown "boomerang shaped" organ. Another awesome thing, in anatomy, is that it looks like a whale. In Native American theology, the whale is the record keeper. Guess what records it keeps!!

According to Chinese medicine, all internal organs work as a team in the body. The liver is considered the "General" or "Chief of Staff" and is also the most emotionally sensitive organ. The liver has one major function, which is to filter your blood. Its weakness is often connected to emotional anger and frustration. It is a gentle, loving General. Remember that. When things come through your filter, the liver uses fat to encapsulate the toxins. This keeps the toxins out of your blood stream. It does that to protect you; it doesn't want a dirty particle to go through your heart or your brain and potentially cause you harm.

Its location in the body is immediately under the diaphragm on the right side of the upper abdomen; thereby, it acts as a filter and prevents the passage of bacteria and particles from the stomach and intestines into the blood. The liver lies on the right of the stomach and makes a kind of bed for the gallbladder which stores bile. Angel, Sunlight, even 10 minutes a day, assists the liver in vitamin D and Calcium absorption. You can do your eye exercises during this time, too. The liver also helps the pancreas with fat metabolism, the synthesis of fatty acids from amino acids and sugars, the production of lipoproteins, cholesterol, and phospholipids and with the oxidation of fat to produce energy. Isn't that cool?

Your liver is the key to regulating high or low blood pressure, cholesterol balance, weight loss, increased blood flow, increased mental clarity, and to get much needed blood and nutrition to your whole body. The liver is among the few internal organs capable of natural regeneration of lost tissue; as little as 25% of the remaining liver can regenerate into a whole liver again. This is predominantly due to the hepatocytes acting as uni-potential stem cells. Studies show that if a person has two/thirds of their liver removed from trauma or surgery, it will grow back to its original size in four weeks time! Isn't that amazing?

Another function specific to the liver is that it produces an enzyme that breaks down fat. So sometimes when we are eating better and exercising more but we still aren't able to lose weight, it might be because there is not enough of this enzyme being produced. So what I have seen happen when people get their liver cleansed, is that they go into what we call a melting effect. The weight melts off automatically and naturally. This is very common.

The liver also acts as a detoxifier. Protein digestion and bacterial fermentation of food in the intestines produce ammonia as a byproduct; this ammonia is detoxified in the liver. he liver regulates thyroid function by converting thyroxine (T4) a thyroid hormone, into its more active triodothyrnine (T3).

Thirty percent of the blood pumped through the

192

heart in one minute passes through the body's chemical factory, the liver. The liver cleanses the blood and processes nutritional molecules, which are distributed to the tissues. The liver also receives bright red blood from the lungs, filled with vital oxygen to be delivered to the heart. The only part of the body which receives more blood than the liver is the brain.

The structural position of the liver as a bridge between the returning blood from the digestive system and the lower part of the body to the heart makes the liver an important organ for the health of the heart. A weakened and swollen or congested liver can obstruct the venous blood flow to the heart. A healthy liver helps maintain an adequate amount of blood flow to the heart and the heart can only pump the blood it receives.

Now Angels, I ask that you not go out and try to do any liver cleanse without making way for the particles to get out. I also ask my Angel Graduates to not share liver cleanse information I give them here at Angel Farms because we do not have nerve endings in our digestive tract that we can control. You have no idea what kind of things such as ropes, worms, and pockets that might catch things and not allow toxic particles to be released from your body safely. Our Cleanse program does not even consider emptying the liver until the seventh day, only if participants are clear. Therefore, I am not including the Liver Cleanse program so as not t o cause harm to those of you who are not willing to do all the deep work first and be educated so you do not cause harm to yourself or others.

Your amazing liver removes toxic substances from your body such as; insecticides, drugs, alcohol, metabolic wastes & harmful chemicals, sending them to the kidneys to be excreted. The kidneys must function properly for the liver to function properly. Your amazing liver also breaks down hormones like adrenaline, estrogen, aldosterone, and insulin after they've performed their function in the body and provides most of the body's heat. It also produces great digestive enzymes. It works with the spleen and the bone marrow to produce red and white blood cells, keeping the functions of the immune system working well. The liver is most importantly the filter for your blood stream. Blood is a liquid organ! A drop of blood contains about 5 million red blood cells. It also contains about 10,000 white blood cells and 250,000 platelets! Do you understand how important your liver is to your health and your life?

The liver creates glucose tolerance factor (GTF), a substance consisting of chromium and glutathione. GTF works with insulin to regulate blood sugar levels. Sugars not needed for immediate energy production are converted into glycogen in the liver. The glycogen is stored in the liver and the muscles, and is converted back to sugar when needed for energy.

When the liver becomes loaded with toxins from food, environmental elements, metals, chemicals, and anger, it becomes clogged, heavier and more sluggish. This causes poor circulation and reduced capacity to carry oxygen and nutrients. As a result, tissue and organ cells are undernourished. Your overall health and vitality depends greatly on the health of your liver.

Angel, did you know that your amazing liver did all that? Remember, your liver is your filter. What would happen if you never changed the filter in your car? Would your car run healthy? Probably not! It would more than likely cough and choke till it couldn't run anymore. The same happens in your beautiful liver. Yet we continue to go through our lives and never clean the filter in our body. Then we can't figure out why we aren't getting enough oxygen and nutrition when we are eating better and we are thinking better, and still, we are not healthy!

Have any of you have ever had an ultrasound done on your liver? You have them the first thing in the morning and they don't want you to eat anything because at night, when you go to sleep, your liver goes into what is called a collapsed or resting state. It flattens, because your liver regenerates at night. So in the morning, they can run the ultrasound over your liver and more clearly see what is in it.

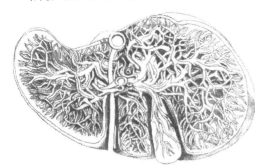

Look at the cross section of the liver. There are thousands of blood vessels. Notice the gallbladder. The liver can handle some plugged up blood vessels for a little while. But if you can imagine anywhere from 2-10,000 or more blood vessels clogged up, how much blood, nutrition and oxygen are you getting through your system? Look at all these blood vessels, thousands and thousands of them! This is a filter and directly affects your circulatory system. The body will keep the majority of blood in the internal organs and sacrifice the extremities first. People start getting cold hands and feet because of less circulation which are symptoms of a plugged filter.

Gallbladder

The gallbladder is a pear-shaped organ located inside your liver. Bile, a substance produced by the liver, is stored in the gallbladder for release into the gut to help digest fat. When you eat fatty foods, the bile becomes saturated with cholesterol, one of the components of bile. Bile digests fat and assists the body in the absorption of fat soluble vitamins, A, D, E. and K, and helps assimilate calcium. Eventually, the excess cholesterol separates from the bile and begins to calcify, forming stones. Gallstones can be formed from substances other than cholesterol, but in the United States about 80 percent of them are composed primarily of cholesterol.

If a doctor ever tells you that they don't cut into the liver to get your gallbladder, they are not telling you the truth. Many people are told that. "Oh, you don't need it. We aren't going to cut into your liver." Yeah, right!

Gallstones

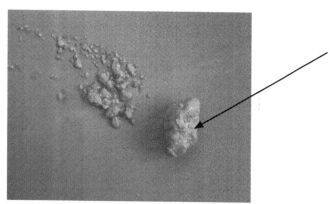

Gall stones themselves may not be the problem. In fact, many people without symptoms are surprised to learn from an ultrasound sonogram or x-ray that they have gallstones. By age forty nearly 2.5 percentage of the population has gallstones. The problems begin when the stones begin to move from the gallbladder into one of the small bile ducts leading to the liver. The pain of a gallstone attack comes when the stone blocks the duct and the duct contracts, most commonly after a fatty meal.

A minor but potentially significant step is to be sure to drink as close to a gallon of water a day as possible. This fluid is necessary to maintain the water content of the bile and help prevent the formation of stones.

Interestingly, it has been found that angels who skip breakfast or have only coffee (re-read how to drink coffee with wisdom) have a much greater incidence of gallstones.

Emotions related to the gall bladder: hardened, abrupt, intense anger. If you have ever had or witnessed a gall bladder attack you would really want to let go of everything that makes you angry!

If you can just start with yourself, imagine the amazing world shift! It can only start with you! You become the beginning of your 144,000. WOW! There would be no more war-no war inside of your body at the cellular level (dis-ease), and no war on Earth. Peace begins within! If you don't go within, you go without.

None of this is happening now in this moment. It is all a past life experience and will you let it go now? We human beings are the only species that continually beats themselves up over something that happened last week, last month, last year, last 5 years, lost 10 years, last 15 years, last lifetime. Haven't you hurt enough? Blessed Angel, when is enough, enough? From this moment on you can choose joy. Tune into your anger and let it go. A miracle is just a change in perception. Be thankful for every breath of your precious life. I am! "Anger is nothing more than an attempt to make someone else feel guilty." (Course in Miracles) Guilt hurts us in the middle of the back. We all know what it feels like to have pain there. Why would we want someone else to feel pain because of our anger?

Liver Day

Angel, now let's get down to the business of letting go of some anger and frustration and resentment. If your life is not working out like you would like it to, it could be that you have some forgiving to do. The next step of your journey is about letting go of old anger and resentments. Your amazing liver has been waiting for you to let it be free. Your thoughts you've held on to really do lead to physical and emotional distress. Are you ready to let it go?

How much do you love other people? How much do you love yourself? Fill your liver with LOVE. We were all created complete. So, now I am going to ask you a question, and I promise you this is not the last time that I will ask this question. On a scale of 1 to 10, 10 being highest, how much do you love yourself? How much does God love you on this scale? 10 of Course!

The more we accept this love for ourselves, the more we can pass it along to others. Loving others is impossible until you love yourself. I want you to understand how important it is that you begin to live your life as a 10. That's what we are here for. Too often we consider ourselves unworthy of love. The danger is when we believe ourselves to be empty of love, we find someone to love us to "fill the void". Ever done that before? Who hasn't? We do not experience true love when we search for love outside ourselves. We experience what true love really is when we release the love that we have accepted for ourselves..

Now I want you to write down the answers to the following questions.

Get out a piece of paper. Write the word Worst across the top of the paper. Write down 10 or more of the worst things that have ever happened to you in your life. Write down people, places, or events that have pissed you off or made you angry. This information is only for you to access your anger. You only have to jot down a word or two for yourself, not the details of the events. Put yourself on this list because you have been most pissed off and angry at yourself.

Turn the paper over and now write the word Best across the top of the paper. Write down 10 or more of the best things in your life. Write down people, places, or events that have been the most loving, happy, joyful, and good times. Put yourself on the list too, because you have always been the best thing in your life. If there is more, write down more, if there is less, write down less.

Now turn your paper over again to the Worst side. I want you to thank God for each and every one of these. Find the gift in each one. What did that person teach you about who you are NOT? What did that place show you about where you want to be? If you have trouble forgiving them, put a mark next to them and we will get back to them later. Take your time on this. I want you to see why this happened to you in your life. You have to see the good in something before you let go of the bad. In order to let go of these "worst" things of fear, hurt, anger, and resentment, etc, you need to see the gift in it. There's a gift for you in each and every one of them. Forgiveness is a very important thing because our livers are the key to our health.

Now let's address those things with marks beside them. How many of the people you have been angry at on your list even know that you are still angry at them? How many of the things on your paper are going on right now in this moment?

You are reading this book and really none of that is going on in this moment. So all of it is what we call 'Past Life Stuff'. Anything that is not NOW is Past Life! Does that make sense? So look at what we are dragging around with us and is causing us pain inside our bodies and in our world. Still! We need to be responsible for what we are dragging around with us.

Do you see the truth that your spiritual progress is at a standstill until you practice true forgiveness? We get stuck, don't we? How do we get past this? Do you see the truth that holding onto anger and resentment hurts you-spiritually, emotionally and physically? I am going to prove that true forgiveness is part of your basic nature. How easy was it for you to forgive MOST of the worst things in your life you wrote on your paper?

We do it effortlessly. When we are hanging onto "the past" we have true problems. Imagine that we have all these 'things' in great big suitcases that we are dragging around with us. Every time we think about that person or that place or that thing or that event—all this energy is adding weight into these suitcases. These things get so heavy that pretty soon they break us! Sweet Angel, this is your opportunity to get the big scissors out, clip off the suitcase and let it all go. What would it feel like to completely let this weight of all your past life go? If it happened yesterday, it is still a past life. How would that be? How many of these things are happening to you right now as you read this book?

I also like to remind you that you can not access your 100% God wisdom if you are still carrying all this stuff with you. You are still in the past. How can we access the true potential of what is possible when we are dragging around this stuff that is so heavy? If it is past stuff, then it means nothing NOW, and to continue dragging it around is pointless, and KILLING US. A great example is my sweet dog Shilo. If someone steps on him he yipes and moves. The

198

next moment he is loving. Humans are the only species that holds on to things that are not happening in the now and still hurting from them!

Here Is How We Do It!

In true forgiveness, there is nothing to forgive because it means seeing yourself and everyone else as a Child of God. What I would like for you to do, if you have any marks on your paper, please take a moment and see these people as Children of God; even if they don't see themselves that way. As children of God, everyone is beautiful and perfect. They just don't know who they really are! But you can love anyway. When we can truly forgive, we move into a great and ultimate power within ourselves called love, and God's love, who loves through us so we are able to love them anyway. We can help them only with our love, but we can't do it with our anger, and our judgment and our hatred. That's why the world is in the mess that it is: our anger, hatred and judgment. Now, can you see each of these people as a Child of God? Can you see yourself as a Child of God? Can you forgive everyone who has ever hurt you in their unknowingness and be free of pain and anger?

How does that feel? Does that feel better? It might feel very light. It's heard in the entire world when you are able to say; "Yes, I see you as you really are, even if you don't." So many people don't know who they are. You can have compassion for them, because you know what feeling all alone feels like, don't you? I call it hell! It hurts when you feel separate from God and you don't remember who you really are.

Now turn your papers over. What is the one common thing that you are experiencing or feeling in all of the very best moments of your life? You are experiencing love and joy. See how that common thread moves through the best and it is the energy of love? Do you see that?

Now, hold the paper with the Best side toward yourself.

I want you to look at your list. Isn't it wonderful to know that you can fill all the rest of the page of your life with this instead of the other? Now flip your page over to the Worst list. I want you to notice your handwriting. Worst side might be smaller writing, tighter writing, and closer together; stiff, jagged, and messier. Feel the energy in the page. Things that are harder for someone to forgive will have more frustration than other items on the list. Turn your paper over to the Best again. The best side will usually be larger print with more straight lines. As people take more time to write the best things in their life, it is more easier and has lots of little loops and character to it.

Can you feel the energy in the page? Feel that? See that? This is what anger does, even in our bodies. It shows up even in our handwriting!

Without the liver there is no life! Therefore: love your liver and treat it well.

What hurts us the most is holding onto grudges, anger, hatred, unforgiveness and resentment in our hearts. These emotions and judgments are self destructive. They eat away at our souls, filling us with resentments and blocking the essence of our true loving nature. No matter how many spiritual principles you have been guided to, unless there is complete forgiveness in your life, we are dying spiritually, emotionally, physically and mentally. We must find another way to love and forgive so we can really experience total healing, true happiness and peace.

In our society, family, and religion, we were taught about forgiveness. Here are some examples of what we think forgiveness is.

Have you ever said to someone in your life, I will forgive you but I won't forget? That is not true forgiveness. Have you ever claimed that you now understand why some people act as they do so you no longer require them to live up to high standards? That is not true forgiveness. There is only one type of forgiveness that we seek. Did you ever hear the incredible story of the Amish people who had several of their little children murdered in their school? The man who did it was mad at God and took his anger out on the small children and then killed himself. The Amish people went to the wife of the murderer and asked if they could help her and her children. They let her know that they were all in pain and together they could forgive and heal.

Their forgiveness had a profound impact on the entire world. Now can you imagine what this world would be like if we could all forgive on that level?

Think about it for a minute, Angel. If we could forgive on a level like that, including inside of our bodies, there would be no room for war. Forgiveness begins by understanding it is not a matter of 'I forgive you' but 'forgive me for judging you in the first place' and that is true forgiveness.

Now I want you to look at your papers and tell me: Of the people who caused you harm or pain in any way, do you think if they had known who they really were, that they would have done things to cause you or themselves harm? They would not have done that. Think about who might have you down on their list. Did you ever cause any harm on purpose? NO! So let them go and let yourself go! Forgive! Dig deep Angel, your liver is counting on you! Who do you need to forgive? What do you need to forgive? Your basic nature is LOVE.

Say This Prayer For Your Amazing Liver Now

Angel's Toolbox

Spirit of Love within me, I now choose to let go of all my feelings of hurt, anger, judgment, and pain caused by anyone, person, place, or event. I choose to see each and everyone as a child of yours and a part of me. Help me to seek out any unloving thoughts and replace them with your Divine Love. Thank you God .

Every master who has walked on this planet has said the same thing: if you live your life in love, you can have phenomenal results. Jesus said it, Buddha said it, Gandhi said it, Mother Teresa said it, and I call her a master too. Quan Yin said it, Mandella says it, etc. Anything that isn't love is something other than love. We need to pay attention.

Do you know that in the Bible in John 15:12, it says, "This is my commandment, that you love one another as I have loved you." Have you heard that one before, Angel? We all know that the Bible has been changed many times. The last time was done in the King James Version, right? Before it was changed, this passage used to say, and I want you to feel this in your Angel heart: "This is my desire, that you love yourself and one another, even as I have loved you." What happened to our society when we took the 'loving self' part out of that equation? How many of you think we have to sacrifice our lives for others so we will be closer to God and yet we leave our 'self' out?

When was the last time you took a hot bath for yourself? When was the last time you really took time to nurture and love yourself? Many people do not do that. Many people in our society have a belief or a feeling, because we were taught this in churches and schools and from our parents and our grandparents, that what we have to do is to take care of our family, take care of our community, etc. but we don't take care of ourselves. And this puts us in an out-of-balance position, without loving our selves, we have pain. Do you know sweet Angel, that you are created complete? There can be nothing added to you to make you more then you are already. We are Spiritual first and we only need to release love to feel healthy, abundant, and powerful. Love must be released from us because it is what we are. We do not have room to receive love from others, we are completely full of love already.

If I said, "I need you to love me, so I will be whole", this would let me know that I don't know who I am. It's a completely different flow of energy that we circulate within us when we know who we are and we love. We receive true love only from God. Only when we allow love to pour from this infinite source, we are loving as all the masters have taught us: "Love yourself, and one another, even as I have loved you." How can you express more love that is within you already? You love because it truly is what you do best. You are a master of Love. Step up and love/live it!

Which side of the paper did you feel most alive after reading? The "best" side, of course!

One of the greatest gifts we have in this lifetime, besides life itself, is the freedom of choice. No matter where we are, no matter what we do, we are love. We can't change who we are. The best moments in your life are when you are in the truest part of yourself: love. Another point about "Commandments": Where does freedom of choice come in when you have to be commanded to do something? Do you hear the contradiction in the word 'commandments? How does love work here? Have you ever looked to the Bible to find the definition of God? I am in full agreement with John who is the only writer in the Bible to define God in three magnificent words. God is love. So simple.

Visualize the energy of light and absolute love coming into your crown chakra, or the top of your head, and then out through your heart.

It comes from a divine source and out. We are a conduit. We ground the love onto this planet. If we are looking for someone to love us and make us whole, then we are lost. We are so lovable that we don't need that.

I give people this challenge all the time. Try to overdo love. Just try to run out of it. You cannot. The more you love, the more it comes. Become an example to be a lover like God and see how that can change your life; without judgment, without criticism. Love cannot be added to you, it can only be released from you. Do you see the truth of that?

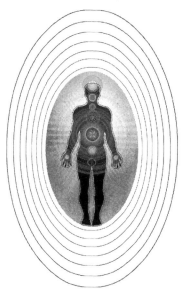

Now look at your energy field. I want you to remember what it looks like. Notice the energy that radiates about six feet off the body in all directions. How do you add love to that? Do you see any holes or gaps or anywhere that's empty? It's not possible, it's complete. That is how God created it. Perfect light. You are whole and complete in all ways. When you allow God's love to come to you and out to others, you are loving as a master. Remember what the masters told us. Love yourself and one another even as I have loved you!

Repeat this: I now choose to open my heart to the full love of God. Letting this infinite love radiate and light up this world, blessing and healing myself and everyone and everything. Every step I take, my footsteps send out ripples of healing love/energy to the the great mother earth and everyone on it. I remember now I am the way, the truth and the light. When I realize this about myself, I am most like you, God. Thank you for showing me who I am!

Now I want to tell you about how your anger is connected to your wonderful Liver. The more anger you access and release, the more things you are going to be stirring up. Guess what your liver wants? It wants the anger out, it wants the stones (physical manifestations of anger) gone. It wants to be able do its 535 different functions! And now I am going to teach you about what some of these functions are.

How does you liver get sluggish and out of balance? Your liver encapsulates toxic particles by wrapping them in fat, to prevent them from reabsorbing into the system which would cause harm to your heart or brain. We call these liver stones and gall stones, which are fat encapsulated particles. Your liver loves you enough to sacrifice its functions in order to not hurt you. It does this as a safety device. The angrier you are, the more stones you have and the less blood flow your body is allowed. The liver will be compromised because you are angry at someone else, or yourself, and anger comes from what you think someone could have done, should have done, or would have done, so immediately it's a judgment. Anger (according to The Course in Miracles) is nothing more than an attempt to make someone feel guilty.

So what does all this anger do to your body? You are plugging up your largest filter with your own anger. Anger creates conditions of high blood pressure and high cholesterol. It plugs up the blood vessels. Your heart has to pump really hard with a limited amount of blood flowing through it to get it to different areas of your body, hence cold extremities. Do you understand, Beloved Angel, that if you have high or low blood pressure, circulation problems, cholesterol issues, and low energy, your liver needs some love? When you are angry you harm your liver and your entire system. No one else but you can affect your liver!

If you really want to never have a heart attack or stroke find ways to be peaceful and learn to not be angry at other people's behaviors. Just forgive them for they know not who they are, they know not what they do. Every master teaches non-attachment. This is how you live in peace.

Remember Angel, I talked to you about how every time

you get angry you depress your immune system by 5 hours and stress your adrenals! You are plugging up your liver with stones because you are still angry at something that isn't happening now!

If you feel the need to scream in a pillow over sexual abuse that happened when you were 14 and you are now 38, you are just aggravating the stones in your liver and aggravating your adrenals. You are experiencing the same old thing which has nothing to do with the NOW. Imagine your past life as a big paddle wheel on a river boat. It keeps spinning and spinning, but the poor ol' wheel is just not getting anywhere! You can't heal it until you let go! These things are not happening now! Be responsible for your earth choices. Empower yourself! Ask yourself now why did I choose that journey? Why would I do that to myself? Stop being a victim and feel the power of Love within to transform all things! Good job, you don't have to do it again!

Body Check! Look at the blood vessels in your arms, legs, knees and throat. Are you having blood pressure, cholesterol, or difficulty staying warm? Is your circulation to your hands and feet flowing well? Notice the color and texture of your skin, and the whites of your eyes. Do they have a yellowish color? Look also at the coloration in your toenails and fingernails. Are they thick and yellow? Are you exhausted and feeling very "heavy"? If you have any of these symptoms, you are experiencing liver overload.

When you release anger from your body, you allow the liver to release stones. I have found that connection between anger and liver stones are the same. We say all the time here at Angel Farms: are you going to create a liver stone over that? Is creating a stone in your body and limiting its many functions, worth being angry? I think not! Let it go and get on with your life!

When you are ready to let go of your anger and liver stones, blood vessels open up and fill with blood, (like turning on a hose that was just trickling, it is now on full blast.) When you unplug the liver, your vascular system opens and works better than ever! The whites of your eyes are whiter because there is more oxygen in the blood, your lips are pinker, and the tips of your fingers, feet and hands are warmer.

Anger Miracle Story

Raven came through the Cleanse and literally had 75 things on her anger list! I had another Angel, Inge from Germany who didn't understand English very well, so I had to go very, very slowly while I was educating the group about the liver and how to clear it, so Inge could understand. I could see Raven getting angrier and angrier because I wasn't in a big hurry. I was laughing inside of myself at God setting up this situation for this woman to have an opportunity to have patience. Shara said something to Raven about money that day and about how it was okay and that she was worth it. She yelled at Shara, "I don't want to hear about money from a 20 year old!" After she left that day she was very angry. The next day she came in thinking we were going to kick her out of the program because she had yelled and been so angry. She was surprised to find us loving her! She said, "You mean you aren't going to kick me out of the program? Guess what? Last night I got it. I got that if I didn't let go of this anger stuff I was going to die and so, I let it go! " And she did. She shifted and it was amazing!

True Healers

True healers are those that live love and feed their Spirit every day. They do not teach with fear! They feed their body good healthy food and water to the best of their ability. True healers are able to hold space for everyone and everything in complete love and non-judgement. Catch yourself thinking. Are you living in your head, not your heart? Did you love your neighbor today? Were you sharp or curt with a member of your Ohana/family? Did you love the flower in your yard as you walked out? Where did you miss an opportunity to love? Because you chose the opportunity to love, so did your 144,000! It's the journey not the destination that matters.

Unhealed Healers

You cannot help another to the truth unless you are living there already! This is called integrity. All of us came in as healers to heal this world of the trauma or the judgment of trauma. We are all here to do that and the time is now! How many times in the day did you love? Were you aware of it? Are you thankful of the beauty around you, grateful for the monumental construction of the universe to hold the space for you in this moment? Instead of thinking, what am I going to do in an hour? You can't have your 'healing center' until you are clear of your drama/trauma in the first place. That's when the healing center will manifest and you will become part of a community of healed healers. Many of our Graduates want a healing center. Start now by getting yourself clear and loving. Do unto others as you would have done unto yourself. You have to start living the truth now. And what's the truth? It's the truth that sets you free. The truth is that you are going to love here on earth, no matter what. You did the other stuff already and look where it got you and where it got our world. So what would happen if you just woke up in love instead?

You still have to take care of yourself in whatever you are doing, Cleansing, holding space, doing energy work, massage, doctoring, chiropractic adjusting, readings, etc. You can easily balance yourself with a walk in nature, yoga and exercise, a hot bath, meditation, a massage, a moment in a hot springs, or even a great smoothie. It is vital you take care of your physical, emotional and spiritual self too, because it keeps you strong and grounded and in alignment with Spirit so you can show up and help other people. Otherwise you can't show up because you are too exhausted. At Angel Farms, we have a requirement that our staff gets regular massages from the massage therapists and they must do their cleansing maintenance. It teaches them to take care of themselves, so they can teach others to take care of themselves. It is important to keep ourselves in balance.

I remember, in the beginning of my journey, wondering, "Can I do it? Can I actually change the world by loving?" It seemed so hard. I didn't know if I could really step up and hold space of unconditional love for everybody. How is that really possible when this person does this and that person does that? I decided to fake it until I made it. I found it to be the easiest thing, it wasn't hard at all. I found the hard part was wobbling into where I had been (and my back would rmind me) and returning to the present time where that was over. I no longer could still see other people as they had been.When people do the Cleanse, I tell them they are not the same as they were 10 days ago. Your family and your friends and your co-workers don't know that. You are going to go back as a different person. How is that going to affect you when you show up and people are going to be judging you via the way you used to be, not the way you are now? You are a different, clearer person. You can become an example of what is possible! People will notice there's something different about you and they will want that. They will feel hope just because you showed up a clearer vessel! Sometimes some of us have to set an example to show that if you love, just you, not every one else, maybe somebody else can do it too. Maybe your best friend or your co-worker can say, wow, maybe if they can do it, maybe I can do it! It just takes enough of us to wake up and say I am going to choose love and joy instead of anger and sadness, because that's what I want for my world and my family.

The Symptoms Of Inner Peace
http://www.expressionsofspirit.com/symptoms.htm

A tendency to think and act deliberately, rather than from fears based on past experiences.
An unmistakable ability to enjoy each moment.
A loss of interest in judging others.
A loss of interest in judging self.
A loss of interest in conflict.
A loss of interest in interpreting the actions of others.
A loss of ability to worry.
Frequent, overwhelming episodes of appreciation.
Contented feelings of connectedness with others and nature.
Frequent attacks of smiling through the heart.
Increasing susceptibility to kindness offered, and the uncontrollable urge to reciprocate.
An increasing tendency to allow things to unfold, rather than resisting and manipulating.

Guilt

Guilt hurts the middle of the back, like hanging ourselves on a cross and guess what, God needs the wood for a higher purpose than hanging you. Anger is not peaceful, not loving, and separates us from who we really are.

If others express anger with you or withhold love in some way, do not let their negativity become a part of your response. Remember you are creating new neuro-pathways! By tuning into another's energy and seeing them transform, you will be able to sense the pain in them. This is why you want to learn to stay in your heart.

If you are having trouble forgiving people, try the following exercise.

Imagine that the next time you talk to them; it is their last day on earth. What would you say? How would you feel? I know you would be able to come from your heart no matter how the other person acted. You would be generous, warm, and loving.

Imagine going to this person who has brought you pain and pretend this meeting will be your last. See how much you appreciate them for who they are, the gifts they have given you, the love they have sent your way. It will be easier to let go of the pain and come from a higher level if you knew this was their last day on earth. Notice how you begin to see wonderful things about them, their light and love. See how they had no real intent to hurt you; they were acting from their own pain or lack of clarity. Perhaps you did something to push a button in them and they simply reacted to a program of pain within the self. You can come from this higher perspective. You can make every connection high and loving.

Picture in your mind the various people in your life, knowing you had only one more chance to be together. If you are not going to be with them again, send them a telepathic message that you forgive them and send them love. Imagine that you have one day left to clear up any messages that you have sent them. Even if they have pulled away and left you, there are still telepathic messages going on and you can clear them up.

Someone recently told me she hated someone. She was asked, if that person was in a car wreck in front of you, would you call for help for them or let them die? She of course said she would assist in any way. She really did not hate.

If someone has died and left you, you may have anger toward them. You can transmit forgiveness through your soul and it will reach theirs. Release the pain within, go to the peaceful higher state when you do connect, sit quietly with them, not rehashing the situation, not going into details, but instead sitting in peace together.

Tell them that you know now, that they did not mean to hurt you, that you understand the contract, and love them. Then, the pain will disappear. While it is wonderful to release others, the one who truly receives the greatest benefit of forgiveness is the one that forgives. Remember to send love to the negative voices that criticize or don't believe that you can have what you desire. Send loving energy every night to your past. In this way you can be a compassionate Angel to yourself. We teach what we most need to learn.

Weight

Did you know that your liver is the key to regulating weight loss? It is the only organ in the body that produces the enzyme to break down fat? That is why the liver can use fat to wrap around dirty particles that might go to your heart or brain and kill you. Your liver loves you enough to sacrifice itself for you. When people force themselves to reduce without having done sufficient transitional therapy to clear early life issues, losing their unconscious defense mechanism can lead to emotional break-downs, depression and even suicidal tendencies. Often such persons see themselves as 'weak and gluttonous' which is probably a learned behavior. One addiction replaces another and they take up addictions to cigarettes and coffee or even alcohol and drugs.

It might be well to question how a person bothered by their weight feels about their friends and colleagues that are overweight. The very person who feels he/she would be more loved if he/she were slender does not apply this principle to carrying for friends based on weight. So the major issue is not the weight but rather self love and acceptance. It is better to encourage overweight people to learn about proper nutrition; and to develop a focus on gratitude for wholeness and health rather than a self criticism concerning lack of perfection in their body image.

Weight cannot be taken off until fat is efficiently burned which requires every nutrient. If you lack any of the B vitamin family, it results in a lag in energy production. Proteins are needed for energy producing enzymes. Fat is burned twice as rapidly when protein is adequate and thus calories are used.

210

Plenty of Vitamin E foods allow for double the utilization of fats! Lecithin helps the cells burn fat. Overweight persons tend to have excessive blood fat and cholesterol which indicates energy is not being produced normally. Excessive blood fat also leads to unnecessary fatigue which leads back to obesity.

The health of the liver is also essential. Liver damage or sluggishness prevents energy producing enzymes from being synthesized in adequate quantities. If protein, vitamin B2 or Pantothenic acids are under supplied, the liver is unable to produce enzymes necessary to inactivate insulin. Excessive insulin accumulates in the blood causing fat to be formed quickly and the blood sugar to fall: hypoglycemia. A person with continuous low blood sugar usually gains rapidly yet stays so ravenously hungry that it is difficult to lose weight. They probably have some healthy parasites too.

When given small frequent meals of the identical food, weight remains normal. Most of the food is converted into energy when small meals are eaten. Large meals overwhelm the stomach and can be dumped into the small intestine without proper breakdown of proteins.

Americans tend to eat 80 percent of their food after 6 pm. One study of people who could not lose weight revealed that they obtained most of their food in the evenings and had no appetite for breakfast. In the morning while their blood sugar was still high from the night before, will power to not eat was no problem. Perhaps even having lunch was not an issue. In the evening, the blood sugar drops and one can be irritable, exhausted and starved. The problem is not eating too much but rather too little. Lecithin's major function is to aid in burning fats. Too little linoleic acid stresses the adrenals which then allow blood sugar to fall and makes weight loss difficult.

Metabolism is mostly carried out in the liver. Sluggish metabolism due to sluggish liver and too much estrogen are contributing factors to weight gain. Daily morning exercise helps to activate the liver. Letting go of anger is also vital for the health of your liver. When the liver becomes more efficient and bile flows better, the weight problem is usually helped significantly.

Here is a poem written by my grandmother whom I consider one of my master teachers. She is 97 years young. I am so blessed to have her in my life. Without her you would not be reading this book and I would not have been able to help thousands of people get well. Enjoy!

90 Year Old Plus Party

by Fern Manning (A True Story)
My Grandmother who just turned 98.

I was invited to a party.
That's quite unique for us.
The only thing that was required
was to be 90 years old and plus.
Since I had all the qualifications
and I'm vertical to-day,
thought I'd go check it out,
and hear what they had to say.
I got dressed up the best I could,
and put on matching shoes.
I even had a pedicure,
for me that is good news.
I got in my silver Camry,
and drove straight up the street
to the Senior Citizen Center,
where all the old folks meet.
I was seated at a table,
with flowers, balloons and such,
they soon brought over four old men,
so that made five of us.
One old guy said he had rested
for three days in advance.
He wanted to make sure he got there,
didn't want o take a chance.
He said his hearing was impaired,
to that there was no doubt.
He was glad his eye sight was fairly good
He wanted to check all the women out.
He said to me-"Do you drive a car?"
I said, "Why yes I do"
He said, I'm really glad to know that sweetie,
now I can ride with you.
I didn't like that very much,
so I thought I'd set him straight
I said, "That's never going to happen friend"
no need for you to wait.

212

A lady who was 99
Came and sat down next to me
She took the Mic and sang a song
she was sharp as she could be
She sang a song from olden times,
about some silk and lace,
It would have sounded better,
if her false teeth had stayed in place.
They served us lunch, that was pretty good,
the hamburger and potato type
I think the broccoli was over cooked
cause it was almost white.
There was a box of oranges sitting there,
the sign on the box said "take"
If you were lucky enough to be 90
you could have a piece of cake.
I made some brand new friends to-day
they were friendly from the start,
no matter how old the body gets,
we are all still young at heart.
I started home with a grateful heart
and said a little prayer,
I said, "Thank you lord for keeping me safe,
and out of that wheel chair.
If God is willing and I'm still here
I'd like to have the chance
to attend the party next year,
think maybe I'll do a dance.

(Isn't she wonderful!
I am so Blessed to have her in my life!)

Chapter 8

Empower Yourself by Knowing and Growing 8 Master Herbs & Minerals

1. Aloe Vera ....
2. Cayenne Pepper ....
3. Comfrey ....
4. Echinacea ....
5. Golden Seal ....
6. Noni ....
7. Tumeric/Olena ....
8. Garlic ....

I am the Breath of Life.
I am Joy.

8th Day
Right Lung Area

"Use healing herbs when you are weak to help you be strong, and food to keep you strong!"

In this chapter I am going to talk about what I call the 8 Master Herbs for you to know and use. This in no way means all herbs are not a gift, yet these 8 Master Herbs are a great way to begin your empowerment for your future. I have been an herbalist for over 20 years. I believe if you have the basic information about these amazing gifts from the Creator you will be safer and healthier. I encourage you to get to know these herbs by planting and using them. Many diseases can be averted and helped with this knowledge passed down from many sources. I have used these and many other herbs for over 20 years with great appreciation and respect for the help they have offered myself and so many Angels. Do not be afraid of the future and your health. You have the ability to help yourself and your Ohana/family easily and with skill. Practice and research the use of these plants and you will empower yourself and others.

Check with your health care provider such as your, doctor, midwife, OB, etc before adding these herbs into your diet.

215

All plants, like all medicines, may be dangerous if used improperly-if they are taken internally when prescribed for external use, if they are taken in excess, or if they are taken for too long of a period of time. I have been taught that food is the medicine and medicine is the food. We use herbs to help us be strong when we are weak and food to keep us strong. These eight master herbs are also food for the body and can help us when we are weak. Be Thankful, Angel, that this knowledge of great master helpers is here for you and I. I recommend you research each herb and give yourself an education about these wonderful gifts.

Aloe Vera

Aloe is a member of the lily family which includes long life healers such as garlic and onion. Aloe plants are found in tropical and desert regions throughout the world, and they are easily recognizable. These large, fleshy, spiny and succulent leaves are popular for their many medicinal properties. The word Aloe is derived from an Arabic word which means "bitter and shiny". The sap has an almost neutral PH value and contains amino acids, vitamins and minerals that make it ideal for soothing skin inflammations. Young specimens are red spotted. The plant bears yellow tubular flowers in summer. The aloes ferox plant is similar to aloe vera and is a succulent plant. The plant is native to Africa, but is cultivated in other parts of the world. Aloe Vera Gel is the colorless mucilaginous gel harvested directly from the cells of fresh Aloe leaf. Aloe pieces are broken off the plant, split or torn open and used directly on injuries. Aloe juice is extracted from the pulp. There is a bitter laxative that is made from the leaf after it dries to a crystalline substance.

Aloe Vera was first mentioned in the Egyptian "Ebers" papyrus around 1552 B.C. Ancient Egyptians had drawings of Aloe plants inscribed in the tombs of pharohs; considering it the 'plant

216

of immorality'. The beautiful Egyptian queen, Cleopatra used Aloe Vera as her personal beauty secret. When Alexander the Great (he conquered Egypt in 332 BC), heard of the amazing healing properties of the plant, he conquered the island of Socotra in order to have the Aloe plant for his army. His crusades took Aloe into Asia.

Throughout history soldiers have sought and carried Aloe for wounds. Aloe has been popular with soldiers on the move for centuries. Spanish Conquistadors discovered the Aloe plant in South America and exported large quantities back to Europe throughout the sixteenth century, making the Aloe plant a foundation of western medicine. Throughout the 18th and 19th centuries, Aloe has remained one of the most popular prescribed and over-the-counter medicines.

The fresh Aloe Vera plant is unique in that it contains the full range of all the most concentrated polysaccharides known. These very large and complex, intricate polysaccharides found in fresh Aloe are responsible for the profound and direct immune enhancing properties demonstrated by scientific research. Polysaccharides (made by body) are manufactured by our bodies until puberty. They are difficult to find from food sources. It has been recently discovered that Aloe is the most concentrated plant source of these mucopolysaccharides (made by plant). These very large and complex polysacchrides have been shown to be directly immune enhancing by being able to survive the digestive process and by being taken up whole and intact into the lymph system. Very rare indeed!

Aloe stimulates macrophages by fitting their receptor sites. The macrophages have a myriad of functions which include: engulfing foreign bodies, releasing growth factor, stimulating tissue production, orchestrating and stimulating function of all cells, regulating immune system response, regulating the inflammation process, (increase and decrease) releasing factors that tell the immune cells where to go, as well as stimulating the other immune cells to release their antibodies as needed. Aloe Vera Gel is widely used for small cuts and abrasions. It seals the wounds, promotes healing and helps prevent infection.

Aloe Vera gel is squeezed from the leaf, and may be used as a natural bandage. Thermal and radiation burns heal faster with less scaring when treated with preparations containing Aloe Vera Gel. But did you know aloe relieves the burden on the immune system, helping the body deal with any dis-ease? Aloe juice soothes digestive tract irritations such as colitis, ulcers and irritable bowel syndrome. Aloe's ability to encourage the release of pepsin, a gastric digestive enzyme, which is normally released when the stomach is full, is a possible reason for its ulcer-healing effects. It is crucial that the structural integrity of the mucopolysaccharides be protected for them to have direct immune enhancing properties.

Aloe is best used when it is fresh and clear, cold pressed and organic of course! I have used aloe vera as a natural treatment of burns and witnessed how it decreases pain and it also reduces scarring every time! For any kind of stomach or digestive issue, I recommend using $\frac{1}{2}$ cup of fresh aloe in the morning $\frac{1}{2}$ hour before drinking your morning water and eating. It soothes and protects the digestive track and protects the soft mucus lining when it has irritations. Other great uses and indications handed down through time:

- Sunburns
- First and second-degree thermal burns
- Radiation burns
- External treatment of minor wounds
- Inflammatory skin disorders
- Acne
- Hemorrhoids
- Psoriasis/Dermatitis
- Anemia
- Helps kill Fungal infections and is a carrier for other herbs
- Constipation
- Poor appetite
- Colitis
- Irritable bowel syndrome
- Asthma-good results in patients suffering when not dependent on corticosteroids
- Diabetes
- Immune system enhancement
- Peptic ulcers
- Nutrition, providing vitamins, minerals, amino acids and enzymes
- Anti-inflammatory agent
- Hastens wound-healing by enhancing cell proliferation
- Breaks down and digests dead tissue, including acne
- Anesthetizes tissue, relieving pain associated with joints and sore muscles
- Stops itching
- Reduces the heat sores

218

USE only the juice of the inner leaves for the anti-inflammatory effect on Crohn's dis-ease. The outside edge of the leaf and the laxative and bitter principles of Aloe must NOT be used by people suffering from Crohn's dis-ease as it causes cramping.

Aloe Vera also stimulates the growth of healthy kidney cells and helps to slow the formation of kidney stones. A strong purgative and stimulant laxative exude from the leaves but can cause cramping. It stops the inflammation and blood supply of tumors. Showed interesting results in preventing carcinogenic compounds from entering the liver and is combined in some cancer treatments. Laxative effect is preferable to use than that of cascara and senna, as Aloe draws less fluid into the large intestine and is less likely to cause electrolyte imbalance. The leaf's inner skin is extracted for use as a very powerful laxative. Aloe has a stimulating effect on the pancreas to produce more insulin and it causes a decrease in cholesterol, triglycerides and sugars.

Aloe Vera detoxification allows:
• an ability to enjoy a wider range of foods
• relief from pain
• an ability to reduce prescribed bulking agents or antispasmodic drugs
• a greater feeling of well-being
• an improvement in the quality of life
• faster healing and repair of damaged skin
• moisture to hold on skin and adds flexibility to retard aging

Topical application of Aloe Vera gel is said to be devoid of complications. Use Aloe with gratitude and trust, you have a gift to help in times of need.

Cayenne Pepper (Capsicum)

This is one of my most used master herbs. Cayenne pepper is produced from the Capsicum Plant- a tender, variable annual with branched stems and simple oval, lance-shaped leaves. Bell-shaped, white to green flowers appear in spring and summer, and are followed by hollow fruits, which display differing colors when ripe. The fruits are used for culinary and medical purposes. Cayenne pepper has a tonic and antiseptic effect, stimulating the circulatory and digestive systems and increasing perspiration. It contains capsaicinoids such as capsaicin, as well as vitamin C. The color of the fruit is due to the carotenoids contained.

Cayenne is a medicinal and nutritional herb. It is a very high source of vitamins A and C, has the complete B complexes, and is very rich in organic calcium and potassium, which is one of the reasons it is good for the heart. The potency of Cayenne is determined by the intensity of its heat. This is determined by the quantity of the chemicals in Cayenne and its resins. The more of these chemicals that are in Cayenne the hotter it is, the stronger it is. The heat is measured in heat units and most Cayenne peppers are between 30,000 to 80,000 heat units. Capsaicin blocks pain impulses. Certain types of nerves in the human body actually appear to have receptor sites for capsaicin. Cayenne is the key that fits a certain lock in the nerves. Many herbalists believe that Cayenne is the most useful and valuable herb in the herb kingdom, not only for the entire digestive system, but also for the heart and circulatory system. It acts as a catalyst and increases the effectiveness of other herbs when used with them.

Ointments containing capsaicin have been clinically proven to help relieve the pain of:
• arthritis
• shingles
• psoriasis
• fibromyalgia

Capsaicin ointment has also become the treatment of choice for numbness and tingling sensation in the extremities as seen with diabetes and pain from skin cancer. Capsaicin also can lower your LDL (bad) cholesterol along with reducing triglyceride levels. Capsaicin can also aid congested bronchial tubes or a stuffy nose. Despite popular misconceptions, hot peppers do not cause ulcers or gallbladder problems.

Internal uses for Cayenne Pepper:
• Improve circulation
• Assists in the cold stage of fevers
• Varicose veins
• Asthma
• Digestive problems such as dyspepsia, colic and flatulence
• Used for laryngitis as a gargle
• As a gastrointestinal detoxification
• Used as a food preservative in the tropics

An amazing cough and sore throat remedy is honey, lemon, and cayenne. Make it thick in order to stick to the throat and as hot as you can handle. It kills pain and really speeds up healing. My daughter had chronic tonsillitis when she was young and could not tolerate over the counter cough remedies. (She would gag) I would make this for her in a cup and give her a spoon to use whenever she needed it. She kept her tonsils and really liked the formula.

External use: When applied topically to the skin, the Cayenne causes a sensation of pain and warmth, which can cause extended reversible insensitivity of the skin, which is useful in treating various forms of topical pain such as arthritis and spasms. Apply externally to sprains, areas that itch, arthritic spots, neuralgia, and pleurisy.

Internal use: Cayenne can rebuild the tissue in the stomach and increase the peristaltic action in the intestines. Cayenne helps the body to create hydrochloric acid; necessary for good digestion and assimilation, especially of proteins. All this becomes very significant when we realize that the digestive system plays the most important role in mental, emotional and physical health, as it is through the digestive system that the brain, glands, muscles and every other part of the body are fed. Emergency uses:

I have been known to carry only cayenne when I hike or

travel. Even in Kalalau Valley in Kauai, people come off a 13 mile hike with crazy blisters on their feet. Staph is well known in the valley and unsafe on open sores. People would hear I had a solution and come to me for help. I tell them that this will burn as I pour it on their wound. After a moment of great heat, pain disappears and no one got staph! I also suggested that they take it internally to help keep the blood clean until their wound was healed.

If a heart attack should occur, it is suggested that a teaspoon of extract be given every 15 minutes or a teaspoon of Cayenne in a glass of hot water be taken until the crisis has passed. Dr. Richard Anderson also knew of a doctor who rushed out into the parking lot and put Cayenne tincture into the mouth of a man who had died of a heart attack while he was parking his car. Within a few minutes, the man's heart started beating again. According to Dr. Anderson, using Cayenne and hawthorn berries together has a most incredible effect upon the heart. A regimen of Cayenne and hawthorn berries for several months will great- ly strengthen the heart, and possibly prevent heart attacks. He states that if an attack were to occur in someone who had followed this regimen, chances are very good that no damage would occur.

If a hemorrhage occurs in the lungs, stomach, uterus or nose, it is suggested that a teaspoon of extract (or a teaspoon of Cayenne powder in a cup of hot water) be given every 15 minutes until the crisis has passed. The bleeding should stop in 10-30 seconds. The reason for this is that rather than the blood pressure being cen- tralized, it is equalized by the Cayenne, and the clotting action of the blood becomes more rapid. Works great after birth, also. Can also help with extreme menstruating issues by increasing blood flow to restricted blood vessels thereby relieving cramping and pain.

How to prepare cayenne tincture and cayenne powder: You will need Alcohol (vodka-80 proof), to extract the medicinal properties of the herbs and to add a preservative to the tincture. Wear gloves at all times when handling the cayenne and be sure to wash your hands very thoroughly as the cayenne stays on your hands!! Care must be taken when handling fresh peppers, as severe eye irritation can occur. Cayenne is a powerful herb and must be used with respect and gratitude.

Cayenne tincture made from fresh organic peppers: Purchase fresh organic peppers from the grocery store and

222

wash them thoroughly. Dry the peppers by hanging them away from sunlight until they are dry. Grind the peppers in a coffee grinder into a powder.Take a canning jar (quart size) and fill it up $\frac{1}{4}$ of the way with the dried Cayenne peppers. Add alcohol (40% or 80 proof) to just cover these powdered chilies or approximately 1 inch in depth of alcohol. In a blender add some fresh chili peppers and enough alcohol (80 proof) to blend this into an applesauce consistency. Make enough of this to fill your canning jar up to $\frac{3}{4}$ of the way full. Top this off with more alcohol (80 proof).

It is ideal to start this procedure on the new moon and let it sit until the full moon. This will take approximately 14 days. Shake it several times a day in these two weeks before straining the liquid on the full moon. You should keep a bag of Cayenne powder in your kitchen; a bottle of Cayenne tincture in your emergency kit and in the glove compartment of your cars, etc. as it can be life saving!

"In my 35 years of practice, and working with the people and teaching, I have never, on house calls, lost one heart attack patient and the reason is, whenever I go in-if they are still breathing- I help pour down them a cup of Cayenne tea (a teaspoon of Cayenne in a cup of hot water, and within minutes they are up and around)."
—Dr. John Christopher

"If you master only one herb in your life, master Cayenne pepper. It is more powerful than any other." Dr. Schulze I agree!!

Comfrey

Comfrey is a stout, bristly haired, perennial herb with thick roots and large tapering lance-like leaves. Purple to pink-white, funnel shaped flowers are borne in summer. The roots and rhizomes are normally used, but the leaves are also used to a lesser degree. Comfrey is a sweet, cooling herb with expectorant, astringent, soothing and healing effects. It reduces inflammation and controls bleeding. Comfrey has been used since the sixteenth century in the external treatment of broken bones and was thus called "knit-bone". Allantoin, the active ingredient, with exceptional healing properties, is absorbed fast and deep into the skin. The healing process is speeded up because of rapid growth of new cells.

Comfrey is a fast growing plant, producing huge amounts of leaves during the growing season; hence it is very nitrogen hungry. Comfrey benefits from the addition of animal manure applied as mulch, and can also be mulched with other nitrogen rich materials such as lawn clippings. Mature Comfrey plants can be harvested up to four or five times a year. They are ready for cutting when about 2 feet high. Comfrey rapidly re-grows; it will be ready for further cutting about 5 weeks later. It is said that the best time to cut Comfrey is shortly before flowering, for this is when it is at its most potent in terms of the nutrients that it offers. Comfrey can continue growing into November. In order to allow the plants to build up winter reserves, as the leaves die back and break down in winter, nutrients and minerals are transported back to the roots for use the following spring. It is not advisable to continue taking cuttings after September.

One of the first herbal combinations I recall using was full of comfrey. The root and foliage of comfrey contain allantoin, a nitrogenous crystalline substance which is a cell proliferant- that is, it increases the speed at which a wound heals and broken bones knit back together. Even old injuries are helped with this master knitter and mender. I had been in a skiing incident (although there are no accidents!) because I forgot to have the bindings checked after sitting in the garage for 3 years. Too excited to ski again! One gentle fall and my ankle twisted completely around. Nothing broke but everything tore! I was in a cast for 6 weeks and a year later it was still swelling up. Sitting on a curb, rubbing the ankle, a Native American stopped to inquire what was up? I told him the story and he recommended B, F, & C, Bones, Flesh, and Cartilage. I started on it that day and it completely healed and has been strong all my life, not weak like I was told it would be. This began my research into herbs. Comfrey is so easy to grow and very beautiful.

A formula for an amazing poultice is what we call a People Pack. It is a combination of 1 part slippery elm, 1 part comfrey root, and $\frac{1}{4}$ part golden seal root. You can add cayenne if inspired. Mix these ingredients with aloe or water or urine if that is all you have and make a paste. Place it directly on the wound and cover it with gauze. It will even suck out blood poisoning. Amazing internal and external use of Comfrey:

• Rashes and Skin problems
• Wounds and Ruptures
• Muscle injuries
• Bruises
• Inflammation of arthritic joints
• Anti-bacterial agent
• Anti-fungal agent
• Anti-inflammatory agent
• Pain relief
• Astringent usage-shrinks soft tissue and contracts blood vessels, thus checking blood flow
• Expectorant
• For expelling mucous
• Stopping bleeding
• Stimulating cell growth
• Cooling effect
• Mild sedative
• Digestive problems
• Wound healing
• Lung issues
• For the digestive tract- helping to cure ulcers and colitis

Help for respiratory problems

Pick and add Comfrey leaves to your blender with enough water to make a paste. Once mixed, place this paste directly on a sprain or bruise and then wrap with a clean cloth. Leave on injury overnight. Comfrey will speed up your healing process. If movement causes you pain, you need to stay still. Comfrey will also help mend bones. It requires, however, that the mending fracture not be used.

Echinacea

Echinacea is a tall perennial with lance-like leaves about $5\frac{1}{2}$ inches long. Purple-pink, daisy-like flowers that smell like honey, with orange-brown centers, are produced in summer to early autumn. Resembling a black-eyed Susan, Echinacea is a North American perennial that is indigenous to the central plains where it grows on road banks, prairies, fields and in dry, open woods. Native people called Echinacea 'snake root' because it grows from a thick black root. Native people continue to use it to heal snake bites. The roots, rhizomes and parts above ground are used in herbal preparations. This bitter herb has some aromatic properties. The root is the active ingredient of the plant although many formulas use only the top part of the plant. Echinacea has been one of the top selling herbs in the Unities States since white settlers adopted its use as a therapeutic plant. Most of the research during the past 10 years has focused on the immune-stimulant properties of the plant. The most important immune-stimulating components of Echinacea are the large polysaccharides, such as insulin, that increase the production of T-cells and increase other natural killer cell activity.

Echinacea, in animal and human studies improves the movement of white blood cells to attack foreign microorganisms and toxins in the bloodstream. Research suggests that Echinacea's activity in the blood may have value in the defense of tumor cells. Echinacea benefits infectious conditions. Echinacea prevents the formation of an enzyme which destroys a natural barrier between healthy tissue and damaging organisms. Echinacea aids in the production of interferon which increases antiviral activity against influenza (flu) and herpes, an inflammation of the skin and mouth. It may reduce the severity of symptoms of a runny nose and sore throat and reduce the duration of illness. Its anti-inflammatory properties may relieve arthritis and lymphatic swelling. If Echinacea is not in your natural antibiotic formula, add it now!

Echinacea is used internally for:
• boosting the immune system thus helping clear up
  chronic infections
• skin dis-eases
• fungal infections
• septicemia-serious blood poisoning
• slow-healing wounds
• chronic fatigue syndrome
• venereal dis-eases
• early stages of coughs and colds
• urinary infections
• respiratory infections
• stimulating the immune system to inhibit viruses and bacteria to
  enter and take over the cells
• bolstering the immune system in cases of HIV/AIDS
• herpes
• acne
• psoriasis
• infected injuries
• gargling for sore throats
• ulcers
• improving skin tone

   The root is the active ingredient of the plant. Many formulas use only the top part and are not as powerful at activating and boosting the immune system as the root does.

Echinacea has/is used for:
• anti-bacterial effects
• anti-viral effects
• one of the best blood purifiers
• an effective antibiotic
• warding off the common cold
• relieving the symptoms of hay fever
• toothaches
• mumps
• smallpox
• measles
• upper respiratory infections
• the common cold
• sinusitis
• staph and strep infections

Echinacea's antibacterial properties can stimulate wound healing topically and are of benefit to skin conditions such as:
• burns
• insect bites
• ulcers
• psoriasis
• acne
• eczema

Echinacea has also been used in homeopathy treatments for:
• chronic fatigue syndrome
• indigestion
• gastroenteritis
• weight loss

You can use Echinacea dried or fresh. It is easy to grow and lovely to have in your world. Get to know this amazing gift to your health and have fun with it!

Goldenseal

Goldenseal has been used since it was discovered in the Americas some 500 years ago. The original purpose for Goldenseal extract was to deal with Staph and Strep infections. Goldenseal has been used to treat most every infectious condition known to man. Goldenseal was very successful in treating cholera during the cholera epidemics in Calcutta, India in 1966 and 1967.

The Native Americans introduced this wonder herb to the early settlers. The root of the Goldenseal plant continues to be used for a wide variety of purposes. Considered a broad-spectrum herb, Goldenseal contains many vitamins and minerals, including the antioxidant vitamins A, C and E, as well as B complex vitamins. Goldenseal also contains the minerals calcium, iron and manganese. Native to Canada and the Eastern United States, goldenseal is an excellent antibiotic which destroys harmful bacteria and germs. It is very helpful against staph and strep. It is very potent for intestinal, antibacterial activity which has many times equaled or outperformed allopathic antibiotics without the side effects. Goldenseal is named for the golden color of its roots on the Goldenseal plant.

When Goldenseal drops are first made, they are a magnificent yellow color and with time they turn green from an increase in chlorophyll. Goldenseal has a soothing and anti-inflammatory effect on mucous membranes and is beneficial for peptic ulcers. Its antibacterial action is beneficial in treating Giardia and amoebas in the intestinal tract.

In Chinese medicine it is referred to as a "bitter tonic herb". These bitter herbs are also indicated to assist with stimulating digestion; it stimulates the gall bladder to secrete bile, thus counteracting sweet cravings. Goldenseal works by purifying the blood and promoting a cleansing action of the spleen, liver, kidneys and bowels. Since Goldenseal root has been harvested extensively, it is nearly nonexistent in the wild. Most Goldenseal available today is grown specifically for use as an herbal supplement. The pure herb, therefore, is very much in demand and well worth the price. Most health food stores sell it in bulk and you can fill your own capsules.

"Goldenseal is probably the premier anti-microbial herb in North America." Cancer Salves, a Botanical Approach to Treatment (p. 129) by Ingrid Naiman. The great natural antibiotic quality of Goldenseal coupled with its ability to combat infectious agents make it very attractive during cold and flu season. Goldenseal soothes and conditions the mucous membranes which are easily infected by colds and flu. Goldenseal helps restore the body after fevers and helps tone the body to maintain good health and vitality to overcome dis-ease. 2 parts Goldenseal combined in a tincture with 1 part cayenne is a wonderful remedy for chronic alcoholism.

The Native peoples of North America used Goldenseal for centuries for:
• all types of dis-eases and ailments
• skin dis-eases
• sores and wounds
• boosting the immune system: assists in fighting bacteria and viruses
•antibacterial uses
• antifungal uses
• antioxidant properties
• detoxifying uses
• a blood purifier
• its superb anti-inflammatory properties to ease inflamed membranes
• its antiseptic qualities
• eye, ear, and nose inflammations
• throat mucous membranes and inflammations
• stomach problems
• aiding digestion
• nausea
• heartburn
• constipation relief
• regulating blood sugar levels
• urinary and uterine problems, especially infections
• controlling uterine hemorrhaging
• promoting menstruation
• relieving congestion

230

- eczema
- poison ivy
- canker sores
- cold sores
- ringworm

How it is used: Goldenseal tea enemas reduce inflammation of hemorrhoid tissue Goldenseal tea is a marvelous mouthwash for ulcerations in the mouth. Drinking or gargling the tea can help with tonsillitis and throat problems. Goldenseal eyewash can reduce inflammation in the eye. The berberine in Goldenseal conditions the walls of the stomach and intestines; it is helpful for diarrhea and gastritis. It works as a mild laxative. Goldenseal is very helpful in stimulating the production of bile from the liver which helps break down fats for easier digestion. Goldenseal is taken orally in tablet or tincture form, and is also applied locally to sores and ulcers. Though generally safe, Goldenseal root should not be taken in very large doses or for more than three weeks at a time. Because of the alkaloids in Goldenseal, gastrointestinal distress may result from long term or excessive use. There should be a break of about two weeks between periods of use. Large doses of Goldenseal can be toxic. Hydrastine stays in the system for a long time and accumulates. It can destroy intestinal bacteria and reduce the absorption of B vitamins over prolonged periods. Avoid large doses during pregnancy and while nursing. Those of you who should use Goldenseal with the advice of your health care practitioner: pregnant and lactating women, children under the age of two, and people on anticoagulant medications.

Use caution with the following conditions:
- heart dis-ease
- high blood pressure
- diabetes
- glaucoma
- lupus (can stimulate into increased activity)
- multiple sclerosis and all auto immune system affunctions (can stimulate into increased activity)
- those who have transplanted organs

Use Goldenseal Drops drops under your tongue to start systemic healing. Topical healing: apply to any area of concern, to help heal most infections. Teeth and gum problems: place full strength drops onto toothbrush. Ear drops or eye wash: People have reported great results with many eye conditions. Nasal spray for colds or allergies.

Noni

Noni, also known as Indian Mulberry, is a small evergreen shrub or tree, usually less than 10 feet high, occasionally up to 20 feet. The large dark green shiny leaves are generally paired, except near forming fruit. Thick and oval in shape, they are deep veined, short-stemmed and 8 inches or longer. The flowers form in globular heads, about an inch long and bear many small white flowers. The flower heads grow to become mature fruit, 3 to 4 inches in diameter. The noni fruit begins green, turns yellow, and has an unpleasant, rotten cheese odor; especially as it ripens to whiteness and falls from the tree. To the Polynesian peoples, Noni is a valuable plant to have nearby their home so they can utilize the many natural healing properties of this remarkable life sustaining plant. Noni's birth place is the Tahitian Islands. Noni has been used for centuries by early Polynesian settlers, and through migration is now growing throughout the Pacific Islands (Hawaii), Asia, Australia, New Zealand and even parts of South America. Noni has prolific beauty; bearing fruit year round. The aroma of its fruit is truly awesome. It is well known as one of the main healing plants among the traditional Hawaiians and they call it old Hawaiian medicine. We use it when we are feeling very sick or very old.

How Noni Juice is Prepared

Noni is truly a remarkable plant! Noni fruit should be picked at its yellow stage. This is the critical picking period and very important as set down through generations from Tahitian Medicine People. For a wonderful poultice for deep cuts and broken bones, take the slightly unripe fruit and pound it thoroughly with salt - this mixture is then placed carefully on the wound. Using salt with Noni on deep injuries helps to speed healing. I do not use salt with Noni except on deep wounds. The ripe fruit can be directly used as a poultice for facial blemishes, (rubbed until the oil disappears), and also to draw out the pus and core from an infected sore or boil, such as a staph infection. In the old days, this was tied on with a bandage of tapa bark cloth.

The fruit can also be washed and placed in a jar for at least five days to a week or more, until the fruit turns to mush. Sometimes the fruit is then placed in drums and allowed to macerate (naturally pressed) for approximately 4 weeks into juice. It is these juices that are strained and filtered for use. This is the traditional method that allows the natural extraction of Noni Juice with all of the Noni fruit's natural enzymes. It just makes itself! I have used Noni every Cleanse since discovering it in 1998 when I moved to Kauai. If you notice the food signature of Noni you will find a cluster of cells on the outside of the fruit. It is a cellular re-generator.

There are those that eat Noni fruit as it ripens, either as a food in times of scarcity or famine, or as a tonic when needed. Other people make a tea using the leaves of this plant - although the tea is not very pleasant to drink. The fruit was used in a recipe for a repeated remedy against tuberculosis, arthritis, rheumatism and the changes of old age. The leaves and bark of the stem were pounded and strained, resulting in a liquid and drunk as a tonic or for urinary disorders, muscle and joint pain.

Noni is used for:
• broken bones (Healing)
• cancers (Immune System)
• diabetes
• fibromyalgia
• high blood pressure
• headaches (Migraines)
• hair Loss
• impotency

233

- immune system failure (Aids & Viruses)
- increasing energy
- indigestion (Constipation, parasites & Diarrhea)
- infections & viruses (Immune System)
- malignancies (Tumors)
- multiple sclerosis
- skin problems –boils and bruises
- toothaches (Gum dis-ease)

Other uses for this amazing plant: the bark yields a red dye, while a yellow dye can be prepared from the root. Both colors were use to dye the tapa cloth of the chiefs of ancient Polynesia.

In Samoa, the flowers are employed in treating sties, while in Tonga; vapor from the broken leaves is used for the same purpose. Also in Tonga, a tea or infusion of the leaves or bark is sometimes used for stomach aches. Ancient Tahitians and Marquesans used the fruit as a tonic for many ailments, such as diabetes, fish poisoning, and stings from reef fish, tonsillitis, abdominal swelling, burns, and many other ailments. Noni leaves were used as a poultice for boils. Simply passing a Noni leaf over a fire briefly and then applying it to the affected area such as boils, cuts, abscesses and inflammations of various types, helps it heal rapidly. The amazing qualities of Noni are hard to describe here. I believe Noni is one of the greatest gifts we have. It may smell funny but the body really loves it. See if it will grow in your area and if not look at our resource guide in the back of this book to get your own.

Turmeric/Olena

Turmeric is a flowering plant in the ginger family. This perennial herb with a large rhizome and large leaves with yellow flowers are a close relative to the ginger plant. The above ground and underground roots known as rhizomes are used in medicinal and food preparations. Bromelain, another property of turmeric, is a protein digesting enzyme also found in pineapples. It enhances the absorption and anti-inflammatory effects of cur-cumin, the best studied active ingredient of Turmeric. Turmeric is generally boiled and then dried, thus turning it into the familiar yellow powder. Cur-cumin made from Turmeric, as well as other substances in this herb, have antioxidant properties, which some claim may be as strong as vitamins C and E. Turmeric is the master anti-inflammatory. It is great for all of you with auto immune system affunctions.

Remember if you have inflammation, be careful with carbohydrates. Only one per day and then rest your pancreas. I have used it often in baths and soaks. Try it! Turmeric has been used extensively in both Ayurveda and Chinese medicine as an anti-inflammatory. It is used to treat digestive disorders and skin dis-eases as well as to assist in wound healing and liver problems.

Turmeric is also known in Hawaii by the name of Olena, a very sacred herb. In our culture we use this herb as a spiritual sanctification along with other herbs, seaweed and sea salt. We use it to create sacred spaces and to sanctify ourselves. Olena is also used for land and house blessings. For land blessings we usually use Olena with other combinations: kino and kinolau (plant bodies) of land and sea and mountain, which we call Hui Kala (gathering forgiveness). The Hui Kala is then placed in the four corners of the land and converge them in the center where an ahu (altar) or Lele (wooden altar) is placed for the blessing. Hui Kala is also used with fresh water (cleansing), salt (purification), Olena (sanctification), and Limu Kala (forgiveness). This is put in a bowl and Pi Kai (with Ti leaf) swirled in the bowl and sprinkled on the people, the land, and any other sacred things. Hui Kala was used to consecrate any desecrated area or thing. Information here is by Kaliko, one of the beautiful Divine beings I get to walk with. He is also one of my head techs at Angel Farms!

In many North Indian traditional wedding ceremonies, turmeric is applied to both the groom and the bride. This is not only to make them look good with fresh glowing skins, but is considered by the Hindus as a symbol of prosperity and as a cleansing herb for the whole body. Pieces of crushed roots mixed with seawater are sprinkled to remove the negative influences from places, persons, and things during ceremonies. Indians, therefore, are no strangers to the multiple uses of Turmeric. It is well recognized as the best anti-oxidant, hypoglycemic, colorant, antiseptic and wound healer. Used in cooking as a spice for over 2,500 years, Turmeric has a bitter, musty flavor similar to mustard. It is this spice that gives Indian curries their characteristic bright yellow-orange color (from the cur cumin pigment).

The healing properties of Turmeric have made it a most sought after ingredient in cosmetics and drugs, as the leaf oil and extract can also be used as a sunscreen and bio-pesticide. Turmeric is used internally as boiled powder, fresh juice, and confection and externally as paste, oil, ointment, and lotion. It is also applied topically for ulcers, wounds, eczema, and inflammations. The roots are pounded and pressed to extract a juice that, when mixed with water, is used for earaches and to clear the sinuses through nasal application. The active ingredient in Turmeric is cur-cumin which, in the body, induces the flow of bile, and facilitates the emptying of the gallbladder and helps break down fats. Cur-cumin is also wonderful for upset stomach, gas, and abdominal cramps. Extracts of Turmeric root reduce secretion of acid from the stomach and protect against injuries such as inflammation along the stomach or intestinal walls and ulcers. Turmeric may help relieve the symptoms of osteoarthritis. It protects against free radical damage, as it is a strong antioxidant and reduces inflammation by reducing histamine levels.

Cur-cumin has a protective effect on liver tissue exposed

236

to liver damaging drugs and is traditionally used for liver ailments. Liver damage resulting from excessive consumption of alcohol or prolonged use of painkillers may be minimized to some extent. Turmeric also protects the liver from a number of toxic compounds and substances such as carbon tetrachloride and acetaminophen. By clearing them from the body; they protect the liver from damage. Studies have shown that Turmeric may help reduce cholesterol and also prevent the internal blood clots that trigger heart attack and strokes. There are promising results on the use of Turmeric to treat cancer, as it is believed to inhibit the growth of lymphoma tumor cells. Turmeric is extremely safe when used wisely. It has been used in large quantities as a food, with no adverse reactions. Be careful though, unusually large amounts of Turmeric consumption may result in an upset stomach. Turmeric's potential anti-clotting effects might cause problems for those with clotting disorders in large amounts. Start slowly and research! A mixture of oils of Turmeric, holy basil, and Noni with the addition of vanilla extract in a base of citronella is an alternative to D.E.E.T. bug repellents, one of the most common chemical bug repellents commercially available and can be harmful to the body.

A wonderful Ayurveda formula of herbs and minerals containing Turmeric as well as winter cherry, Boswellia, and zinc significantly reduces pain and disability. Turmeric has been shown to be helpful for Atherosclerosis in preventing the build up of blockage of arteries preventing platelet build up along the walls of an injured blood vessel thus preventing blood clots and artery blockage that can eventually cause a heart attack or stroke. Turmeric also lowers cholesterol levels and inhibits the oxidation of LDL ("bad") cholesterol. Turmeric has shown great results in helping prostate, breast, skin, and colon cancers. Turmeric is as effective as corticosteroids.

Do you remember, Angel, that your adrenals are the organs that release your natural steroids to suppress white cell production in your body? Turmeric can be a great help until you are practiced being in the Now! Weekly bath oils with Turmeric are used by South Indian women. The result is beautiful skin and hairless bodies! In South India, it is considered very auspicious and therefore, is the first item on the grocery list. It is a bitter herb with a pungent smell with astringent, antibiotic, and anticoagulant properties. Turmeric is an antioxidant, antimicrobial, and a cytotoxic (fights tumors).

It also assists with digestive problems, skin complaints, the respiratory system, circulatory disorders, menstrual problems including painful menstruation, and liver dis-ease and jaundice. It reduces the risk of stroke and heart attacks and is a master anti-inflammatory for all forms of inflammation.

In Chinese medicine it is used to:
• invigorate the Qi (life force)
• relieve menstrual pain
• remove stagnation
• lift depression

Turmeric blended with oil applied topically is wonderful for injuries
• minor wound management
• sores
• ringworm
• athletes' foot
• bruises
• sprains
• cosmetic use: during traditional East Indian ceremonies
• colds: Turmeric boiled with milk and sugar and consumed orally
• stimulating breast milk flow: Poultice of Turmeric is applied
 directly on the breast

For seasonal colds and influenza with a runny nose, immediately administer honey mixed with Turmeric, or Turmeric mixed in milk to soothe and to help you feel better. Have fun with turmeric and remember it will turn your fingers yellow!

Garlic

Eat Leeks in March and Wild Garlic in May. And all year after,
physicians may play. — Old Welsh Rhyme

Garlic is a species in the onion family, Alliaceae. Its close relatives include the onion, shallot, leek, and chive. Garlic has been used throughout history for both culinary and medicinal purposes. The garlic plant's bulb is the most commonly used part of the plant. With the exception of the single clove types, the bulb is divided into numerous fleshy sections called cloves. The cloves are used for consumption (raw or cooked), or for medicinal purposes and have a characteristic pungent, spicy flavor that mellows and sweetens considerably with cooking. The leaves and flowers on the head are also edible, and being milder in flavor than the bulbs, they are most often consumed while immature and still tender. The sticky juice within the bulb cloves is used as an adhesive in mending glass and china.

Among the herbs for healing, garlic stands supreme. It has a remarkable range of medicinal properties. Word of its healing properties has been handed down by priests, physicians and herbalists for thousands of years. Writings of the early civilizations of Egypt, China, Greece and Rome contain many references of their medicinal use of herbs and garlic received the highest praise. Any Egyptian medical papyrus from around 1500 B.C. listed twenty-two garlic prescriptions.

Garlic seems to be perhaps the greatest wonder drug of all, a truly indispensable medicine. Imagine a single pharmaceutical drug that could prevent heart attacks, reduce cancer risk, lower cholesterol, lower blood pressure, improve digestion, and act as an antibiotic. Garlic was in use at the beginning of recorded history and was found in Egyptian pyramids and ancient Greek temples. There are Biblical references to garlic.

Garlic is nature's wonder drug. While modern research is confirming this ancient tradition, don't expect to hear much about it from "conventional medical doctors". Vitamins and other supplements are not nearly as effective as raw garlic. The best source for proper nutrition comes from food; the garlic clove itself.   Garlic contains hundreds of minerals and nutrients. It is very likely that garlic's effectiveness and safety comes from these ingredients working together in concert.

In first century India, garlic was used to prevent heart disease and rheumatism. For centuries Chinese and Japanese physicians have recommended garlic for alleviating high blood pressure. The use of food as a medicine has always been important. Dr. Albert Schweitzer used garlic against cholera and typhus. Intravenous garlic has been used to treat serious infections of the brain.

(China) In WWII, garlic was used to ward off septic poisoning and gangrene. Candida is caused by a fungus. So is tuberculosis. They are both on the rise, perhaps due to the overabundance of antibiotics used in animal feeds. At the turn of the century, doctors reported remarkable cure rates from eating, inhaling and smearing garlic ointment on the chest which was the best treatment for tuberculosis. Fresh garlic has been used to immunize animals against tumor development or to reverse it. It has wiped out breast cancer in mice! It is a powerful antioxidant in reversing liver damage and works the same way as expectorants and decongestants.

The pungent property of garlic irritates the stomach and signals the lungs to release fluids that thin the mucus, enabling the ordinary lung processes to expel it. Regular doses of garlic help keep susceptible persons from developing chronic bronchitis. It keeps mucus moving normally through the lungs. Polish physicians use garlic to cure children suffering from recurrent and chronic bronchitis and bronchial asthma. As a food and a spice, garlic is used widely in both the East and the West. Scientific studies show that garlic can "deactivate" carcinogens, prevent the growth of cancerous tumors, and stimulate the formation of glutathione which detoxifies foreign materials. Garlic contains allicin which has antibiotic and anti-fungal properties. People call it a natural chemotherapy drug because of the way it destroys cancerous cells. It is especially preventive of colon and stomach cancers. One of garlic's components, ajoene, is very toxic to malignant cells. The maximum benefit is achieved by eating raw garlic.

Garlic can be as effective as many modern antibiotics, without the dangerous side effects. What's more, garlic is an antiviral. Antibiotics are ineffective against viruses. In fact, in all of modern pharmacology, there are no effective antiviral drugs. This has important implications for AIDS patients, and in preventing colds and influenza. Garlic nose drops have proven to be 100% effective in preventing influenza in animal studies. Considering the danger of allopathic flu inoculations, of which one of the side-effects can include death, this is welcome news.

Eaten regularly, raw onions and garlic decrease the clotting tendency and increase the body's ability to dissolve clots. NO need for baby aspirin and its potential side effects. Garlic is also highly effective in lowering cholesterol and high blood pressure and it boosts immunity. Raw garlic dramatically augments the immune system's natural killer cells and should be the first line of defense against infectious diseases and Cancer. It is a powerful antioxidant. Garlic destroys bacteria; it is a broad spectrum antibiotic against a long list of microbes that spread diseases including:

- botulism
- tuberculosis
- diarrhea
- staph infections
- dysentery
- typhoid
- fungal infections
- colds and influenza

Garlic is truly a gift. Use it often. It is also a great way to heal warts. Slice a thin piece of fresh garlic and squeeze it to release juices. Place the slice on the wart and put on a band-aid. Do this for 3 days and watch what happens. If you get to the source, they will all disappear.

Angel Tool Box

I recommend that everyone have in their medicine cabinets: one people pack, one B F and C, one pain ease, one infection fighter, one bottle of cayenne, and one bottle of lavender oil. You can grow and make your own! Make a garden with these 8 Master herbs and get a good practice of helping your body when it is in need. Check out vsnatureworks.com and your health food store for help.

Honorable Mentions

Kava Kava or Awa Awa

Grown on the Hawaiian Islands, it has a lilac odor, and is used as a local anesthetic, diuretic, and a douche for vaginitis. It gives a tingling type of sensation to the mucous membranes. The root makes a particularly potent, fermented drink, very different from alcohol, somewhat psychedelic and rather pleasant, inducing mild hallucinations. Kava is sedating and is primarily consumed to relax without disrupting mental clarity. Kava is chewed by some to relieve symptoms of throat pain, as Kava produces a "numbing" effect on the tongue and throat. The Kava produces an effect similar to that of a chloraseptic spray. As a sleep aid, the drinker does not experience any mental or physical after effects. This sleep has been reported as extremely restful and the user often wakes up more stimulated than he or she normally would. If you are having trouble sleeping this is a great non toxic gift to you. Here on the Big Island we love Uncle Robert's Awa Awa bar and all of the Ohana there too. Visit them if you can.

Valerian

Valerian got me out of a neck brace in 15 minutes! This is the master muscle relaxer. I have been hooked on this magical and stinky herb ever since. Valerian is a hardy perennial flowering plant, with heads of sweetly scented pink or white flowers which bloom in the summer months. Guess where Valium came from? Why not stay with the source? The dried rhizome and roots of this herb are used medicinally as a muscle and nerve sedative, and as a remedy for hysteria and other nervous complaints. Boiled with licorice, raisin, and anise seed, it was used as an expectorant for phlegm in difficult coughs and lung congestion. Its odor is very unpleasant to humans and quite delightful to cats.

White Willow

Hippocrates wrote in the 5th century BC about a bitter powder extracted from willow bark that could ease aches and pains and reduce fevers. This remedy is also mentioned in texts from ancient Egypt, Sumer, and Assyria. The bark of this tree contains salicin which is related to aspirin and used as an anodyne, antipyretic, astringent, detergent, tonic, anti-periodic, and antiseptic. Internally, it is good for rheumatism and arthritis; externally, as a hydrating lotion or wash to clear the face and skin of pimples, pus-filled wounds, eczema, or burns. A solution of the bark with borax acts as a deodorant wash for offensive smelling perspiration. I use white willow for bone injuries and muscle pain and spasms.

Master Journey Herbs

There is a great deal to say about the Master Journey Herbs. These herbs were given to us directly from the Creator, and are here for humanity to develop and increase our spiritual perceptions.

Ayahuasca

Ayahuasca is any of various psychoactive infusions or decoctions prepared from the Banisteriopsis spp. vine, usually mixed with the leaves of dimethyltryptamine-containing species of shrubs from the Psychotria genus. The brew, first described academically in the early 1950s by Harvard ethnobotanist Richard Evans Schultes, who found it employed for divinatory and healing purposes by American Indians of Amazonian Colombia, A notable and puzzling property of ayahuasca is that neither of the ingredients cause any significant psychedelic effects when used alone; they must be consumed together in order to have the desired effect. The vine is considered to be the "spirit" of ayahuasca, the gatekeeper and guide to the otherworldly realms. How indigenous peoples discovered the psychedelic properties of the ayahuasca brew remains a point of contention in the scientific community.

Those whose usage of ayahuasca is performed in non-traditional contexts often align themselves with the philosophies and cosmologies associated with ayahuasca. It takes everyone to a place of Infinite Love. The religion Santo Daime uses it. While non-native users know of the spiritual applications of ayahuasca, a less well-known traditional usage focuses on the medicinal properties of ayahuasca. Its purgative properties are highly important (many refer to it as la purga, "the purge"). The intense vomiting and occasional diarrhea it induces can clear the body of worms and other tropical parasites. Thus, this action is twofold; a direct action on the parasites works to kill the parasites, and parasites are expelled through the increased intestinal vomiting and diarrhea that is caused by these alkaloids. From years of experience it does NOT get rid of all parasites! It is recommended to purify one's self before any journey by abstaining from spicy and heavily-seasoned foods, excess fat, salt, caffeine, acidic foods (such as citrus). Remember to stay well hydrated, and make your mantra be to Let Go Of Everything! All you have left is Spirit and Yourself.

What a gift! I have grown immensely from Ayahuasca journeys. They are really Spiritual sacraments. I was even brought to Hawaii and taught many healing modalities in my journeys. I do not believe they should be done on a regular basis. Even the shaman only did it for certain reasons and to access information. I have seen a weakness in Iris reading with long term use. They have the ability to take you farther than you can go yourself into the realm of the Beloved. Research and seek knowledge of the Shaman and the herbs. This will give you more information in order to make an educated choice for yourself and see if this is the avenue to show you your fears and help you see through the illusion.

Peyote

Peyote is a small, spineless cactus. It is native to southwestern Texas and through Mexico. It is found primarily in the Chihuahua desert among scrub, especially where there is limestone. Well known for its psychoactive alkaloids, particularly mescaline, it is used world wide as a supplement to various transcendence practices including meditation. Peyote has a long history of ritualistic and medicinal use by indigenous Americans. Its pink flowers bloom from March through May, and sometimes as late as September. The effects last about 10 to 12 hours.

Peyote is reported to trigger states of "deep introspection and insight" that have been described as being of spiritual nature.

In addition to psychoactive use, Native Americans used the plant for its curative properties. They used peyote to treat such varied ailments as toothaches, pain in childbirth, fevers, breast pain, skin diseases, rheumatism, diabetes, colds, and blindness.

The U.S. Dispensary lists peyote under the name Anhalonium, and states it can be used in various preparations for neurasthenia, hysteria and asthma. Screening for antimicrobial activity of peyote extracts in various solvents showed positive microbial inhibition. The principal antibiotic agent, a water-soluble crystalline substance separated from an ethanol extract of the plant, was given the name peyocactin.

Peyote is known to have been used since the middle of the Archaic period in the Americas by the people of the Oshara Tradition in the Southwest. In 2005 researchers used radiocarbon dating and alkaloid analysis to study two specimens of peyote buttons found in archaeological digs from a site called Shumla Cave No. 5 on the Rio Grande in Texas. The results dated the specimens to between 3780 and 3660 B.C.. Alkaloid extraction yielded approximately 2% of the alkaloids including mescaline in both samples still intact! This indicates that native North Americans were likely to have used peyote since at least five and a half thousand years ago. Specimens from a burial cave in west central Coahuila, Mexico have been similarly analysed and dated to 810 to 1070 AD. Documented evidence of the religious, ceremonial, and healing uses of peyote dates back over 2,000 years.

The Native American Church started in the 19th century. American Indians in more widespread regions to the north began to use peyote in religious practices as part of a revival of native spirituality. Its members refer to peyote as "the sacred medicine", and use it to combat spiritual, physical, and other social ills. Concerned about the drug's psychoactive effects, between the 1880s and 1930s, U.S. authorities attempted to ban Native American religious rituals involving peyote, including the Ghost Dance. Today the Native American Church is one among several religious organizations to use peyote as part of its religious practice. The Navajo Nation now has the most members of the Native American Church.

The Beloved Native American Church in Northern California,

gave our family, and Angel Farms, an appreciation ceremony. With the Peyote as the guide and gratitude as the intent it was the most amazing ceremony! Over 30 Graduates joined the ceremony and many said it was the best journey to another level of consciousness. I believe this happened because they were ready. So many clear vessels! Hardly anyone had to "get well" Wow! I include this information as a possibility to take you to another level when you are ready. Check the resource guide for more information.

"Thousands of people have, by one means or another, come to the conclusion that psychedelic plants are profound tools for the exploration of the inner depths of the human psyche." "Food of the Gods" by Terence McKenna.

I am thankful for all the shaman's who I am honored to know, love, and be witness in their journeys, who have Cleansed at Angel Farms.

Marijuana

Marijuana has been used as an anodyne, nervine, aphrodisiac, and appetite stimulant; for coughs, pains of gout and arthritis, d.t.'s, hysteria, mental depression, and morphine and chloral hydrate addiction. It can be smoked, eaten, or made into a tincture or salve. There have been no conclusive studies that marijuana is addictive; therefore, if someone does not have it available, there are no withdrawal symptoms. Remember to not smoke between 9 a.m. and 1 p.m. and 9 p.m. to 1 a.m. daily to protect your lung regeneration.

Never hold onto the smoke. Studies have shown no more THC is absorbed if you hold on to it. It just blows capillaries in the lungs! Give your body and lungs a break from it often and remember all things in moderation. This herb is widely used for cancer pain relief and is used to help relax and assist with nausea and appetite balance. In many states including Hawaii, the majority have voted to legalize Marijuana, usually 7 plants per person. The Federal government is still choosing to dishonor our choices. What do you think about that, Angel? Standing together makes a difference. Please vote for everyone to have another natural option in our health care and pain relief if they choose. Make sure it is organic and with permit, grow your own with love.

Magic Mushrooms

Called teonanacatl ("the Flesh of God") by the Aztec and Mazatec Indians who have been using it for milenna to produce divinely inspired visions and to reveal the future. Mushrooms were served to the Spaniards at the welcoming feast in the court of Montezuma. Some of them saw visions of the future, while others became frightened and committed suicide. The Spaniards, being Catholics, tried to stamp out the use of the mushroom- it interfered with their (the Spaniard) belief that in swallowing their host of bread and water they, and only they, could eat the flesh of God. The Indians went through, and still do to this day, lengthy purifying ceremonies before they partake of the mushroom. For them the eating of the mushroom is a holy and sacred event, it cannot cure, but it can foretell the future and give advice. Psilocybin has been used in the rehabilitation of criminals and in the treatment of chronic alcoholism. These master journey herbs assist in the awakening of our awareness. Be careful not to judge them or use them without great respect.

Important Minerals

Epsom Salts

I believe this information about Epsom salts will help you in many aspects of your life. It is easy to get and easy to use and is not toxic to you or your environment. Your liver likes the extra magnesium too. I find almost everyone is low in magnesium and in order for the body to properly heal it needs this very important ingredient. Enjoy!

Epsom Salts, or magnesium sulfate, the scientific name of Epsom Salts, are so named because of the early discovery in the mineral rich waters of Epsom, England, back in Shakespeare's day in the 17th century. Epsom became known as England's first spa town. In those early days, folks came to drink the waters as a purgative, while these days we prefer to soak the aches, pains, and toxins out in a bath, although Epsom is still used as an ingredient in stomach medications and as a laxative. The term "salt" probably refers to the specific chemical structure of the compound, although many people mistakenly assume it refers to the crystalline structure of Epsom Salt. It has an appearance similar to that of table salt.

Magnesium

Magnesium, the other major component of Epsom Salt, has a demonstrated calming effect and plays a role in the activity of more than 325 enzymes. Because both magnesium and sulfates can be absorbed through the skin, many parents report that giving their child a warm bath with 1-2 cups of dissolved Epsom Salt just before bedtime helps extend the child's sleep cycle and ease digestive function. This mineral product is "the ultimate foot soak," easing achy muscles, smoothing the rough patches, and absorbing odors.

Magnesium is the second most abundant element in human cells and the fourth-most important positively charged ion in the body. This low-profile mineral is so very vital to good health and well being. Magnesium, a major component of Epsom Salt, helps to regulate the activity of more than 325 enzymes and performs a vital role in orchestrating many bodily functions, from muscle control and electrical impulses to energy production and the elimination of harmful toxins.

You may have a magnesium deficiency if you have symptoms of heart disease, diabetes, stroke, osteoporosis, arthritis and joint pain, digestive issues, stress-related illness, or chronic fatigue. The average American male gets just 80% of the magnesium required for good health, while females get only 70% of their recommended levels. Nutritionists say Americans' magnesium levels have dropped more than 50% in the past century.

A variety of factors contribute to the nation's magnesium deficiency. Intensive farming practices deplete magnesium from the soil, and magnesium is not a standard component in most fertilizers. A diet that would have supplied enough magnesium a century ago may not supply enough today.

The average Americans eat diets far less healthy than their ancestors ate. The typical modern diet, rich in fat, sugar, salt and protein, not only contains less magnesium than a balanced diet does, but these same foods actually accelerate the depletion of magnesium from our systems.

Calcium

Calcium can only perform its role in the cells when sufficient magnesium is present. Calcium drains magnesium from the body if our magnesium is low. Studies indicate that taking a calcium supplement without ensuring the body also receives enough magnesium can therefore amplify the shortage of both nutrients. Researchers have found that most Americans have five times as much calcium as magnesium in their bodies; the proper ratio for optimum absorption of both minerals is about two parts magnesium to one part calcium. Magnesium can be ingested as a nutritional supplement.

Here are some additional recommendations: Add one or two cups of Epsom salts to warm bath water for a soothing and stress-reducing soak. Massage a handful of Epsom salts over wet skin to cleanse, exfoliate, and soften the rough spots. Use a warm salt-soaked compress to reduce swelling from scrapes; use a cold compress to take the sting out of insect bites. Feed Epsom salts to your plants, vegetables, and lawn for greener grass and big, healthy vegetables.

Researchers and physicians report that raising your magnesium levels may improve heart and circulatory health, reduce irregular heartbeats, prevent artery hardening, reduce blood clots, and lower blood pressure. It can also improve the body's ability to use insulin, thereby reducing the incidence or severity of diabetes. It can flush toxins and heavy metals from the cells helping the body to eliminate harmful substances which will ease muscle pain. It can improve nerve function by regulating electrolytes. Calcium is the main conductor for the electrical current in the body, and magnesium is necessary to maintain proper calcium levels in the blood.

Guess what stress does to your magnesium levels? Excess adrenaline and stress are believed to drain magnesium, a natural stress reliever, from the body. Increasing magnesium also helps prevent or ease migraine headaches! Magnesium is necessary for the body to bind adequate amounts of serotonin, a mood-elevating chemical within the brain that creates a feeling of well being and relaxation. Don't forget, Angel, that 90% of serotonin is absorbed in the gut! Studies show that magnesium is an electrolyte, helping to ensure proper muscle, nerve and enzyme function and is critical to the proper use of calcium in cells. It helps prevent heart disease and strokes by lowering blood pressure, protecting the elasticity of arteries, preventing blood clots as well as reducing the risk of sudden heart attack deaths.

Increasing sulfates also reduces inflammation to relieve pain and muscle cramps and improves oxygen use in the body. It aids in the formation of proteins that line the walls of the digestive tract and helps detoxify the body's residue of medicines and environmental contaminants. Magnesium, the key component of Epsom Salt performs more functions in more systems of the human body than virtually any other mineral. Can you believe you probably have it in your cupboard right now!

While increasing your magnesium levels, Epsom Salt also delivers sulfates, which are extremely difficult to get through food but which readily absorb through the skin. No wonder we love hot sulfur springs to soak in so much! Sulfates serve a wide variety of functions in the body, playing a vital role in the formation of bone tissue and joint proteins. They stimulate the pancreas to generate and regulate activity of more than 325 enzymes, making digestion and insulin more effective. It can ease stress and improve sleep and concentration and help muscles and nerves function properly.

Although magnesium is absorbed through the digestive tract, many foods, drugs and medical conditions can interfere with the effectiveness of this delivery method. Soaking in an Epsom Salt bath is one of the most effective means of making the magnesium your body needs readily available.

Important Information
About Magnesium & Epsom Salt
Have fun with more great uses of Epsom Salt.

Have fun with more great uses of Epsom Salt. Locally it may be used as a treatment of an ingrown nail: Daily soaking of the afflicted digit in a mixture of warm water and Epsom salts and then applying natural antibiotics such as Echinacea.

Mixed with your favorite deep conditioner it adds body to hair.

Dissolved in a bath, Epsom Salt is absorbed through the skin to replenish the body's levels of magnesium. Magnesium ions relax and reduce irritability by lowering the effects of stress related adrenaline. Helps regulate the electrical functions that spark through miles of nerves.

Lowers blood pressure. Researchers have found that magnesium also increases energy and stamina by encouraging the production of ATP (adenosine Triphosphate), the energy packets made in the cells. Experts recommend soaking with Epsom Salt at least three times a week to look better, feel better and have more energy.

For compresses: Use 2 cups of Epsom Salt per gallon of water for sore muscles, bug bites and splinter removal.

For soaking: Add two cups of Epsom Salt to warm water in a standard-sized bathtub. Double the Epsom Salt for an over sized garden tub. Popular for easing muscle pain and fading bruises.

Foot bath: Add a cup of Epsom Salt to a tub of warm water as a popular balm for aching feet.

Laxative: Consult the package directions for instructions.

To exfoliate: Mix 2 cups of Epsom Salt with ¼ cup of coconut oil and a few drops of lavender essential oil. Use the mixture to gently scrub away dry skin patches.

Facial: Mix ½ tsp of Epsom Salt into cleansing cream for a deep-pore cleansing. Gently massage on skin. Rinse with cool water. Pat dry.

Spa treatment: After showering, gently massage handfuls of Epsom Salt over wet skin to exfoliate the body. It's the same treatment many great spas use!

Studies show plants love magnesium and sulfur, the two components of Epsom Salt because they are: a critical mineral for seed germination vital to the production of chlorophyll, which plants use to transform sunlight into food and aid in the absorption of phosphorus and nitrogen, two of the most important fertilizer components. They make plants grow bushier and help them produce more flowers.

Although magnesium and sulfur occur naturally in the soil, they can be depleted by various conditions. Unlike most commercial fertilizers, which build up in the soil over time, Epsom Salt is not persistent so you can't overuse it. Tests by the National Gardening Association confirm-roses fertilized with Epsom Salt grow bushier and produce more flowers, while the compound makes pepper plants grow larger than those treated with commercial fertilizer alone.

House Plant and Garden Uses

Houseplants: 2 tablespoons per gallon of water; feed plants monthly.

Tomatoes: 1 tablespoon per foot of plant height per plant; apply every two weeks.

Roses: 1 tablespoon per foot of plant height per plant; apply every two weeks. Also scratch $\frac{1}{2}$ cup into soil at base to encourage flowering canes and healthy new basal cane growth. Soak unplanted bushes in $\frac{1}{2}$ cup of Epsom salt per gallon of water to help roots recover. Add a tablespoon of Epsom Salt to each hole at planting time. Spray with Epsom Salt solution weekly to discourage pests. Shrubs: (evergreens, azaleas, and rhododendron): 1 tablespoon per 9 square feet. Apply over root zone every 2-4 weeks.

Lawns: Apply 3 pounds for every 1,250 square feet with a spreader, or dilute in water and apply with a sprayer.

Trees: Apply 2 tablespoons per 9 square feet. Apply over the root zone 3 times annually. Garden start-up: Sprinkle 1 cup per 100 square feet. Mix into soil before planting.

Sage: Do not apply! This herb is one of the few plants that doesn't like Epsom Salt.

Homemade Skin Mask: Apply the mask to damp skin.
Normal to oily skin, mix:
1 tablespoon of cognac
1 egg
$\frac{1}{4}$ cup of nonfat dry milk
Juice of one lemon
$\frac{1}{2}$ teaspoon of Epsom salt

Normal to dry skin, mix:

$\frac{1}{4}$ cup of grated carrot

$\frac{1}{2}$ teaspoon of mayonnaise

$\frac{1}{2}$ teaspoon of Epsom Salt

Oily hair: Control the oil and dandruff that usually accompanies it. Mix 2-3 tablespoons Epsom salts with $\frac{1}{2}$ cup of shampoo and store in a plastic container. Massage about a tablespoon of the mixture into your DRY hair. Add water and shampoo as usual. Be sure to rinse thoroughly.

Hairspray: Combine 1 gallon of water, 1 cup of lemon juice, and 1 cup Epsom Salt. Combine, cover, and let set for 24 hours. The next day, pour the mixture into your dry hair and let it sit for 20 minutes. Then shampoo as normal.

Hair Volumizer: Combine equal parts of deep conditioner and Epsom Salt. Warm in a pan. Work the warm mixture through your hair and leave on for 20 minutes. Rinse.

Epsom salt may not taste so great and honey helps, but isn't it nice to know you have such a great resource that is inexpensive, good for the environment, and good for you!

Chapter 9

The Responsibility of Being An Earth Angel

If not you, then who?
If not now then when?

9th Day
Lower Right Side

Your Freedom of Choice

When I ask anyone what do you really want? They always answer, Freedom! We only get freedom when we know who we are and realize the connection between the Earth, each other, and God.

When I was around 10 years old, I learned at my church that we were all given freedom of choice. Wow! Freedom of Choice. I wondered, what does that mean? Well, as usual I asked my Beloved horse, Sunshine. We came to a 4 way stop sign. As I stopped and looked at all the directions, I had an epiphany. I could go right, or left, forward, or turn around and go back and I would still have the opportunity to love and always be loved. I realized there was no wrong direction! It has made moving and changing easy for me, knowing that every direction has love/God in it. Do unto others as you would do unto yourself; love them and love yourself. What does this really mean? It is so time to get responsible.

Many of us don't think of choice as a spiritual gift. We believe choices are burdens to be endured, not embraced. And so they become burdens. But after breath, is there a more precious gift than freedom of choice? Consider for a moment that there are only three levels of awareness. You are either unaware you are unaware, aware you are unaware, and aware you are aware. You may not realize it, but your life at this exact moment -it doesn't matter who you are or where you are-is a direct result of choices you made once upon a time. Choices you made thirty minutes or thirty years ago.

Does the thought of having to make choices in order to span

the distance between your dreams and their coming true scare you? Actually, if you just decide to get out of bed, show up to make breakfast, get the kids to school, and get to work on time, you've already made more than three choices, and it's not even nine o'clock in the morning! Most choices we make are unconscious. We get up to pee, stretch, and tune into our bodies mostly unconsciously. It is when we become conscious in all we do that life becomes at peace. Dreams are a part of our lives. Without them we could not create and we would have nothing to look forward to. Keeping freedom of choice and present time awareness is truly living as a seed of God and not the seed of man. Angel, please note that following your dreams and what makes you happy are the best choices you can make. You can have complete trust that you are making the correct decision. Stop doubting yourself or your guidance. God/love is with you always and seeks to express itself through you. Aren't you amazing!

Freedom of choice is an interesting concept, isn't it? Do we really have freedom of choice to come into this life? Yes! Absolutely! Do we choose our parents? Yes! Do we have freedom of choice as children? Mostly not! This is why we, as children, see this time as unfair and feel so abused. Does this sound familiar? This is our stage in life to be guided by those that have chosen to be our earthly guides for us. Parents, grandparents, teachers, the good advice we get from strangers, these are our earthly guides. Spiritual guides and angels are always there to assist and protect us even when we fall down the stairs. I have witnessed so many amazing stories from my Graduates in 20 years and how just being here is a miracle. Some have been run over, been hit by cars, banged their heads really hard, or had all kinds of illnesses that heal. It is always a wonder to me that we even survived childhood! Thank your wonderful guides for all that they have taught you and thank yourself now for the Angel guide you have become. Can you see how you are the guide for many in your life?

Do we have freedom of choice when we do not know who we are? Not really. It is only in our awakening that we can access our freedom of choice. And then, what choice do we have but to love and is that really freedom of choice? What do you think, Angel? Are you living from freedom of choice or someone else's story and dream? As Angels, enough of us have learned individually that the world has suffered enough on every level, and now we can choose to beam up!

Freedom of Choice gives us the option to choose who we

walk with and walk away from those who are not holding a more loving, healthy, and aware frequency.   This does not mean that we have to condone or approve of other's unloving or unconscious behavior, but it does mean that we do have to love them. We must stay healthy in this process, and love is the way.

"If you can't say something nice, don't say anything at all". I teach and live that gossip is the number one killer of an Angel. I have seen people sitting in hot springs and heard them talking about another in a counter-productive and unloving way. I go over to them and say," Excuse me, Beloveds. I choose to stand in proxy to the person you are talking about, and now you may continue. Everyone chokes. I guess they really forgot they were talking about God/Love and themselves, too.   Whoops!   Remember that when you are talking about another you are really talking about yourself. You might want to speak a more loving language because your cells are listening.

Are you the starter of the rumor mill? Do you crave someone else's mishaps and mistakes? Do you relish in the thought that someone else has a more messed up life than you? Look at how many "reality" TV shows are on now! Are you addicted to drama and trauma? Do you get off on tragic stories, by repeating them often, or the possibility of a tragedy? If someone falls off a playground slide do you assume the worst first? Do you assume they have a broken neck, concussion, or their teeth are knocked out before you even assess the situation? Some of you do these things and you are not really fun to have around in an emergency. Where is the freedom of choice in this? When does a mistake get to happen and be seen for its Divine blessing: a lesson? How is a person supposed to grow and become more aware of their divine self without the lessons life teaches us? Do not judge yourself or others so harshly, Angel. From the time of conception until we are adults, we are strongly influenced by the feelings, thoughts and attitudes supplied to us by others who love us, teach us, (including the media) and interact with us on a daily basis. Whenever children develop non acceptable behavior, the ancient Hawaiians would temple lomi the children and counsel the parents because the behavior was a mirror of the energy of the family.

The person who is made to feel he is constantly making mistakes will automatically embrace the feeling of guilt for being. One incorrect perception leads to another and another until the person feels absolutely worthless. When a feeling or thought validates what we already believe to be true, the matching emotion becomes

257

ingrained in the person. All this happens on the subconscious level.

Our choices can be conscious or unconscious. Conscious choice is creative, the heart of authenticity. Unconscious choice is how we end up living other people's lives. "The most common despair is ...not choosing, or willing, to be oneself," the nineteenth-century Danish philosopher Soren Kierkegaard warns us, "[but] the deepest form of despair is to choose to be other than oneself." This is how we hurt the one we forget to love. Ourselves.

An ancient poet said, "There is a field between right and wrong, I will meet you there!" We live in a world defined by duality-light or dark, up or down, success or failure, right or wrong, pain or joy. This duality keeps us in perpetual motion. Like a pendulum in an old clock, we swing back and forth through our emotions. Creative, conscious choice gives us the power to stop swinging and remain in balance, at peace. Be still and know who you are. Remember your tool to stay in the now!

Most Angels, are petrified of making choices. This is because we don't trust ourselves because we judge our past choices. I like to ask my Angels when they are being too hard on themselves, did you love? They all say yes! Even in the hardest moments of your lives, you loved. You did not get it wrong. Forgive yourself NOW! The past is the past- it is over! Did you learn from your "mistakes"? My daughter Shara says that life isn't fun anymore when you are not learning. Learning always creates mistakes and you learn FROM them. You become a more aware person with every choice you make, good or bad, because in each one you find out who you are a little more. I had a teacher that said you are punished by your sins not for them. Making better choices is part of waking up!

So you married the wrong man. Became a teacher instead of a country and western singer. You didn't finish college, join the Peace Corps, or move to New York. If you had, your life would have been different, but not necessarily better. That's because we, not our outer circumstances, are the catalysts for the quality of our lives. Be sure to not look back at your life with regret, it hurts your bones, and remember only the love goes on.

I have met many who have had such difficult childhoods that they chose not to have children. Some judge those people for not having children and some judge others for having children. When did it become OK for us to judge others by their choices? Honor everyone and your own choices without attachment to outcome and watch where love shines through anyway. Be aware to not judge your own journey, either.

Have you ever asked yourself, "How could I have been so stupid?" Our lives are not entirely shaped by right or wrong choices, thank God. There have been wise choices, happy choices. Brilliant decisions. We just don't remember many of them. Certainly we don't give ourselves enough credit.

God's Image

God is both masculine and feminine, and in God's image, every person is half female and half male energy. We come in with the predominance to be one or the other, because of our choice in the womb. Men like Larry, that can cry at Hallmark commercials, show us compassion and strength at the same time. I can be very masculine. My attitude is let me try hammering, building, or fishing, and if I can't do it, you can help me. Larry can counsel people in a very gentle, compassionate, and more feminine manner and still be a man. If you are a man saying women are all weak or inferior or a woman saying men are all aggressive and dominating, you are not accepting that part of yourself, or God for that matter!

The Gentle Art Of Blessing
By Pierre Pradervand

On awakening, bless this day, for it is already full of unseen good which your blessings will call forth; for to bless is to acknowledge the unlimited good that is embedded in the very texture of the universe and awaiting each and all.

On passing people in the street, on the bus, in places of work and play, bless them. The peace of your blessing will accompany them on their way and the aura of its gentle fragrance will be a light to their path.

On meeting and talking to people, bless them in their health, their work, their joy, and their relationships to God, themselves, and others. Bless them in their abundance, their finances...bless them in every conceivable way, for such blessings not only sow seeds of healing but one day will spring forth as flowers of joy in the waste places of your own life.

As you walk, bless the city in which you live, its government and teachers, its nurses and street sweepers, its children and bankers, its priests and prostitutes. The minute anyone expresses the least aggression or unkindness to you, respond with a blessing: bless them totally, sincerely, joyfully, for such blessings are a shield which protects them from the ignorance of their misdeed, and deflects the arrow that was aimed at you.

To bless means to wish, unconditionally, total, unrestricted good for others and events from the deepest wellspring in the innermost chamber of your heart: it means to hallow, to hold in reverence, to behold with utter awe that which is always a gift from the Creator. He who is hallowed by your blessing is set aside, consecrated, holy, and whole. To bless is yet to invoke divine care upon, to think or speak gratefully for, to confer happiness upon - although we ourselves are never the bestower, but simply the joyful witnesses of Life's abundance.

To bless all without discrimination of any sort is the ultimate form of giving, because those you bless will never know from whence came the sudden ray of sun that burst through the clouds of their skies, and you will rarely be a witness to the sunlight in their lives.

When something goes completely askew in your day, some unexpected event knocks down your plans and you too also, burst into blessing: for life is teaching you a lesson, and the very event you believe to be unwanted, you yourself called forth, so as to learn the lesson you might balk against were you not to bless it. Trials are blessings in disguise, and hosts of angels follow in their path.

To bless is to acknowledge the omnipresent, universal beauty hidden to material eyes; it is to activate that law of attraction which, from the furthest reaches of the universe, will bring into your life exactly what you need to experience and enjoy.

When you pass a prison, mentally bless its inmates in their innocence and freedom, their gentleness, pure essence and unconditional forgiveness; for one can only be prisoner of one's self-image and a free man can walk unshackled in the courtyard of a jail, just as citizens of countries where freedom reigns can be prisoners when fear lurks in their thoughts.

When you pass a hospital, bless its patients in their present wholeness, for even in their suffering, this wholeness awaits in them to be discovered. When your eyes behold a man in tears, or seemingly broken by life, bless him in his vitality and joy: for the material senses present but the inverted image of the *ultimate splendor and perfection which only the inner eye beholds.*

It is impossible to bless and to judge at the same time? So hold constantly as a deep, hallowed, intoned thought that desire to bless, for truly then shall you become a peacemaker, and one day you shall, everywhere, behold the very face of God.

We are all teachers and we are all students in this world. We draw certain people into our lives so we can have the exchange of teaching and learning. Ask yourself, "What did life teach me and awaken in me to who I am right now, and how can I not love my beautiful self?" As soon as you start doing this, you start staying more in the now, because you look at the past and say, "Wow this is what I learned, and now I can be your teacher. I don't have to go through the same pain, because I already did that, and aren't I thankful for me?"

How many of you Angels believe that you are responsible for another person's happiness? How many of you believe you have to sacrifice yourselves for others in order to be good enough to be with God? Get over it! You are not responsible for their happiness. They are responsible for their own happiness. You are responsible for your own. I see so many in terrible pain in their shoulders and upper back. Sound familiar? Ask yourself, If I am not happy, who is? When I am happy, who is? How would you like everyone on the planet to answer that question?

When you are happy, who's happy? Everyone around you is happy. When you are not, who is? Mankind was created to have great joy… not great sorrow, struggle, pain, manipulation or control. It's about great joy. Guess what? If you are not having great joy, your soul will find another way to joy and love, even if it has to check out. If you really want to be in the body, and you really want to love it because it's a delicious experience, then you really might want to choose love.

Your children are not yours. They are God's. If you can-not look at them and be thankful they chose you to be their parent, (and be really thankful because they could have chosen anyone else in the universe and they chose you,) don't you think you are pretty special? Maybe you should look at them again and say, "Thank you for choosing me. I understand that you are on temporary loan from God. I am so blessed and honored that you chose me, and I am open to your master teachings." I am truly thankful for my children, now adults and amazing parents themselves.

Ideas on how to work well with a computer

Many of us spend the majority of our day in front of a computer. When we spend the day in our brain, we are not in our body. This produces an automatic fight or flight response within us. Our entire body is in a state of contraction all day long. There are several things we can do to remedy this situation. First of all, if possible, use a bouncy ball instead of an office chair to sit on. This allows you to continually move your body. It moves the lymph, and your body never contracts, but instead moves and flows, and by the end of the day-you'll feel great! You can also shrug your shoulders to your ears and take an in-breath, then slowly drop your shoulders and take an out breath. Do this three times in a row once every 30 minutes and the difference will be remarkable! When you take a break outside, remember to do your eye exercises in the sun.

Tool Box Time
Eye exercises are very easy.

This comes from Ayurveda. Medicine that is over 1000 years old. Without contacts or eye glasses, look at the sun and then close your eyes. Begin to rotate your eyes up and down, side to side, make a figure eight a few times, hold the eyes up and count to 10 and down and count to 10. Do this for 5 minutes a day and you will be amazed. This helps stimulate the brain, strengthening the retina and keeps your eyesight from weakening. It also stimulates your liver because it stimulates vitamin D production, and even makes your bones stronger. Many people work inside for years of their lives, and they don't get enough sun, so they are not producing enough vitamin D through sunlight. Sunlight for at least 30 minutes daily keeps the brain, eyes, bone marrow, spleen and pancreas in alignment, because they all need a healthy dose of Vitamin D every day!

On Quitting A Habit

I teach and live that you can be addicted to only two things. Water and Loving! Everything else in moderation and variety.

Watch your thoughts: they become your words,

Watch your words: they become your actions,

Watch your actions: they become your habits,

Watch your habits: they become your character

Watch your character: it becomes your destiny!

If you need to stop a habit, put a soft hair tie around your wrist. Every time you want to break a habit; a less than positive thought about abundance, or cigarettes, or even speaking unkindly, you can snap the hair tie on your wrist and then kiss your wrist, (because you don't want your body to think you don't love it) simply as a reminder to the brain to pay attention, because you are shifting this thought pattern. This brings you back into your body and into the now time where you want to make the choice that is more clear and more healthy.

If you would like to quit smoking and that familiar craving comes along, go ahead and honor your body; that this is your choice and you want it. Just light up and stand in your bathtub! Listen to your brain as it starts talking to you. Your brain will say "This is really weird. Why are you doing this?" Talk to your brain and tell your brain you are done with this and want to change it. Next time, you can stand on one leg or on top of the toilet, or you can do something weird that you don't normally do...something that you have never done at the same time. Most people smoke when they wake in the morning or with that first cup of coffee, and these are habits. Change the habit. Go ahead and do it, but do it somewhere else. The brain will say, what are you doing? It starts talking to the neurons, "Oh we are doing something different now." It really works.

I've had hundreds and hundreds of people who have successfully stopped smoking, over-eating, etc. by doing the hair tie habit breaker. Another option is to put sticky notes up on your fridge, your bathroom mirror, your car, or computer to remind yourself to go do your eye exercises, not smoke, belly breathe, etc. Every time you see them, they will remind you of your new healthier choice.

Remember to take a breath and get into the now

moment, and say "What do I see, hear, smell, taste, and touch, and thank you for allowing me to have a straight back, or to quit smoking." God will always say yes, if that is what you want but it's the habit that needs to be broken. It's not hard. You do it because you want to be a better, healthier you, and you want a better world, and if you are better, the world is also better.

You are the one determining your happiness. When you accept yourself and accept what is, you can change it, you can make improvements. You need not wait for others to change. Your change will create an atmosphere for others to improve also. You are NOT responsible for changing anyone but yourself. As you are liberated from your fear, your presence automatically liberates others of theirs. Do you understand how important you are? Shifting ourselves creates an environment of understanding and forgiveness of self and others. When understanding abounds in us, it is easier to let go of blame and judgment.

We can honestly accept everyone, including ourselves, exactly where and how we are in this moment. We cannot know what feelings they experienced at birth that have affected their life. We don't have the same inner dialog nor were we disciplined in the same way. Our assignment here on earth is not to judge or blame but to FORGIVE. Remember most people do the best they can based on their perceptions.

There is nothing any of us can do about the past. It is gone forever. It is each of our choices whether things from our past keep us in bondage or if we step into the NOW, opening the door to freedom. That is why it is so important to feel positive feelings, think positive thoughts, use positive words and eat the correct foods. Unresolved negative feelings are on a subconscious level. There is no need for any of us to spend one more minute playing the guilt or blame game.

"No man is free who is not master of himself."
—Epictetus

Acceptance means actually honoring yourself
as you are now.

264

Toolbox—Mindfulness

To become the master of your thoughts and feelings, instead of letting them master you, an intense desire is necessary. You first can practice recognizing mindless chatter and un-loving self talk. As you learn to focus on what you are saying to yourself-this shifts you into awareness. Sweet Angels, please honor yourselves for your good intent! It is what counts. Paying attention to what you are thinking and quieting those thoughts are a key to consciousness. The goal is to become aware when you are doing something while being fully present (not thinking about what is next). Then you are in the meditation of your life. Everything is quiet and peaceful and what comes out of your mouth is the language of your quiet heart!

If you hear the phone ringing at 3 am and it wakes you out of a deep sleep, what comes to your mind? Do you think something awful happened or that someone died? Where does your mind go before you answer the phone? Say the phone awakens you and then stops ringing. Now what are you imagining? What are you projecting?

This is an example of being mindful of your inner dialog. Whenever something unexpected comes, such as a strange message from your boss requesting a meeting or that leaves you wondering; watch your internal dialog. Listen to what comes up in you.

Are you thinking you are being called in for a raise or for praise? Do you think you are in trouble? What is your imagination whipping up for you? Is your body stressing? Instead of letting your thoughts and feelings run away with you which creates all sorts of excuses or blocks and keeps you from moving forward, choose to see this process of shifting your thoughts and feelings as practice, just like the practice in learning a musical instrument or a new skill.

Positive emotions create bodily sensations of openness and expansiveness; inviting the world in. The body is relaxed even though emotions such as joy are energizing. Developing body wisdom through doing *The Cleanse* allows you to tap into what is really going on vibrationally. Positive feelings invite unity while negative feelings invite isolation.

You know when your life is working when: You enjoy loving and satisfying relationships with family, with friends, and with yourself. Are you happy and peaceful most of the time? Do you enjoy optimum health?

Take a big Belly breath. Exhale your breath while making a sound Hum. out and listen to your mind. Notice how the sound distracts the mind. Follow your breath and breathe slowly and deeply from your belly. Tune into your senses: What do you hear, smell, see, taste, and feel right now? Where I am, God is, where God is, I am. Change the tones and feel the chakras bathed with sound. Your mind remains quiet! Isn't the silence of the mind awesome? Keep practicing. It is worth the effort.

Gratitude Prayer

In gratitude, please repeat often: Thank you for supplying me with this opportunity to live life to the fullest and to learn to love unconditionally. Thank you for this great blessing and opportunity! I feel alive and vital! I am now ready, willing and able to accept what I need to learn, and understand what was necessary from this experience to grow and develop and expand my reason for existence on this earth. Yes! Yes! I AM health! I AM happiness! I AM joy! I AM unconditional love!

When most of us experience suffering long enough and have had sufficient misery while going through it, we become more teachable and ready to eliminate misery, no matter how much effort or dedication it requires. We become willing to be more mindful of what we are thinking; we become more willing to become private investigators and figure out what makes us tick.

Love heals

Whatever the problem, love is the answer. Whatever the fear, love is the answer. Love is all there is. Whatever the question, love is the answer." Think of your day to day activities and interactions. How much time do you spend defending various positions that make you feel right, worthy, okay, etc.? The Course in Miracles says would you rather be right or happy? When you no longer feel a need to defend yourself, that is, when you accept yourself, the body can naturally relax.

266

Being tolerant and accepting of the experiences that challenge and teach us, allows our growth experiences to no longer be hard.

Loving others as they are and seeing them perfect as they are allows them to grow and unfold at their own rate. Sometimes you are the more conscious one and you are the ONLY one who can see another's divine perfection. When you do not see the situations in your life, or the life of others, as being perfect, there is no energy for anything to change. Encourage yourself to have faith that when we are doing our part, we are taken care of.

When we are mindfully conscious of what is taking place in our lives and are willing to shift from the role of victim to master, our mindfulness will motivate us to make wiser choices daily and cause us to grow in a way that we gain experience, comfort, and peace for our Being. The core of each of us is the same, unconditioned consciousness, the Divine. See the divine in others. When we accept ourselves as we are, we increase our ability to change. The Eastern greeting Namaste means "The Divine in me honors and salutes the Divine in you."

**"IF YOU WANT TO BE ONE OF THE CHOSEN,
ALL YOU HAVE TO DO IS CHOOSE YOURSELF."**

On the Pain Body

God is trying to communicate with you through your body and pain is one sure way to get your attention. Illness can be understood as a lesson you have given yourself to help you get to know who you really are. Health is enhanced in people who engage in work and relationships that satisfy them. 90-100% of physical health problems have psychological roots! People are used to turning their pain and hurt over to someone else to fix or using drugs to numb/hide it. Beloved Angel, there is no pill to consciousness, and consciousness is the way to health. Antidepressants stop a person's emotional process. Tears of joy and tears of sorrow have different chemical compositions. Joy and Sorrow are parts of how we process. By allowing a full emotional release, the body/mind/spirit can feel cleansed and free. Insights will come up. Long buried self understanding returns as we are finally at peace with painful events of the past even after years of intellectual misunderstanding. On days or moments when you feel wonderful, ask yourself what thoughts, activities, and people enhanced your energy flow. On days you find yourself tired and irritable at the end of the day, ask yourself what thoughts, activities and people drained your energy. If you are caught up in a spiral of negative feelings, you are out of touch with inner guidance and thus giving too much attention to what you don't want. To turn it around: Acknowledge the feeling without making a judgment. Know the feeling is there for a reason; acknowledge it as a teacher coming to you with a message. Spend $\frac{1}{2}$ minute on identifying a cause, if nothing comes, move on for now. Ask 'What do I want?" Shift the focus back to positive thoughts. State what you do want out loud. Affirm with gratitude that you already have what you want. Know that what you have asked for is on its way to you now! Remember that impatience is the original sin. It is the journey that matters not the destination.

Angels Be Selfish- Do you know that the bible has been changed many times? I discovered that Jesus really said in John 15:12 This is my desire that you love yourself and one another as I have loved you. What happened to our society when we took the love yourself part out of the equation? Don't put everyone before you. If you do service to others under obligation, it creates exhaustion and resentment. Say no to what doesn't support you in your essence of joy. It is never too late to say NO to those things that drain you and YES to the positive situations and people that replenish you. Though you may have been terrified or abused as a child, this early abuse will not affect your body unless you start to believe you were entitled to a different life. The mindset that you were intentionally abused and violated creates the dis-ease.

Many people think they make the world better by helping other people. Truthfully the best gift we can give the world is to become more conscious ourselves. When we raise our vibration, we bring many with us. The Hopi knowing says 144,000 are directly affected by our choosing love instead of judgment or sadness, or sacrifice. When we wake up, so do many others! Doesn't that give you hope for the world? If you knew you had only 6 months to live, would you stay in your current job? Would you stay with your current partner?

As children, we first functioned primarily from the right brain, from the feeling/intuitive side. As we explored and we were told NO continually and we were punished, eventually our child minds reasoned that if we wanted to forgo pain, we needed to shift to the left brain using logical thinking and analyzing. In elementary school, children are bombarded with left brain activities; with rules, regulations, reading, writing, and math. To succeed they must function from logic. Feelings are not usually validated. Their desires to explore and reach out have been squelched. The goal is to return to your child-like innocence (feeling/intuitive side). Then you have the capacity to change the world within a moment.

Are you going to choose a world of love and gratitude or a tortured world filled with discontent and impoverishment? According to Buddhist teachings the world is constantly changing and nothing ever changes. Vibrationally speaking, the energy of vibration must go on forever in continuous motion. Understanding that everything exists in this one moment gives each of us hope and brings light to our lives. No one need be troubled by the past. We can know that the future can bring anything one wills it to be. You, in this moment, hold the key to everything Divine and loving. Are you willing?

Your response to a situation held inside you is a feeling. If you express it verbally or physically, it manifests as an emotion. Everything about you is energy. Feelings and thoughts are energy. Your feelings and thoughts are matter. Matter cannot be destroyed but it can be altered or CHANGED.

Deepak Chopra says that negative feelings obscure the truth of our being and cover up the memory of perfection in our perfect blue print. Negativity creates a false self. Thought consists of atoms, tiny amounts of pure energy. Waves of energy slowed down into non movement solidify; that's matter. The closer together the vibrational frequencies, the higher the vibration and the closer that matter is to its source. Thus positive energy is closer to the source and negative energy has wider frequencies, making them further from Source. The closer you are to your Source, the more peace you experience, the more joy you will feel, and the greater your capacity to love. Many people truly experience these characteristics, I do!

Breathing technique:
find a comfortable place, sit down,
relax and close your eyes.
Take a deep breath through your nose and let it out slowly through your mouth. Take another deep breath the same way, only this time hold your breath at the top of the full inhalation for 3 counts; and then let it out slowly through your mouth.

It is important to be single minded and diligent in getting to peace in the mind. God talks to us through our body. Anytime we find ourselves holding onto resentment or not forgiving, it might be that we experience pain somewhere in our bodies. Notice where you hurt as it will help you uncover the unloving thoughts and feelings you are holding.

Do you believe that you could have a disease from someone in your family? An example of this is heart disease or cancer. Angel, does that make you powerful or powerless? Powerless of course! Guess what? That means it is not true! You are powerful beyond measure. Own your journey and then you can change. You have never, ever, been a victim. There is a part of you that can never be touched or harmed by any earthly experience. Remain in your center and stay empowered!

Everyday Work And Everyday Living

When someone says or does something that triggers you, you can train yourself by being present in the moment and having the awareness that you have been triggered. Then breathe deeply, relax, put a smile on your face and a smile in your heart, and you will avoid creating more negative energy with this person or with this particular issue in the future.

It is indeed possible to live in joy and love at all times. You can be "in charge" of your emotions and not be a victim. The lower conscious levels of hate, envy, jealousy, and greed can become love and joy when you realize that you are the one in charge of your emotions, not the other way around. You can learn how to not be affected by the moods and behaviors of the people you connect with each day. People can bring you down and make your life harder; however, this gives you the opportunity to send them light and love. After all, we are all one. Every time you send unconditional love to someone else, you are positively affecting yourself and the whole universe. Isn't that awesome?

Think of how you want to feel and begin to visualize yourself feeling that way. If you are in a difficult situation, send LOVE! Love heals and protects you. Feel thoughts that encourage growth and expand your heart. Life seeks energy, awareness, and love; remember that any given situation teaches you more about who you are. By holding wholeness and unconditional love and support for those around you, you are teaching them experientially about who they truly are.

The idea is to stay in a high space of peace and unconditional love toward all. It is important to forgive yourself if you wobble into a reaction that is not free and loving. As soon as you catch yourself, take a few deep breaths, center yourself in your body on the earth and send out love to yourself and to everyone. Keep forgiving the parts of you that get triggered. Beating yourself up mentally or emotionally will only create more situations for punishment. All we really want is love anyway. The attention we are trying to get is just a cry for love!

 **Every morning, practice balancing and centering yourself before you go to work and interact with others.**
The more you do this, the faster you will get at it. Remember your deep belly breath. Do at least 15 breaths in the morning and 15 breaths at night, or anytime you need to recenter throughout the day. The breath relaxes the diaphragm and therefore relaxes the nervous system, bringing you physically into a state of peace. See yourself joyful and present, able to assist and lift all those around you. See yourself sending out love to everyone you see with your eyes during the day. Anything you want to happen that day from happy co-workers to a call from a loved one; visualize and feel that happening. Anyone you have been challenged by, send unconditional love now from your centered place and tell them telepathically that you desire peace, love and the highest good for everyone. Forgive everyone and send love instead. Forgiveness clears you and creates a pathway for healing and transformation. This is one of the best gifts you can give yourself!

Remember in "What the Bleep" where Joe Dispenza is talking about creating your day? To succeed and come from the highest joy, you need to come from a centered, calm place. Awareness of your body, thoughts and emotions allows you to discover the effect other people have on you. Many of you make yourself wrong when you feel depleted by people. We have all learned various people pleasing patterns. It is important to be aware of your internal dialog. Maybe you are thinking you are not trying hard enough to please a co-worker or client or that you didn't do the right thing or make your point clear enough. Create around you an atmosphere where the other person can embrace and allow their perfection. You cannot save anyone. We all must save ourselves. Remember your job is to be a clear vessel, so keep on embracing love, forgiving yourself, and

271

centering. Many people like to focus on Master Teachers because their energy is uplifting and transforming. Take a moment and try it!

Intuition Development

Learning to trust your intuition is just learning to trust what naturally resides in you. How do we develop our intuition? Pick up an object such as a crystal or stone. Do you sense a feeling, color, word or image? Do you become highly emotional or do you create mental images and pictures? There is no right or wrong. As you learn how you operate, you will know how to access the information you desire. Feedback is very important; actions create reactions. It is important to observe what reactions your actions cause. If you have been tuning into energy and you are beginning to get data such as feelings and thoughts back, please record them in your journal. Journaling really helps to develop your intuition. Your journal is your road map through your processes, experiences and emotions. It is an opportunity to know yourself better and to access your higher, wiser self. The only way you can truly be of service to others is to know the difference between your "stuff" and their "stuff". Many healers are what I call unhealed healers. We must clear our own stuff before we can assist others to clear their stuff.

You may be considering your own business in the future; this can be challenging as there are many hats to wear and much to do. Often you will put in long days. Knowing yourself is very important. Any work you do can be an awesome ride if you constantly embrace joy and truly see everyone, including yourself, as whole and healed-no matter what!

Remember to forgive the parts of you that fear or judge. These parts need to be loved into the present and into unconditional love. The critical voices in your head that may be echoed by those around you at times need to be loved. Remember to see them as children that need love. Honor the journey. If you love yourself for who you are, you are living in the present time, which is a gateway to personal power. If you love only who you will be or what you will have at some date in the future, then you are out of your body, living in the future that you cannot affect until it becomes present time-kind of like a greyhound chasing an imaginary mechanical rabbit around a track.

Look at who you are. Compare it to who you want to be. Ask yourself if they match. Ask yourself if what you want is really in alignment with who you truly are or if you are carrying someone

272

else's 'picture' of you and empowering it as more real than your own desires and needs. The more you can clear yourself of other people's programs, expectations and pictures of you, the more powerful you will become. Maybe, beloved Angel, you are ready to step into that; that you are ready to become you. I teach all the time at Angel Farms to not give a shit, literally, what people think about you. Mother Theresa said, "It has never been between you and them anyway, it has always been between you and God!"

Beliefs And Judgment: Working With Others

What is your natural stance when you approach other people? Do you see them as truly whole no matter what physical dis-eases they may be expressing? Do you respect them? Do you honor the journey that brought them here? Approaching people with compassion and tolerance will enable you to gather useful information. When you sense something that does not fit with your known reality, you will need to see that many people think differently and believe in different things without making them wrong. I used to imagine that I was the only one here on earth. I saw myself as being really bored!

Tolerance means you can accept many different viewpoints and love people for who they are. Tolerance allows you to embark on an enormous adventure! Each person has a unique way of looking at the world. If you can discover what is unique, what is free, open and loving about everyone you know and meet, you will discover new ways that you may become more free, open and loving..

How to see the future and create the best future

Imagine your desire to decide upon a path. This could be anything you deem as important to you. You think of one choice and you notice your breathing has grown shallow, your body is somewhat closed and you feel discomfort in your stomach. These are signs from the future (your Higher Self) that are telling you about this path. If when you think of a path you feel heavy inside, your body is telling you there is a better way to do it. Keep imagining possible future realities until you have a light joyful feeling. If in the time frame you have for this visualization, you do not find a future reality that brings joy to you, call forth the highest good and ask to be inspired with a joyful answer. The universe answers when we ask, so ask! Always talk and share a positive, possible future!

Interpreting What You Receive

Write down your impressions in your journal! After you have brought all the information in and recorded it, sit and read and review it. You may find doubts coming up. It is important that you do not let the doubts stop you. Thank them and let them go. Do not criticize yourself. This is true for almost everyone. As long as your heart is open, you can trust what you are sensing. How do you know if your heart is open? Does it feel tickled and happy or not?

Unless you know how you think when you are alone, you will not be able to recognize the effects other people have on your thoughts. You may feel suddenly tired or happy or charged with energy or drained, anxious or angry. Pay attention to the differences. Learn how to not be drained but activated by your connections with people. The first step is to become aware of when someone's presence leaves you drained, even in a very subtle way.

Awareness of your body, thoughts and emotions allows you to discover your true self. We are all one. We are all in telepathic contact with each other constantly. Watch for feelings of identifying with others, wanting to save them from situations or illness or feeling responsible for their healing. LISTEN TO YOUR INNER DIALOG. Are you thinking that you are not trying hard enough or didn't say the right thing or didn't make your point so they 'got it'? Remember back to "What the Bleep". You need to form new receptor sites to have a different experience.

Be gentle with yourself. Focus on your positive aspects and gifts. Do not make yourself or the other person wrong. You cannot have a healing connection if you see yourself as wrong or lacking. If you are feeling bad about a relationship, say to yourself, I am perfect as I am.

Check in with yourself constantly and notice if you feel good. Do you feel high or do you feel inadequate? As you heal and change the drama within yourself, you will find that you no longer attract those negative lessons over and over. There is no reason to put yourself in a situation where you feel unloved or undervalued.

You may feel that you owe your time and energies to others or that you are obligated to give them attention. If you do, you may find others in your life crying out for you to come take care of them while you are working with your own life. Do you believe you must offer love, support, and care to everyone? Loving someone does not mean making their feelings more important than your own. If you study the lives of highly evolved beings, you will see that there are many ways to be loving to others, including speaking bluntly with compassion and love.

Being committed to your higher purpose and loving to yourself is the highest priority. In your day to day contacts, know that you do not owe anyone your time or energy. Your time and energy are gifts you choose to give. How you use your time and energy will determine how you will evolve in this lifetime.

When you notice that you are feeling depleted in any way, notice if you are leaning forward, trying to reach others, begging for their attention or feeling drained, unappreciated, unacknowledged, or unsupported, it is time to ask yourself why you remain or respond to these types of situations.

TO DISSOLVE FEAR, TURN AND LOOK DIRECTLY AT IT. FOR WHAT YOU FACE, DISSOLVES IN THE LIGHT OF CONSCIOUSNESS.

If you seek an answer, just ask, and then listen. You can never do anything that is not in some way an attempt to bring more light into your life. It is important to take the time to go back and change your vision, release and forgive yourself and see what you learned. If you knew your motivation, you would know the driving force behind everything you do. If you focus on a specific thing to bring you what you want, the universe can truly begin bringing abundance in many ways. See everyone as expanding and growing and you will see yourself that way also.

If you ask for guidance, trust the messages that come into your mind. If you hear people speaking of negative things, immediately send them positive pictures and change the conversation. Faith is a higher vibration. If you find yourself in doubt or criticism: Forgive yourself, dust yourself off, and love again. Everyone wobbles out of love sometimes. It is being human!

Every comment you make is direct energy either towards the past, present, or future. You project energy every moment. If you want a better future, speak of it, picture it, and say it to others. Only you can create it for yourself, it is the greatest power that you have been given.

Responsibility for the Earth/
Chief Seattle's Message to the World

In 1854 President Franklin Pierce made an offer to buy Indian Tribal Lands in the Northwest. Chief Seattle, leader of the combined Duwamish and Suquamish tribes, answered the President with the words below. It is widely considered the most moving and profound statement on the environment ever made.

"How can you buy or sell the sky, the warmth of the land? The idea is strange to us.

If we do not own the freshness of the air and the sparkle of the water, how can you buy them? Every part of this earth is sacred to my people. Every shining pine needle, every sandy shore, every mist in the dark woods, every clearing and humming insect is holy in the memory and experience of my people.

We are part of the earth and it is part of us. The perfumed flowers are our sisters; the deer, the horse, the great eagle, these are our brothers. The rocky crests, the juices in the meadows, the body heat of the pony and the man...all belong to the same family.

We will consider your offer to buy our land. But it will not be easy.

This shining water that moves in the streams and rivers is not just water but the blood of our ancestors. The water's murmur is the voice of my father's father. The rivers are our brothers. They quench our thirst. The rivers carry our canoes and feed our children.

We know that the white man does not understand our ways. One portion of the land is the same to him as the next, for he is a stranger who comes in the night and takes from the land whatever he needs. The earth is not his brother, but his enemy, and when he has conquered it, he moves on. He kidnaps the earth from his children and he does not care. His father's grave and his children's birthright are forgotten.

He treats his mother, the earth, and his brother, the sky, as things to be bought, plundered, sold like sheep or bright beads. His appetite will devour the earth and leave behind only a desert. There is no quiet place in the white man's cities. No place to hear the unfurling of leaves in spring or the rustle of an insect's wings. But perhaps it is because I am a savage and do not understand. The clatter only seems to insult the ears.

And what is there to life if a man cannot hear the lonely cry of the whippoorwill or the arguments of the frogs around a pond at night?

276

I am a red man and do not understand. The Indian prefers the soft sound of the wind darting over the face of a pond and the smell of the wind itself, cleansed by a mid-day rain, or scented with pinion pine.

The air is precious to the red man, for all things share the same breath...the beast, the tree, the man...they all share the same breath. The white man does not seem to notice the air he breathes. Like a man dying for many days, he is numb to the stench.

If we decide to accept (your offer to buy our land), I will make one condition...the white man must treat the beasts of this land as his brothers. I am a savage and do not understand any other way.

I have seen a thousand rotting buffalo on the prairie, left by the white man who shot them from a passing train. I am a savage and I do not understand how the smoking Iron Horse can be more important than the buffalo that we kill only to stay alive.

What is man without the beast? If all the beasts were gone, man would die from a great loneliness of spirit. For whatever happens to the beasts, soon happens to man. All things are connected.

Whatever befalls the earth befalls the sons of the earth. If men spit upon the ground, they spit upon themselves. This we know...the earth does not belong to man. Man belongs to the earth. This we know. All things are connected like the blood which unites one family. Whatever befalls the earth befalls the son of the earth. Man did not weave the web of life. He is merely a strand in it. Whatever he does to the web, he does to himself.

Even the white man, whose God walks and talks with him as friend to friend cannot be exempt from the common destiny.

We may be brothers after all. We shall see. One thing we know which the white man may one day discover...our God is the same God. He is the God of man and his compassion is equal for the red man and the white. This earth is precious to him, and to harm the earth is to heap contempt upon the Creator.

The whites, too, shall pass; perhaps sooner than all other tribes. Contaminate your bed and you will one night suffocate in your own waste. But in our perishing, you will shine brightly, fired by the strength of the God who brought you to this land and, for some special purpose, gave you dominion over this land and over the red man.

That destiny is a mystery to us. For we do not understand when the buffalo are all slaughtered, the wild horses are tamed, the secret corners of the forest heavy with scent of many men and the view of the ripe hills blotted by talking wires. Where is the thicket? Gone. Where is the eagle?

Gone. The end of the living and the beginning of survival."

Be the change you seek to experience in your world. How are you doing with Styrofoam? How are you doing with the things that are unhealthy for ourselves and our earth? We have been given dominion over the earth. Have hope Beloved Angel, that your cleaner choices change the world. How much trash did you pick up today? If you do it, so do 144,000 others. It starts with YOU!

Silent Observation

Whenever you go into a new job, or any significantly different direction in your life or work, it is important to remember that "silent observation" will teach you more than anything. When you are speaking, it is impossible to listen. When you are listening, you are learning, when you are speaking, you are not. If you can understand the concept of silence, it can be your greatest teacher. There are many programs world-wide in which you go into silence for the entire program. Learning is accelerated when the art of listening comes into play. As an example, we use Silent Observation with our Apprentices at Angel Farms. The following is an example of using this art in the work place, as well as any new setting involving learning something new. Only then can you go within and discover parts of yourself that can benefit from this learning experience. Silence allows for your greatest teacher, your higher self, to be heard. Listen well, and you will have found your foundation for your learning. "Go within, or go without."

When I was almost 1 year old and my sister almost 2 years old, we were taken by my 19 year old father, away from my mother. He hooked up with a woman to care for us while he worked and she did not want children. She forced us to sit a room for many hours per day and to not move or talk. She had threatened us to never tell our father by killing our little dog in front of us. I spent many, many hours in quiet silence for many years. As I grew older and healed my stuff, I asked myself, why would I choose this journey? WOW! I realized how completely comfortable I am with silence. It is like an old friend. Many can not even turn off the TV at night, right mom, because they are so uncomfortable. Silence has helped me be the healer I am, and I am a great one! I have owned my journey and carry no blame or ill will towards those that helped me be who I am. Silence has been one of the greatest gifts in my life. It can be for you too, but I recommend meditation and nature to access the Creator in silence.

Your greatest lesson is to learn to hold a space of unconditional love and honor for the process. This requires that you keep your attention on your immediate surroundings for the entire process. This is developing the witness in you who walks hand in hand with others on their journey. Part of this is about knowing how to sense when others need personal support, and when they don't. People will unfold their wings at their own pace, and everyone is different, so remember to be a gentle and supportive presence for them to rely on.

I also request that you do a daily meditation at sundown. This is to open up your intuitive mind. Intuition is a large part of your Higher Self which allows you to be guided directly. Trust in you, for that is your seed. You can always have a day of silence.

Be spiritually intuitive. Pray for guidance in all that you do. If you pray for happiness, he may give you blessings, but the happiness is up to you. If your intuition can be properly applied, it can be the most powerful tool.

Tell Me What Life Is

Life is about BALANCE- you have four legs of a chair.
Each represents one Spiritual, one Emotional, one Mental, and one Physical. Each one has equal importance and if one leg of your chair is weak or missing your chair will fall over.
Life is about PRESENCE. Try to go into tomorrow or yesterday and have a drink of water in them. Not possible because neither one exists. Being present is all we have.
Life is a CANVAS. You can create anything.
Every moment is fresh.
Life is about CHOICE. Choosing love or fear, we all know what fear feels like. Try love instead. It feels much more familiar.
Fear is illusion. Choose your essence. LOVE!
Life is about LAUGHTER. Everything changes.
Life is PEACE. To create a world of peace means no more war inside and therefore no more war outside. You are the one we have been waiting for. Hold this vision of PEACE
Life is UNIQUE. Have you ever seen the same snowflake, leaf, flower, face, or eyes?
Everything is unique and special and different.
Life is about LOOKING into someone's eyes and seeing God there

looking back; including your own eyes.

Life is a JOURNEY. We all came with a vision of heaven on earth. The Journey is to create that now by seeing it whole already.

Life is being RESPONSIBLE. It is waking up from illusion that you are not God. You Are! So be responsible for who you are.

Life is like a MOUNTAIN. It is always changing and yet always there.

Life is about ELEMENTS AND ATOMS.

You can fit all the matter in your body on the end of a pin. All the rest is space, God Space. It is everywhere and everything. You are always SAFE and surrounded by God's love.

It is not possible to be separate from God.

Life is about AWAKENING.

The infinite wisdom that dwells within you is the Wisdom of God. Enjoy your wisdom.

It is God's gift.

Life is about PURPOSE. Your purpose is to love like God loves; unconditionally and without judgment.

BE like God and you will know that you ARE!

Life KNOWS there is no duality.

There is only God and God is Love and therefore so are we!

Life is about TRUST.

It is letting go of control of anyone or anything.

It is about following your heart!

"I am a mountain; I will stay and remember,
I will follow you with my love. I am the mountain;
I will stay and remember,
I will follow you with my love." —By Rumi

I forgive myself today for thinking that I have done anything wrong in my whole entire life
(Repeat 3 times).

Guess what Angel, you didn't get it wrong because even in the hardest moments of your life, you loved. It may have been a puppy, a butterfly, or a rainbow. Your love came through anyway. What a master of love you are! You are doing an awesome job of letting go.

Do you have any fears left? Why bother? Are you good enough? Yes, absolutely! Do not judge one breath of your sacred journey of love as bad! Or anyone else's. Remember, Where I am God is, and where God is, I am! There are no accidents and no victims, only co-creaters with God. What you focus on, you create. Create only love. Forgiveness is knowing there is nothing to forgive because it means seeing everyone and yourself as a child of God. Never judge another until you have walked 1000 miles in their moccasins and you would judge them not. Honor who you are! Get responsible for being an earth Angel. Whenever you look in the mirror, look deeply into your/ God's eyes and say, "I am the way, the truth, and the light." Then beam it. If not you then who? If not now, then when?

Chapter 10

Using This Knowledge In Your Daily Life

Angel Farms Cleanse Information

10th Day
Right Kidney, Right Hip

I loved therefore I am
I love therefore I am
I am love therefore I am
I choose love and joy
In every thought, word, and deed.
When I love,
I am most like you, God
Thank you for your gift of
Unending love.
Thank you for
Your gift of me!
Have great joy in your journey of love.

I know everything IS God
"I don't limit the IS"

I have been talking to you about your wonderful body and how it works all the way to the cellular level and how your emotions, thoughts, and actions affect your life. In the last 9 chapters, I have taught you about your organs, how they function, and how they can be in perfect balance. Can you see it, Angel? Can you see how they can be in perfect balance. Can you see how holding on to the past affects your future and your health? I want you to take this knowledge and incorporate it into your life and LIVE! You have come so far in your journey. Now is the time for you to experience heaven on earth. Follow your bliss and walk in love!

My one goal for writing this book is for you to have a full understanding of who you are and why you are here. Without your wonderful physical body, you are not able to see rainbow colors or to smell a plumeria or rose. You wouldn't know what the snow or rain gently falling on your skin felt like. You couldn't taste a home-baked apple pie (with ice cream, please!). You couldn't hear the sound the waves make when they kiss the shore and sometimes blow you kisses. What a wonderful gift from the Creator and the Earth and every cell in your body, to give you this delicious experience! Thank your cells! Thank your being! And above all enjoy your life! From my heart to yours!

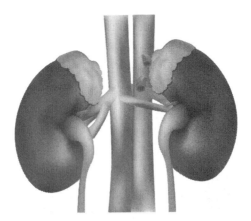

Now, Angel, I want you to remember what I talked to you about in chapter one. Your amazing kidneys have gotten so much stronger and healthier as you are releasing judgment on the world and those who have caused you anger, hurt, and sadness. I want to talk to you about any leftover judgments you may have at yourself. Are you happy with yourself? On a scale of 1-10 how much do you love yourself? How much does God love you? 10 of Course! Do you smile at your "mess ups"? Do you laugh at yourself because you are funny? Just do it! Love yourself! Honor yourself! Pick yourself up, dust yourself off, and RADIATE love and light! That is all you are! No one can stop you from beaming out light and love! This is your essence. How can love do something "wrong"? You/God/Love can't! So forgive yourself and move on with your day. Love your kidneys for the wonderful gift they give you!

Remember your kidneys process 50 gallons of fluid every day! $\frac{1}{4}$ of your blood is filtered every 15 minutes! Larry reminds me that this is all of our blood every hour! Are your kidneys important or what? Is not letting go of judgments of yourself, any person, place, or event, in the past, now or future worth being in the house of the living dead, called kidney dialysis?! The kidneys are the last filtration system to your beautiful heart through your largest internal vein called your aorta that is the diameter of a garden hose. Your right kidney will hold the judgment toward yourself. Will you let it go, Now? Do you understand you are a seed of God and not the seed of Man and you did not do it wrong. You just did not understand and did not remember who you were. You still loved anyway. Bless yourself and your kidneys. It is the last piece!

Skin

I have not said much about the skin which is also known as the third kidney. The skin is our largest body organ. In one square inch of skin there are four yards of nerve fibers, 600 pain sensors, 1300 nerve cells, 9000 nerve endings, 36 heat sensors, 75 pressure sensors, 100 sweat glands, 3 million cells, and 3 yards of blood vessels. When we touch something we send a message to our brain at 124 miles per hour! Each cell in your body has an estimated 6 to 8 feet of DNA chain! Water is a key to healthy skin. 50,000,000 of the cells in your body will have died and been replaced with others, all while you were reading this sentence! If you have skin issues, look at your judgments at yourself and drink more water. It will help!

Angel's Toolbox

Spinning your cells into perfection

Pretend this cell is a playground. Using your finger, what would you do in this playground that would be fun? Go in and notice colors and textures. Notice the skateboards, mazes, balls to bounce on, hair like filaments, (could be!). Notice the chain of the DNA in the middle of the nucleolus. Now, close your eyes and find a cell in your body that does not look like this one. Now, do whatever your imagination can think of to help that cell look like

the wholesome cell. (Examples; vac-
uum, dust, clean, brighten or polish
colors, smooth textures, lighten, etc.)
Now, follow the chain of the DNA
to the center of the nucleolus and
see a light switch there.   Turn it
on! See the cell light up!! It Glows!!
Ask the cell to begin to spin in a
clockwise   direction.   Now   repeat

to all surrounding cells. As I say to one, I say to all, SPIN!
Feel all the cells remembering their wholeness! Do this daily and feel the cellular regeneration. Remember to honor and
love all your cells. (order a color cell photo-angelfarms.com)

It is important to know that the number one hip replacement
is the right hip! (Read information in chapter one on hips.) This is
also about fear of major change or movement; big things like house,
job, or relationship. It also affects the area of the colon that at
Angel Farms we say the 'big boys' like to hang out. I have seen them
six feet long. Yes! Worms. They get all the good food coming in from
the small intestine that empties in front of your right hip at the
illeo-cecal valve. This area can sometimes go for a long period of
time without receiving proper nutrition. We have had over 400 right
hip surgeries scheduled before the Cleanse, and have not lost a hip
yet. The hips can come back when they are properly fed and we have
peace in movement. My Angel, Raphael, got to walk his daughter up
the isle instead of being in a wheelchair. My Angel, Fred, said he was
going sailing in Panama with his daughter, not him and his old shit!

Daily Requirements for Good Health
7 vegetables
2 fruits
2 proteins
1 starch
One gallon of water
Love Yourself Unconditionally

Keep it simple and fun. This can be done in one salad,
one soup, or one meal. Have a lot of variety and try not to eat
the same things everyday. Your teeth and taste buds turn on

communication in the body. Include these tastes daily; bitter, sour, astringent, salty, pungent, and sweet for your greatest health. I recommend you do a weekly soft food day to rest your digestive system. At Angel Farms, we have found our soft foods nutritional program speeds up the rejuvenation process because this food is easily identified and absorbed by the body. We witness people getting younger every day. Wrinkles disappear, eyes change, irises get clearer and whites get whiter. Sometimes hair changes from gray to full color in 10 days!

The Cleanse at Angel Farms is actually written in the dead sea scrolls found in 1946. I am so honored to be fulfilling my purpose and witnessing such profound transformations of the phenomenal, Body, Mind, and Spirit.

One of the hardest things I experience in my life is when I have people come and do this amazing Cleanse and then wobble! Why would they awaken to this powerful force of love in and around them and all of a sudden they decide to go back into unconsciousness? Is it because it's too hard of work; it's too hard to hold it alone? Is it too hard to say I am going to be the only one I know that's going to step up and love right now? It doesn't have to be! Loving is so much easier than hating and judging and much more healthy for your Divine body! Try it and see for yourself, Angel, it is loving that you do the best! It is when you are most like God/Love.

If You Wobble

Remember the toys, weebles wobble but they don't fall down? As practicing Earth Angels sometimes we wobble. Sometimes we have human experiences and not God experiences. Sometimes we are grumpy or irritated and express ourselves in an un-Angelic way. If this happens catch it, forgive yourself immediately, apologize if necessary, and get on with your loving.

A word about I am sorry. Again say and feel the words I am sorry in your body. Can you feel it bend your middle back? Remember the two most powerful words in the universe are I am, they mean God and call forth creation. Sorry is a habitual, pain inducing word we call upon ourselves. Try, I apologize, instead and teach it to your loved ones. If they or yourself say I am sorry, just say cancel that, and apologize instead. Don't hurt yourself when you wobble.

We, at Angel Farms, had a guy come in recently that had full on lung cancer with one week to live. He was in a constant

287

court room fight for 40 years. In and out of courtrooms weekly, that would make anybody not want to breathe again. He got lung cancer and we put him through the Cleanse. His hair and his beard changed color and he looked 30 years younger. He could now breathe too. He came in for a follow up 2 weeks later. I could see he was still holding on to the fight! I told him that we didn't put all this effort and energy into him, to see him not let go. "I don't want to watch you kill yourself when you don't have to. I love you too much." Angel, if you are still living in a place that doesn't make you happy, move! Whatever you are fighting for instead of loving, is it worth it? Do it or Die! He passed 2 months later. He did not choose to let go of the fight. He is, however, free of it now.

Beah, a good friend and my transcriber, says "my guide White Eagle says the same thing. He says to find your joy or you are OUT of here! He's been really, really saying that the past year or so about people. When I am talking to him about somebody or thinking about somebody, he just says, if they don't find their joy, if they don't love the earth and love being here, then they will go somewhere else. Without joy, the vibration is not high enough to stay." Pau! Lesson over, next! Some people are what I call do overs. This means that they have not contracted or taken the opportunity to let go of life's hurts and pains in this lifetime. Remember, Angel, this is a journey of God in another. This part of God decides to not know itself in this lifetime. Do not judge God in this person's journey either. Upon dying, they all always return to love. I have had many caregivers come and do The Cleanse. They repeatedly say that the last words people say are, "Oh, love really is all there is!" And then they take their last sweet breath. They can then do it over if they choose. God/Love does not let them judge themselves.

In the Bible it tells the story of Jesus in the wilderness. Even Jesus wobbled for a moment. Jesus felt alone and probably overwhelmed. It happened in the temple once too. He came upon people disrespecting a sacred place and in anger he threw everyone out! This shows us that we too get overwhelmed and angry but we can also quickly return to our true selves. He remembered his divinity and came back into alignment with God/Love and committed himself to the Creator. ("Father, why has thou forsaken me", and later he said, "Into thine hands I commit my soul.") You can do this too! He said this too, "Father, forgive them for they know not who they are; they know not what they do. "Say to yourself right

288

now, I forgive every person, place, and thing for anything that I thought they did wrong to me. I choose not to judge one breath of my journey or anybody else's as bad. Not one sacred breath of it.

Now you have a choice, do you want to be right or happy? Do you want to be healthy or sick? Do want to be hateful or loving? Do you want to be full of fear or love? Do you want to wake up every day free or worried about things like, where's my money going to come to pay bills? Where's my partner? How am I going to speak to my neighbor down the street who did this to my dog? All these crazy examples of what life unfolds for us so we can show up and love. Either we do it or we don't. Therefore we either have peace or we don't. We've got to do it anyway!

As you grow from the lessons and knowledge in this book, you are becoming a clearer vessel in your awareness. People around you, your community, family, and friends, are still going to see you for who you were, not for who you are now. You are waking up, you are aware of who you are and who God is. You are walking in love and you are choosing better things for your body, better things for your household, better things for your community, and better things for your world. You are a master of love, an Angel!

Speaking a Loving Language

The core of each of us is the same, unconditioned loving consciousness, the Divine. See the Divine in others. When we accept ourselves as we are, we increase our ability to change. The Eastern greeting Namaste means 'the Divine in me honors and salutes the Divine in you.'

Sending your partners or your children out of the door with a, 'be safe', or 'watch out for strangers', or 'it is unsafe out there', is another very unconscious practice. Say to yourself (Be safe and watch out.) How does your body react? Do you bend in the middle of the back? This is what perpetrators look for. A bent and hiding child or person. Now say, "Have fun, radiate light, smile." How does that feel? Notice your back. Feel the strength. Send your loved ones out empowered and ready to radiate and shine! Always send them out with love as the force to be reckoned with and not fear. Let me give you an amazing fact about how safe we really are! On September 11, 2001 in New York, there was a potential of 20.000 people per building that's, 40,000 plus 3 airlines of about 300 each, that's 900. That is approximately 40,900 people that could have crossed over on that day. Less than 4000 crossed! Everyone else did not go to work or board a plane or were guided to leave the buildings. That means over 36,000 people were kept SAFE!

The ones that passed created at least one major earth event! This is one reason I tell people I am thankful for George Bush! Read on, please. On Tuesday, September 11th after the twin towers had fallen, he got on TV and asked for our prayers. Good job, George. Then he called forth a National Day of Prayer to be held that Friday. Against much adversity from fearful people, he insisted it had to be done. The first minister was some lady in Washington that said, "We will show you, we will choose love here!" I was so thankful. Within one hour the entire world governments held space for silence and prayer! Russia stopped, China stopped, Africa stopped, Europe stopped, All Nations stopped and held space for peace. This had never happened in the history of our world.

Many times in public places I hear gossip or negative talk about others. I tell them, Beloved, I am going to stand in proxy to the person you are talking about and now I am here, you can continue! They usually choke and don't say another negative word about anybody else. I remind them that who you are talking about is actually yourself, and just maybe you want to speak in a more loving language. There is only one of us here called, God. They get it. Things can always be done in a loving way and we never have to put up with unconscious and unloving behavior around us. There is another way to speak the language of a Master of Love.

Do we want to see someone ranting and raving in the airport when we have the opportunity to help them and to help their immune system? By helping others put more gratitude in their attitude and pointing out what you are grateful for helps in every situation. If you want a better future, speak of it, picture it, and say it to others. Only you can create it for yourself, it is the greatest power that you have been given. We are all inherently worthy and precious by virtue of our existence. We have nothing to prove.Most people think they make the world better by helping other people.Truthfully the best gift we can give each other is to become more conscious ourselves. The only way you can truly be of service to others is to know the difference between your "stuff" and their "stuff". Many healers are what I call unhealed healers. We must clear our own stuff before we can assist others to clear their stuff. It doesn't matter how long it takes to become conscious. We are all unique in our journey and choices.

One of my dearest friends, Rosemary, is a caregiver. We were talking about judgment and how easy it shows up in everyday life. Someone had said to her, "What do you mean you loved that woman in a wet diaper all day?" Ah! Rosemary knows it's all about another opportunity to love more than you did before and set an example for others. Rosemary says, "It's a challenge." I say it is a challenge too.

We said we are the ones we have been waiting for, right? Consciousness is not always easy to hold, but we must do it. In order for me to maintain my health, maintain my peace, maintain my breath of life, I have to do this; what other choice do I have? In our reality as humans, we already did the fear and the judgment and the criticism and the hatred. We have killed each other and we have hated and murdered each other. We have done harm to ourselves and to each other and to our Earth, because it is all connected. Most of the time, it takes a big trauma to put us on our path to who we really are more quickly. Those things bring us to our intent. It can be the death of a loved one, a divorce, an illness, a car wreck, or a chronic health condition. Because of the trauma (pain) God is trying to get our attention, so we can remember-and God (sometimes in the form of pain) really WORKS!

Prophecy 2012

Let us understand that 2012 is the end of the Mayan, the Hopi, the Aztec calendars, and the beginning of the new millennium. Jesus said, "The lion shall lay down with the lamb and peace shall reign" and he didn't say 'maybe'. He said it shall!

The Hopi knowing says 144,000 are directly affected by our choosing love instead of judgment or sadness, or sacrifice. When we wake up, so do many! Every time you choose love, so do 144,000. You matter that much, Angel! We love you for your gifts that you bring!

In the Isiah papers found in the Dead Sea Scrolls, Isiah asks God to see the future. He sees devastation, fires and floods, disease and illness, poverty and starvation, polluted water and food. He cries! Why would we do that? Then he has another vision. "The water shall spring forth from the desert and food shall rain abundant upon the land and the blind shall be made to see and the deaf to hear and no more disease shall walk the earth again."

Wow, Angel, did you hear that? One vision is created in fear and One in love, What do you choose? No disease means no fear to create pain and separation again! Eastern Master's philosophies feel that the awakening of the world will happen in the United States of America. The Masters are watching us do this because this country was formed under God. It has been prophesied that this is the country it will come forth from and spread throughout the world. If we don't awaken our own hearts, how are we going to fulfill the prophesy that we came here to do?

If you are reading this book, you have to understand you are a part of the solution not a part of the problem. What is faith? Faith is when you have come to all the light you know and you are about to step off into the darkness of the unknown. Faith is knowing one of two things will happen. There will be something solid to stand on, or you will be taught how to fly! Faith takes us to the knowing but not everybody has reached the 'knowing' yet. As you awaken, you will realize the message of love has always been here. Many scriptures, even old rock and roll songs, ancient poetry, and messages left carved in stone speak of the return to love. If you listen to the message with love, it is about having no judgment of one person, place, or situation as less than a God doing a journey of whom it isn't, to whom it is. The knowing that you are as a seed of God, and not the seed of a tomato, is always held for you by more than you can count. Even I know who You are!!

How will you know if you are aware? You know you are becoming more conscious when what occupies your attention is love, joy, peace, and light. You look around and see beauty everywhere, even in death, even in pain, even in destruction, even in fear. Inwardly you securely feel that all is well and you are peaceful in this moment. Even when someone comes in with stage 4 cancer, your focus is loving them. You do not concern yourself with what ifs. You are not here to fix it! When you are focused on love and being present, nothing else can exist.

Heaven on Earth

Angel's Toolbox

Visualize this earth with clean air, blue skies, rainbows, clean, clear, refreshing water everywhere. See the earth as abundant, clean, and vivacious. See all the people as Angels: healthy, youthful, vibrant, wise, peaceful, abundant, free, expressing their essence of beauty, love, and laughter. Imagine your creative power assisting all of us in the manifestation of this

292

Heaven on Earth.THANK YOU ANGELS FOR FULFILLING YOUR PURPOSE!!!

Everyday work and everyday living

It is indeed possible to live in joy and love at all times. Practice Being Godlike and less Human-like until you are living at least 90% in Love. Allow yourself 10% Humanness so you remember to be gentle and kind to yourself. You can be "in charge" of your emotions, and never a victim. The lower conscious levels of hate, envy, jealousy, and greed, can become love and joy when you realize that you are the one in charge of your emotions, not the other way around.

After all, we are all one. Every time you send unconditional love to someone else, you are positively affecting yourself and the whole universe. Isn't that awesome! Remember thoughts that encourage growth and expand one's heart. Life seeks energy, awareness, and love; remember that any given situation teaches you more about who you are. By holding wholeness and unconditional love and support for those around you, you are teaching them experientially about who they truly are.

Every morning practice balancing and centering yourself before you go to work and interact with others.

The more you do this, the faster you will get at it. I also recommend that my Angels place their hand on their belly and breathe into their hand lifting it with their breath. Do these 15 breaths in the morning and 15 breaths at night. The breath relaxes the diaphragm and therefore relaxes the nervous system which brings you physically into a state of peace. This is one of the best gifts you can give yourself. To succeed and come from the highest joy, you need to come from a centered, calm place. See yourself joyful and present, able to assist and lift all those around you.

See yourself sending out love and light to everyone you see with your eyes during the day. Radiate!!! Anything you want to happen that day from happy co-workers to a call from a loved one; visualize and feel that happening. Anyone you have been challenged by, send unconditional love now from your centered place and tell them telepathically that you desire peace, love and the highest good for everyone. Forgive everyone and send love instead. Forgiveness clears you and creates a pathway for healing and transformation. You cannot save anyone. We all must save ourselves. Remember your job is to be a clear vessel, so keep on embracing love, forgiving yourself, and centering yourself.

If you love yourself for who you are, you are living in the present time which is a gateway to personal power. If you love only who you will be or what you will have at some date in the future, then you are out of your body, living in a future that you cannot affect, until it becomes present time. Watch out for this because of your amazing immune system. Worry will kick your butt!

Be gentle with yourself. Focus on your positive aspects and gifts. Do you believe you must offer love, support, and care to everyone? Loving someone does not mean making their feelings more important than your own. If you study the lives of highly evolved beings, you will see that there are many ways to be loving to others, including speaking bluntly with compassion and love. Being committed to your higher purpose and loving yourself is the highest priority. You can never do anything that is not in some way an attempt to bring more light into your life. In your day to day contacts, know that you do not owe anyone your time or energy. Your time and energy are gifts you choose to give.

Here is a simple meditation I did for years that changed my life.

Everywhere you go, see yourself as God because it is not easy to transcend umanness, I tell my Angels Fake it til you make it. I paraphrase Mother Teresa with you learn to not give a shit (Literally) to what others think about you. It is not between you and them. It is always between you and God. And that is all good! If you can find a dark room, close the door and have a lit candle and mirror. Look into your own eyes in the mirror without blinking for as long as you can. When your mind has a thought, just thank it and return to the focus of your eyes. Look until you see God there and God will look right back at you. You will find that all you have to do is realize who you are. Also realize God in your mother's journey, your father's, sister's, neighbor's, all plant's and animal's journeys and the President's journey! We cannot judge one breath of

God's journey as bad.

Teach yourself and your kids to see the goodness in all people. Live this lesson in your life. When we are surrounded in goodness, we won't react in fear to what comes our way.

Making Better Choices

When we are mindfully conscious of what is taking place in our lives and are willing to shift from the role of victim to master, our mindfulness will motivate us to make wiser choices daily. I want you to understand that you must start making different choices. You can choose to drink good water instead of a soda. You can choose an organic food instead of a chemically grown one. You can go for a walk instead of going to watch a movie. You can plant some flowers instead of cut down a tree. If you read a book, listen to music, go to a meeting, or go to church and it doesn't make you feel good inside, uplifted and more full of love; turn it off, put it down, and walk away and make a different choice! If you don't, who is going to?

It can offer so much freedom in your life when you realize that you chose your family to teach you who you are not. There are so many great teachings on how to be or not to be in life that your family taught you. They taught you how to raise your kids, how to get along with friends, how to relate to your partner, how to conduct business, even how to drive! Are you doing it differently from your parents? I am!! Thank your family for showing you who you are and who you are not! When we awaken and become more forgiving and more understanding, then we draw our other family, our spiritual family. We may still walk with our blood family but not on the level that we walk with our spiritual family. I can tell a lot about a person's consciousness by the Ones they walk with.

Surgeries And Healing And What If You Don't Shift

Surgeries and healing: There is an emotional cause for every dis-ease. Sometimes our bodies are unsuccessful in communicating their message to us, and we go to medical doctors and have surgeries. That is part of our journey, no judgment. Cancer is the best example. If you don't address what you are hating and what is eating you up, or what gave you the tumor in the first place, cutting it out won't solve the problem in the long run. The message will reappear, most likely as cancer, in another part of your body. If you are curious about a condition you have had in the past, try looking in Louise Hays book, Heal Your Body, Heal Your Mind or Karol Truman's book, Feelings Buried Alive Never Die. They list several probable causes for many dis-eases. Read down the list and see which one applies to you. Remember that Angel Farms was created to help people work through their issues so they don't have to hurt anymore.

If you don't question a choice that a physician might make that doesn't ring true within yourself, and you are asking the physician to "fix" you by giving you a pill to make you better and you are not willing to look at why you are sick in the first place, how are you ever going to change your world? If you are always essentially saying through your actions, "You do it for me, I am too lazy, you do it for me, I don't want to be diligent in the work of my consciousness; you do it for me." You will remain a power-less victim. NOT! You just think you are but I guarantee you this is not true about you! Own your journey so you can change it!

It is your birthright to be healthy, happy, and free of pain and sorrow and struggle, manipulation and control. It is your birthright to live a life of peace and comfort, happiness and without struggle. Struggle is optional. It is not about surviving, or giving up the comforts of life. It's about finding balance in your experience and not taking anything in excess. Simplify!

How To Help Your Family In Consciousness

Make the information easily accessible, like putting a book in the bathroom, but not forcing it upon them. Introduce the healthy foods they are not ready to eat yet, but maybe in a little while. You step up and you start teaching it anyway to whomever is in front of you. I had a teacher who told me that the more conscious you are, the more responsible you are for every con-versation Spirit puts you in, which is all day long. Even if the person isn't ready, you are still responsible for the conversation. You leave them feeling better than they did when they first came to you or met with you. This works in the physical too! As you leave a room, ask yourself if you left it better because you were there.

It is not about forcing it down peoples' throats. It's about putting it in front of them and living it anyway. I remember times when Larry used to say, "Cindy you are so far out there. You just don't know what the heck you are talking about when you are talking about this God stuff all the time." He wasn't the only one who said this. When a person is unconscious, they are trying to stay grounded into the world they believe to be real. We are really waking up to be spiritual beings on the planet; divine beings in physical incarnations. It's not about forcing people who aren't ready. They aren't done with the journey of who they are not, that part of their and God's journey.

When our children go into a serious situation with drugs or alcohol or other wreck less behaviors, situations where they are in a journey of finding out who they are not, we can step back and hold the space and say we know who they really are. We know that divine child we held in our arms. 'You are the gift to this world; you are the hope for humanity, thank you for choosing me to be your mom or your dad. Thank you for making a difference in this world. Thank you for being my master teacher. I don't have to be responsible for your journey, that's between you and God. I am here to love you, to be thankful for you, to know you are part of the unfoldment of the awakening of the planet, and you might not know this about yourself, but I know it about you.' Knowing is like the rock of Gibraltar, no matter how hard the wind blows, you can't blow it over. It is solid.

Present time awareness and how to get others to it

In order to bring someone to present time, conscious in the moment with you, invite them to open up to all their senses. Open them to smell, touch, taste, sight and sound. Get them out of their head enough to be in present time. Wow, do you smell this flower? Aren't you thankful for this smell? A hug and a squeeze also activates the skin and its senses to present time. Hugs help! People are generally in a state of unconsciousness, until something happens to make them finally wake up, stand up, and be in the now.

Sleep

The one reason people can't sleep is because the brain is too busy thinking, thinking, thinking, instead of relaxing and being. They are not in present time and therefore unable to process what is up in the moment. It must then be taken to dream time to process. You can't sleep when your brain is moving. Before you go to bed, read a page or a sentence of a good spiritual uplifting book, something by Deepak Chopra, or Tolle, or Abraham-Hicks, Gregg Braden, Marianne Williamson, Wayne Dyer, Rumi, Tagore, Hafiz, or any love teacher, or this book. Take some spiritual food into your dreams and you are going to sleep better and wake up at peace. Eckhart Tolle says when you lose touch of inner stillness, you lose touch with yourself. When you lose touch with yourself, you lose yourself in the world.

Toolbox for dowsing to be God-like.

All of us can project our energy 6 feet all around us and know what is in front of us. Blind people do it this way so they don't run into things. Dowsing is expanding your energy with consciousness. When Shara and Anthony were young, Larry and I taught them how to dowse. They would be able to dowse deer 3 miles in front of us and they became very accurate. It just takes practice like anything. Everyone can do it.

I call whales in close to the shore so I can look them in the eye. I send messages like: I love you and I would love to have you come close to me and dance! I imagine their big eyes like a black paper plates looking at me. I see myself looking them right in the eye. I allow them to feel my energy and see my light on the beach. I ask them to come as close as they possibly can so we can have our breath together and so I can laugh and watch them play. Always, they just come, sometimes within 500 yards off the rock wall where it is really deep. They just come and hang out, they blow, and jump! We laugh and clap. It's all about projecting your energy to incorporate what it is you want to have that experience of. Call it in! It's so much fun!

Over the years I have met many Angels who see colors in the auric field of others. This can be a great tool for healing. It is important to understand truth about this also. We are all from the same Source. Every time you look at a rainbow you are seeing what we really look like and even in the same color order. Our fields are actually opalescent in color and we all carry the full spectrum of light. Remember we are light Beings! Dowsing works here too. We have an etheric field that comes about 3 inches off our bodies that helps hold our matter together. It is usually blue in color and can be felt directly off the body by gently running your hand about 3 inches off any one's body. If a cold or hot spot is detected in that field, then something is going on in that particular area of the body which can sometimes be helpful to locate before an illness takes hold. It is very important to understand that there is always an emotional or Spiritual disconnection going on and can be quickly adjusted with awareness to the issue.

12 Ways To Remember You Are An Angel

1. Go into the Sun every day for 5-10 minutes for your eye exercises (without glasses or contacts locate the sun and close your eyes) With eyelids closed-move your eyes left to right, up and down, circles, etc. This will not only strengthen your eyes and eyesight, but will also activate the liver to release vitamin C and A!

2. Drink one gallon of water every day to keep your body and mind fully hydrated

3. Remember to chew your food (Drink your food, chew your liquids)

4. On a scale of 1-10, love yourself a "10", because you're worth it!

5. Pretend that you are like God until you know it's true!

6. Laugh at yourself because you are funny.

7. Love your body-it is your first act of creation on this planet. Honor your creation!

8. Keep yourself out of the illusion of fear: Fantasized Emotion Appearing Real

9. Use your senses of hearing, sight, smell, taste, and touch to pull yourself back into the now.

10. Remember the mantra; where I am, God is, where God is, I am

11. Don't judge one breath of your journey as bad. Don't judge anyone else's either.

12. Allow yourself 10 percent grace in all things; it keeps you out of judgment.

The key to the mastery of this life is that what is going on in your head is going on in your heart, and it is coming out of your mouth. There is no interruption in the flow. You are speaking the language of your heart. You have mastered this life.

TO DISSOLVE FEAR,

TURN AND LOOK DIRECTLY AT IT.

FOR WHAT YOU FACE,

DISSOLVES IN THE LIGHT OF CONSCIOUSNESS.

If is feels hard, remember the Huna teachings
EWOP (Everything's Working Out Perfectly).
Some days are just EWOP days. Quiet your mind.

WHEN YOU ARE DOING THE DISHES,
THAT'S YOUR MEDITATION.

WHEN YOU ARE GOING TO THE BATHROOM,
THAT'S YOUR MEDITATION.

WHATEVER YOU ARE DOING,
BE PRESENT IN THAT MOMENT
WITH THAT TASK
AND IT BECOMES YOUR MEDITATION.

Life is the meditation.
Live like an Angel of Love,
A Master of life, and a seed of God.
It only takes a few. Are you one of us?
Remember you are a "10" forever.
And I know who You are!!!

Cindy's Life Story

When I was almost 1 year old and my sister Vickie was almost 2 years old, my real dad, at 19 years old, left my mother and took us. He had 2 suitcases and 2 little girls and went to California or Arizona and got together with this woman who was to take care of us while he reestablished his life. He actually got a puppy for us. She killed the puppy in front of us and told us that if we didn't listen and obey her, the same thing would happen to us. Every time he left, she put the toys up and we had to sit back to back in chairs and we couldn't talk or move all day long, until Daddy came home. Then the toys came out and everything looked normal to him. This went on for years. One day, when I was about 7, he came home and the toys where still in the closet. When my father found out what this woman had been doing to us, he immediately took us to Ogden, Utah.

We never saw this woman again. I never had to heal anything with that woman. I had no feelings about her. I somehow understood our contract. She was a part of me and my sister and she helped to develop the master healers which we are today. We are the only ones in our family that have touched so many lives in the ways that we have, worldwide. Would we be that way if we hadn't done that journey? Absolutely not.

He set us up with his mother, my paternal grandmother, whom I hadn't met yet. He left us there saying, "Don't let anyone know the girls are here and I will reestablish another job and home and be back for them."

Then I had a situation happen at my grandmother's house that changed my life. My grandma had 13 children and was very grandmotherly and she was real happy to have us. The first night that we were there she gave us cheese with dinner. I just couldn't do cheese, yuk! I couldn't tell her that I didn't like cheese so I put it under the table. I didn't know what to do with the cheese and I was so afraid after coming out of an abusive situation and I was unsure how to behave. Would this cause me pain and harm? Then, we went up to bed and I started shaking! I thought she would come up and kill me for putting cheese under the table. I shook and shook and shook! I couldn't sleep because I was very afraid and I got up and sat at the top of the stairs. I knew she was going to come up and kill me so I might as well be ready. Grandma walked past the bottom of the stairs and saw me sitting there and then she came up. Now I am really shaking. Oh my gosh, she is going to come and get me!

This is called projection, but all I had known was scariness and abuse and if I got out of line, I was going to get hurt. So she came up the stairs, this big woman, with big bosoms, she scooped me up, sat at the top of the stairs and just rocked me for what seemed like forever. It was the longest time I had been held in my life thus far. She just rocked me and held me and then she said, "Honey, you can do anything you want here and nobody will hurt you. You can do anything here and I will always love you. You can't do it wrong here. It's okay." Grandma just held me and hummed and said it was okay. And I remember it being the first time in my life that I had felt safe. Wow! I was a whole different kid after that. She always gave big hugs and was always thankful to have me there.

We started going to school in Ogden, Utah and when school pictures were taken, one of the kids in my sister's class took the picture and showed my maternal grandmother, in Eden, Utah. He was her grandnephew! She asked him, who is that little girl? He said her name is Vickie. She called up my mother immediately who lived in Spokane, Washington at the time and said, "I found the girls and they are right here in Ogden!" My mother had detectives looking for us for years.

My grandmother Fern went to my grandmother Myrtle and said, "I have not seen the girls for years. Please let me see my grandchildren." My grandmother Myrtle could understand because she too had missed us dearly. She said, "Of course, but you can't tell anyone where they are." My grandmother would pick us up for short periods of time. She bought us shoes and I remember having a big lollipop, the first one of my life; we just loved having grandma come and take us. Then when she got the visit up to an hour, she took us to the airport and flew us to Spokane. Grandma's have to do what they feel is right. I am not in judgment of any of it. It's just the story. Then in the airport in Spokane my sister and I met my mother whom I didn't remember at all. We were 9 and 10 years old then. Vickie had a vague memory of her but not much.

My real dad found out where we were and came to get us. Our parents were having a tug of war with us in the doorway. I will never forget it because it was so weird. They were arguing, "I am taking my girls!" "No you are not, I just got them back!" I was holding my dad's hand because I loved my daddy. Vickie had attached to my mother and she was okay to stay with her. Vickie and I were holding hands and were not to be parted. My sister and I were very close and still are to this day. We had survived that situation together and I am very grateful. We had each other's back so to speak.

They finally got it together and they came to the resolution that my dad would help us through school and college and that we were going to stay with my mom. My mom had remarried by then to my step dad, Paul, who became my dad. He was a beautiful, beautiful man. He didn't always get along well with my mother but it wasn't easy to get along with my mother. He never treated us differently. We became his and remained his until he passed. He saved me, by stepping up and making me feel special, I am very thankful for him.

We stayed in Spokane for awhile. Some twin girls that always got me into trouble lived across the street and then Paul would spank me with a belt. One day I said, "Dad, if you don't believe me that I did not do what they said, then who will? Why would I continue to choose this same thing when I know what's going to happen and it's going to hurt? I wouldn't do that. I did not do this nor have I ever. Why are you believing someone over me?" And he looked at me and said, "Wow, I believe you! "And he never ever raised his hand to me again. That was really beautiful. I never lied to him.

We moved to a small town in Idaho when I was about 11. Living in that very small town with a population of 81, I was introduced to the Mormon religion. I am a graduated Mormon now, I call myself spiritual but not religious.

My girlfriend and I went out riding horses daily. One day we got bored and decided to blindfold our horses and ride all day. I was so amazed that my horse Sunshine, was so tuned in to a deeper level in me. I was aware of how she listened with her body and totally trusted me. She taught me so much. I consider my horse ,Sunshine, one of my master teachers. I didn't realize when I was young that not everybody talked to animals like I did or understood them. I thought that was really weird. I found out not everybody can, but everybody has that ability, some are just not awakened to it. I probably accessed that in my quiet time. I could hear her completely clear. I don't know if it was God that I was having these awesome conversations with or my horse (Sunshine). Does it matter?

My parents didn't go to church but they sent us on the weekend, on Sunday. Both had been raised Mormon. One day I went to church and heard that only Mormons were going to Heaven. I was devastated by this because my best friend was Catholic. I was at my grandma's house at that time. I was in tears, "This is so sad Grandma. Chris will never make it to heaven." She said, "Honey, not everything you hear in Church is true." I said, "It isn't?" She said, "Of course it isn't and you will know in your heart when it is." I was very happy! My grandmother, whom I loved beyond all things at that time, gave me permission to question everything, and boy did I.

A couple of weeks later, I found out that God loves us bigger than words can speak it and I could feel that was true in my heart. I went home and got on my horse. I said, "WOW Sunshine, God loves you bigger than words can speak it." It hit me in my heart, and I felt an opening in my heart.

"Wow! I love you more than words can speak. Sunshine, that big beautiful willow tree that we can hide in and nobody knows we are there because it goes all the way to the ground." I felt another big expansion in my heart. I love that willow tree bigger than words can speak it. As we were cruising along, a meadow lark didn't even stop singing as we walked by. God loves that meadow lark bigger than words can speak it in any language. Wow! It hit me! All of a sudden, that was the day I knew that someday I would be a lover like God; I would love it all like God. It was an epiphany for me! I felt in my heart that I could truly love like God. And it never went back down again.

When I was about 12 years old, I started questioning a lot of things. At church one day, I found out we had this thing called Freedom of Choice. Wow! I was riding Sunshine and we got to a crossroads and I said, "Sunshine, do you know what freedom of choice means?" I could go left, I could go straight ahead, I could go right or I could go back the way we came. In every direction I have the ability to love something. God loves me no matter what direction I go. Look how free we are with freedom of choice; it was an epiphany! Nothing is going to stop me now, it doesn't matter what anybody says or what anybody thinks, I can love and it doesn't matter which direction, I can't do it wrong.

Then we found out about the 10 commandments. I was told if we don't follow these commandments we will never get back to God. I talked it over with Sunshine. No, that didn't feel right in our hearts because how can that be freedom of choice. NO matter what, God would not stop loving us even if we did a whoops. It doesn't matter, it wouldn't mean we wouldn't be loved or have the opportunity to love in whatever direction we go. That didn't make sense because that is not freedom of choice.

Freedom of choice felt right in my heart but the commandments felt a little weird. In most religions you are taught to go to your Bishop, Pastor or Minister and ask these questions when they come up if you don't get them answered in church. Of course I went to see the Bishop. I was probably the only kid who did stuff like this to him.

I said, "Hey Bishop, somebody made up the commandments to scare us because how does freedom of choice work this way? What does it mean that if you do adultery or stealing or do this coveting and then God will cast you out? If you don't follow this, there is no freedom of choice in that, so the commandments are not right." He said, "Cindy, you have to have faith that what we tell you is true." And I said, "No I don't. My grandma said if it's not true in my heart, then it's not true. This isn't true, and I know it." He said, "What are we going to do with you?" And I said, "Well, you might as well love me like God does."

I have found that all Christians believe this story and probably some people who are not Christian, it doesn't really matter. Here's another story we have all heard or been taught. Jesus said I will go and show them the way and the Glory be Thine. Satan or Lucifer said, I will go and show them the way and the glory be mine. And God/ Love had a war and lost the war, and 1/3 of God's own creation, that it loves bigger than words can speak, was cast out of heaven. The Devil and 1/3 the host of heaven. I, being 12 years old, couldn't imagine that God would care more about glory than about love. Love is much bigger than glory. So making another appointment, I went to the Bishop, and said, "Hey, Bishop somebody made up the Devil to scare us. How does love work this way? How does God who is love all of a sudden just not love 1/3 of its own creation and cast it out from its love?"

"How is it possible that the Creator of all that Is, which is love, just stop loving 1/3 of its own creation just because of Glory. I believe love is much bigger than glory. So you know what Bishop, I think somebody made up the Devil to scare us." And he said, "Cindy, if you choose not to believe in the devil, he is going to sneak up and get you." And I said, "I hope he does, because I have some questions for him." And he literally took hold of his chair and shook and he said, "I am going to call your parents." How many of you have felt weird about these things too? I have found many of us questioned and were told to believe anyway.

Clearing entities comes from this age old story of the devil. All of you Angels who are reading this book and still believe in the Devil ask yourself this question, "Does it come from fear or from love?" Then choose again. I hope and pray that you let go of that fear because no one's out to get you except yourself and God. Nothing is here to say that you did it wrong or tempted you into something that you weren't here to experience, so there are no accidents and no victims and no Devil. Let it go. If the world lets that one go, how much more love (and less fear) will we have?

Many people on the planet believe there are entities or lost beings that can stick to us after we die; that they might not cross over but rather get stuck in between. Some people call these entities or ghosts. Some people go around clearing others of all this stuff. There is even radon emissions that will clear all of these things out of your house at a certain time, or whatever. The key to realize is that this simply isn't possible. I had a lady named Doris who came to me when I was in Utah. Doris was sobbing and rushed over to see me because one of my teachers had made her fingers into a cross shape and held them out in front of this lady, telling her she couldn't work with her because she had entities around her. I couldn't believe my teacher did that.

I was under the illusion at that time that there really was evil in the world. I picked it up from some of my teachers who told me this is how you clear people so it doesn't get stuck to you. I had this paper with a symbol and words for Doris to repeat after me. I said to Doris, "We will just clear you and then we will do a session to see what is going on." As I go through this process to clear her and as she is repeating something for me, I hear God say, 'Cindy, look at this beautiful angel in front of you.' I looked and agreed. Then God says, 'Exactly what kind of glue would I use to stick an entity to a seed of God?'

I stopped dead in my tracks, 'What?' And meanwhile Doris was waiting for me to say the next thing she is supposed to repeat, and I am not saying anything because I was having a different conversation. And then I heard this laughter, like rolling thunder that said,' Elmer's maybe?' I said, "Thank you Doris." I took the paper and I ripped it up and I never did that again. I realized how silly it was. How do you stick an entity to a seed of God? No glue would work. It's all God. It's all love. It's all the creative force of the universe having the experience of who it isn't and who it is and in between, waking up. It's not evil; it's not wicked. People only act according to who they think they are and most of them don't know who they are, so forgive them.

I went to my mom when I was 13 and asked her if I was

adopted. I couldn't understand why they were so crazy! There was so much screaming and violence. It was a hard time. I was pretty sure there was a mix up at the hospital. She yelled at me, and reminded me that she carried me for 9 months!

Now I laugh because at Angel Farms so many of us feel like we came into the wrong family. We wonder what happened here and how did I end up in this space? I must be from a different planet; these guys are from some place else. We are not alone when we feel like we were adopted or somebody misplaced us. It just means you already came in more aware than your earthly family, that is part the journey of it.

During hard moments, I always felt this energy up close to me, right up next to my body. They were so close to me, I would get under my covers at night to change. Like they couldn't see through the covers! Ha, Ha. I wasn't afraid of this energy, I knew they were my family. Have you ever felt your multitude that walks with you? I knew they were holding me very close so it would be okay. I felt like a princess. They were watching over me! They were right in my field.

At 14 years of age, I was in the Temple in Boise, Idaho. When I was in the dressing room, getting ready to leave on the bus, I had this presence come over me. It began on the top of my head and traveled all the way through my body, and it was so, so blissful. It was a magical thing as I felt the presence of God literally wrap itself around me and it just held me, and held me, and held me. They came to knock on the door, "Cindy the bus is loading." I didn't want to speak or move, I didn't want the presence to go away. I went timeless, I don't know how long. Knock knock knock-everybody has to load up on the bus. I never said a word. One of the teachers came to the door and said, "Cindy, are you okay?" At that moment I felt it begin to lift from me. I am very sure as we made the long journey home, I never said one word.

At age 16, I was in Washington with my uncle where he and 2 other partners had started a blind ski school at Snoqualmie Pass. I went up there and I was going to be an instructor with the school. I had never skied before and I had 2 weeks to learn! In order to be an instructor, I had to do this test. They took me up the mountain to the top and I had to ski down. I saw where I was going and so I had a big issue with the ski down!! When a person is blind, they don't see all that! At the top of the mountain, a lady put a blindfold on me. I think to myself, I can't do this, I am not very good at it, I just learned how to ski, I have never been up this high! All this stuff went through my brain and my legs were like noodles. Then

I remembered that moment when I put that blindfold on Sunshine and she immediately went into trust. I felt if she could do it, I could do it! I felt her give me so much support! So I settled into the process, and I trusted like she did. I skied down the mountain, looked back and said, wow, look what I did! It was very empowering. It was one of the most profound things in my life to work with blind kids on that level. They taught me much more than I taught them.

One of things they taught me was how to speak a different language on levels that are unseen. They taught me how to appreciate the sense of sight, to be able to say what snow really looks like, other than it's white, but the depth of it, and the colors in it, and the sparkles in it, and the gift of it. I wouldn't have been able to do that if I hadn't learned how to really trust from Sunshine.

I am not a victim, I am a goddess. So many people believe that if we let go of our stories, what will we be? I call it FREE! If you don't have a story to tell about what happened to you in your past, who would you be? Exactly! You would return to your childlike innocence and perfect divine wholeness. Most people stare blankly at me and giggle when I ask that question! I tell them they could still talk about the birds and the flowers and the bees and smells and the tastes and the yummy-ness of life and they would no longer be attached to a story that they think defines them. You would be in present time (without past) and feel that you are indefinable. If you hadn't had that journey would you be who you are? I would say no. Youand I are the way we are because of our journeys, not despite them.

When you own your own journey and stop the blame that someone did or did not do something, then you can change it. You will realize you are no longer a victim and that you are powerful beyond measure. You will understand, I am the creator of my journey and God did it with me, why would I create that journey? Why would I do that to myself? Why would I choose sexual abuse, why would I choose to be beaten, why would I choose to sit in a chair year,after year, after year? You know what I got from it was profound!

In those long hours a day I learned quietness. I learned how to travel. I remember traveling. I have visited places as an adult and I have already been there, but not in this body. I went all over. When you are quiet enough, you can leave. This gift to shut up and do my work in this world, was profound. People are afraid to be alone because they are afraid of the silence. The biggest

310

issue is that people never shut up. I have helped over 4000 people worldwide get well. (Nearly 1/2 to 2/3 of the people who did the Cleanse wouldn't be alive today). Every breath of my journey was worth the effort to be able to touch so many lives with miracles.

When I was 18 years old, I met this sweet and handsome guy, Larry, at a Tuesday night auction in Jerome, Idaho that my mother made me go to. He asked me out Friday, and then again on Saturday, and then we talked about getting married! We just knew! Five months later on a break from college we eloped to Las Vegas together with Larry's sister Carolyn and her partner Mike. We then called Larry's parents at 2:00 am and let them know. We have been so blessed to find each other and create our lives together. I do recommend the union of marriage because it makes glue. It is not so easy to walk away when you are upset or angry. It is worth it to love and be thankful for your partner. Having a partner is the most wanted experience I have found from people at Angel Farms. People really ache for a partner to share their life with. As I write this Larry and I have just celebrated our 30th year of loving each other. I like to say that Larry has made this my best lifetime ever.

My love for him and my friendship with him has been the key; we always laugh together. We have the same common interests and that really helps. We have had the same jobs most of the time. When we didn't share the same work, it was hard, and those jobs didn't last very long. It's been really interesting to look back over our lives, our 30 years together, to see that we have chosen to be together 24/7. We have our time apart here and there but mostly we are together. We do better together than we do apart.

After we were married and both going to college at CSI in Idaho. (community college-College of Southern Idaho) we took classes together and we competed for the best grades. It was so fun. Did you get your homework done? In our sociology class, we decided to find out about marriage, what worked and what didn't. We decided to do our thesis on this. We went around and interviewed 50 people that had been married 25 years or more. We made up this whole questionnaire. We even interviewed Larry's parents who had just celebrated their 25th anniversary. Prior to this time I had never seen a marriage that worked. In all my life I had never seen a happy couple who had been married more than 25 years other than Larry's parents. When I first met them, I thought, is this for real? Now I hear people say that about Larry and me; are you guys for real?

We did the survey. We correlated all the information. We studied how relationships work and why. What we discovered was that the number one ingredient for a truly great relationship is friendship. If you are not friends with each other, you cannot have a healthy relationship. The second thing we learned from the 50 people we interviewed was that when you are angry or upset, you have to be very careful not to call each other names or say things to your partner that you wouldn't say to your best friend. Sometimes best friends have quarrels but they don't call each other names that they can't get over. Name calling is really destructive in a relationship. Even though some people had differences in religion, they still had a happy marriage, because they could allow each other to find their own way to God without being caught in religion.

We learned to speak a good language to each other, to be best friends and to have a weekly date night, even while our children were young. A couple has to keep a priority on the relationship because the children are temporary. The number one major disruption in the relationship happened when the children left home. Many marriages ended after 20 years because they had nothing left in common. Some couples spent so much time with children that they forgot each other. That was a really big thing for Larry and I. We did not let that happen.

Another thing that really helped us during those times when we just couldn't agree with each other because we are different people and we have different thoughts on things. Larry and I would say to each other, "You know what? I can't agree with that but I am going to agree to disagree. Okay, I agree, we can disagree on this one." No problem and then there is no argument. That's a really good tool. You can agree to disagree and still love each other.

When I found, in the past, I had concepts I wanted him to know and he wasn't open to them yet, I put the book in the bathroom about Abraham Hicks, or Deepak Chopra or Gregg Braden. Men love Gregg Braden and Deepak Chopra too because they work with a lot of intellectual stuff even though it's spiritual. What I found was that Larry would read something I had left in the bathroom and say, "Guess what, Cindy?" And I would say, "That is so cool Larry, thank you for sharing that with me!"

In 1983 Larry and I were driving down the road in Jerome Idaho, going about 50 miles per hour. Shara was 14 months old and I was 3 months pregnant with Anthony, I heard very loudly, 'Get her out of the car seat now!' I looked over at Larry and said, "What

312

did you say?" He said, "I didn't say anything." I thought, that's weird. I turned around, and she was getting a little fussy, I was a new mom and an avid believer in car seats, but I listened. I thought that was too loud to ignore. If Larry didn't say it, then who said it?

So I took Shara out of her car seat, put her in my lap, looked up and said, "Oh my God, Larry, he is not going to stop!" There was a 16 year old girl who ran a stop sign; she never looked. Larry, with some amazing help from the unknown, went between a cement barrier on a bridge and a stop sign right next to it. We flew across the bridge and went into the water. I hit my side and the water came in the back of the car. I found out many years later that Shara actually saved Anthony's life because I was holding her and she lessened the blow to my abdomen. I had 9 miscarriages after Anthony. He hung in there after the car wreck, which is a powerful reason why he is supposed to be here. I wasn't doing anything excessive the other times I was pregnant and miscarried. The backseat was totally in the water. I would not have had time to unbuckle her and get Shara out. If I hadn't listened and cooperated with the guidance, she wouldn't have made it. The other side was smashed up against the wall on the other side of the canal. She definitely would have drowned, I might have drowned too. That was one time I heard it so clear. I had no idea it was going to happen. Sometimes it comes really, really clear.

In the car wreck my back bent in the middle. My pain began. From 1983 to 1989 I lived in what I call Hell. The only thing the AMA had for me was to break my back and put two titanium pins in it and it would keep me out of pain. I could not let them break my back and again I am glad I listened. In 1989 I was lying on my living room floor with a neck brace on and I could no longer care for myself or my family. I was angry, mostly at God! I was ready to go into the desert and give it up to not hurt anymore. Have you ever felt like that? I saw a ladies' face come to my mind and as a last resort I called her up. She brought her massage table and everywhere she touched me was like a rock. She asked, "Why are you holding onto all this pain?" I was mad anyway and said, "That's the most ridiculous thing I have ever heard! Why would anyone hold on to this kind of pain on purpose?" She said, "Maybe you don't have to." I said, "What are you talking about?" She told me about a ten day Cleanse. I thought I was all cleaned out already. She asked, "Are you still in pain?" I said, "Duh!" She said, "Maybe you don't have to." I started with her the next day. Guess what, 10 days later my back was straight and I was out of pain! I was my first miracle! I studied with this amazing healer and became her last student.

My first client that I had, was Bo. We were working on some advertising work. We were driving around, and I had been studying iridology with one of my teachers. I noticed these spots in Bo's eyes. I told her about my Cleanse and that I was still in training but that I could help her. She Cleansed for 4 days with me. She had to go up to Salt Lake City to a emergency meeting and she got sick and ended up in the emergency room. They did an emergency colonoscopy on her. Usually they prep the person and do the procedure the next day. The doctors told her she was full of cancer. She went in the next morning to discuss options. The doctors told her that they were going to start her on chemotherapy and radiation. They gave her 6 months to a year to live. She was a single mom, 38 with 4 children. She looked at them, and said, "No, I have found another way." She got back in her car and drove all the way back to my house.

As she told me her prognosis, I was thinking, oh my God, I don't know anything. She's ready to start Day 5 of her Cleanse. What am I going to do? I can't help her. I am brand new at this. This is my first one. God, why are you sending my first client to me with colon cancer and a 6 month life prognosis? What's up with that?

I heard very clearly, 'Cindy, you know there are no accidents.' And I knew that was true, from my own journey. I responded,' yeah, I know.' I knew this meant this is all divinely perfect and I am not doing this alone, I had all the help I needed. "Bo, I will take you on. You have to know I am new at this and I am learning. I can only do this with you; I can't do this for you." She said, "Of course, it's my journey. I have been guided that you are the one who is going to help me through this." My first real lesson as a Colon Hydro therapist and Healer! We are all responsible for our own healing and no one can "heal" us but ourselves! When we are ready the teacher/student will come. I said, "Awesome. I have been guided that you are the one who is going to teach me a lot." I worked with her daily for 6 months. It's the longest time I have worked with someone. It doesn't take me that long now, but I was learning. I figured she was my PhD.

Four days prior to making the decision to Cleanse Bo, I was in Harmon's Grocery Store in St. George, Utah. I was doing my grocery shopping, just in my own little bubble. All of a sudden there was a woman standing in front of me with a long white dress with some kind of weird tie that crossed over like a big rope. She had long beautiful hair. She handed me a book. She said, 'Cindy you are ready for this.' In my infinite wisdom at the time I said, "Huh?" She told me a lot of information. She told me that I was on the right path and that my intent was right. She said that I was doing exactly what I said I was going to be doing and that I had many with me and to trust the journey. She told me there was information in the book that I would need. She said she would see me again. I found out many years later in a mission in Oceanside that she was Elizabeth, John the Baptist's mother. Her picture was up on the wall in the mission. She walks with me even now. I looked down at the book and when I looked up, she was gone! Why would this woman dressed in long flowing robes be in the grocery store? That was my judgment. I was puzzling on this. And then she just disappeared. I went to the front of the store and walked back and forth between the two entry/exits knowing she couldn't get out of the store without me seeing her. I walked back and forth, back and forth. People didn't appear and disappear in my world at that time. It was really trippy. I was new at all this.

I started studying the book. It taught me a lot about Chakras and color meditations. The book was called THE WOMEN'S BOOK OF HEALING by Diane Stein. I learned about crystals and therapy. Every time Bo called with a symptom I would look it up in my book. Then Bo would do it, and she would get better. I was learning all these tools and techniques as she was guiding me through her own journey.

About 6 months later, we had Bo better but not all the way healed. She was completely clean but she still got very, very tired. Then she would rest for a few days but then feel symptoms again. Prior to this she had been hit by lightening which blew her cowboy boot open and caused a lot of burning in her spleen. Physically this might have been one of the reasons why she had cancer, but I believe you can't get cancer unless you hate, judge or have revenge for somebody in your past. If something is eating you up, it is called cancer.

We held hands and we said a prayer and we asked for a miracle. "Okay, God we have done everything we know and everything we have been guided to and now we are just going to call forth a miracle because we don't know what else to do from here." We said thank you and giggled and talked. I went home. The next morning, Bo called. She asked, "Cindy did you make a doctor's appointment for me with Dr. Hagen's office?" I said, no, but I knew who he was because he was one of my advertising clients who was an internal specialist. "They just called me to confirm an appointment for 10:30 tomorrow morning." I said, "Well, who made it?" She said, "I don't know, but I will call you back."

She called everybody she knew including all of her family members who knew she was going through this journey. Nobody knew anything. She even called the doctor's office and asked who had made the appointment for her. The two ladies said they had just been sitting there talking about it. They said they were the only two that booked appointments in the appointment book. They said it was in neither of their handwriting and added that they never put the phone number under the name either. Neither one of the ladies had written Bo's name or number in the book!

Bo called me back, told me the story and asked me if I thought she should go. I said, "Yes, it sounds like the makings of a miracle to me." She went and told this doctor what she had been diagnosed with and what she was doing to treat her condition. He kinda poo-pooed her, putting his hand up flowing it through the air. Then he said, "Let me check you for one thing." And he checked her for Giardia and found it all through her system. Giardia is a microscopic parasite that comes from ingesting bad water. She didn't have cancer anymore, she had Giardia. The lingering symptoms were Giardia. He gave her Flagil for 14 days. Thank you Flagil! She was all better. She raised all her four children. She got happily remarried. She lives in Moab and that was almost 20 years ago now.

I ask that you release any judgments from medicines. It's really important we don't judge the things that helped us survive in our journey, so we are able to wake up to NOW. Please don't judge the doctor either. Doctors are there for a reason and all they are trying to do is help. Hold them to their original intent to help. They still go home and kiss somebody. So they still love. Please be aware that doctors are on your health care team but not totally in charge. If a physician hears your symptoms and immediately makes a conclusion of how bad it could be, please find another doctor. They must stop planting seeds of fear before they even have test results back. I think this is absurd. Listen to your own feelings, too! If a doctor recommends a test and it doesn't feel right to you, then get a second opinion! Doctors have created a world of "conditions". Don't let yourself be a statistic!

I had been doing the Cleanse for about a year when I began to question if this was really big enough. I felt I was here to touch a lot of lives and I didn't think this Cleansing was big enough. White Eagle, one of my great Native American teachers, came to my house and said, "Spirit just kicked my butt to get over here. What's going on with you?" I explained that many strange things were coming to me and I felt I had really big things to do. He asked me what my intent was. My intent still hadn't changed. My intent was that my work becomes the worship. I wanted to help people understand that they didn't have to hurt anymore. It was not necessary to carry the pain anymore. I have helped many to know they have a choice. I have helped many to stop hurting. White Eagle told me that the reason all this came to me, is because my intent was true. He continued, "You have to understand that every time one of us comes to consciousness, meaning we remember to walk as the seed of God and not the seed of man, on earth, we take 144,000 with us!" That's how important each and every one of you are. One of us has to choose to wake up and love and trust for the other 144,000 others to do it too. It does give us hope for the world. Not everybody has to wake up but enough of us have to. The earth will shift by itself. According to the Isaiah papers in the Dead Sea Scrolls, only 8,000 need awaken for the world to shift. I hope this book is part of that which shifts it. Are you the One we have been waiting for? I think you ARE!!

Did you know that 2012 is the end of the Mayan, the Hopi, and the Aztec calendars from which our modern calendar is based, and the beginning of the new millennium? Jesus said it best: "The lion shall lay down with the lamb and peace shall reign" and he didn't say "maybe." Teachings and messages of truth have always been here. When we listen to the messages with love, it is about having no judgment of one person, place, or situation as less than love. Then we'll have an opportunity to remember who we really are. We are all One and we are all parts of the Beloved One, who is love.

This knowing of whom you are a seed of God and not the seed of a man is always held for you by more than you can count. Even I know who You are!!

Most of the time, it is a big trauma that will focus us on our path to who we are. It could be the death of a loved one, a divorce, an illness, a car wreck or a chronic health condition. Whatever the journey is, it is all the same thing. We are the God, the creator of all of it-having an experience of who we are not, so we can eventually remember who we are. The trauma (pain) is God trying to get our attention, so we can remember-and God (sometimes in the form of pain) really WORKS!

Beginning of Path and Trust

I have a funny story to share now. I was in Utah. This was way back in the early part of this life journey. I went to a yard sale and I saw that this lady had all these conscious books. She was selling all this stuff, she had all these great shoes that fit me and I found out that she had painful migraines. I went over to her and said, "Hey sweetheart, I can help. I do this awesome Cleanse. Pain is just God trying to get your attention and you know what, you have the opportunity to be absolutely well and touch a lot of lives." I made a judgment in that moment thinking that she had actually read and was living the truth of some of those conscious books. This is what is so amazing about these awesome books and yet people read them and they still hate their neighbor or they still try to control their partner's way that they do the dishes or something, which is ridiculous. So really they don't know how to live it yet. But I thought that she was there because she had all these great books.

She said she would do the Cleanse. We sat there and made an appointment for her to get started. Then I paid for my stuff. We decided we would reduce her Cleanse price for a sewing machine trade and some other things I chose. As I was leaving, my heart was completely full and I said to her, "You know what? God loves you no matter what." I knew that migraines were about self judgment. I proceeded to tell her how God loved her and didn't judge her. Immediately she jumped in and said, "Yes, God does judge me! Yes, God does judge you too. I am not coming to do the Cleanse if you think that God doesn't judge us." And I thought, Oh no! I was very hard on myself. I felt really bad for God. I thought I had let God down. I was so sorry, I missed an opportunity to have one of your beloveds live pain free and not hurt anymore. I missed an opportunity because I opened my big mouth and talked about your great unconditional love and to help another to live a pain free life! I had no doubt that the Cleanse worked. Look what it did for me and my back. I didn't have to have my back broken and have pins put in it. 10 days later, I was free! That means if I can be clear, so can everybody else on the planet. I am very clear about that being true. I felt really bad. I got the big stick out and I went wham wham wham wham—like we do in the silliness of our human self that thinks it did it wrong. I was still learning, I was new at this.

I went over to my girlfriend, Shalona's house. I said Shalona, "I did this terrible thing, I feel so bad, I let God down." Shalona said to me immediately, "Cindy did you forgive yourself yet?" And

I got it. Instead I changed my way of thinking, to oops what did I learn from this? I forgave myself immediately because I didn't want to carry it another breath. What I got from this experience in my quiet time with God was that it wasn't this lady with the migraines time to be well yet. It was her message from Creator, the seed thought that maybe she didn't have to hurt. Maybe there would be hope for her too but she wasn't ready yet to let go of her stories and her old painful judgmental journey. That's why we don't want to push people into consciousness or drag them along with us.

It was good lesson for me. I am not responsible for another person's happiness or their health. I am responsible to love first and forgive myself if I think I did it wrong and to love them no matter what. That's easy! When you forget to love and you think you did it wrong, just say Oops! Follow this example I use all the time at Angel Farms. Pretend that you are a little child just learning how to walk, maybe 9 months old, and you fall down. You can't even verbally talk yet but you are learning how to walk. Are you never going to get up again? Are you just going to stay on the floor. Are you going to just keep crawling? That's not the way it works. You get up again, dust yourself off and keep on walking.

Practice Oops and whoops. Whichever one works for you, it doesn't matter, you wobbled, you stepped out of love for just a moment but you caught it. You step back into love.

Repeat this; In this moment I forgive myself for thinking that I did it wrong, and I step up and love again instead. I am not hard or critical of myself anymore. I don't hurt myself again because I thought I didn't get it right. I will keep stepping up until I am strong enough that I don't wobble again; strong enough that I can say now I can become the lover like God.

"On awakening, bless this day, for it is already full of unseen good which your blessings will call forth; for to bless is to acknowledge the unlimited good that is embedded in the very texture of the universe and awaiting each and all."

—Pierre Pradervand

In the bible it begins with God created heaven and earth. Do you believe that? Then count down 31 lines later and it says all that God created is Good. That would be you and everything else. Bless you!

I want to say, here's what I know is true. Here's what I am choosing to live, whether you do or not is up to you. Still you are divine in your essence and you will rise to it someday whether you do it here on this physical plane or you cross over and you get it, it doesn't matter. We all will return to love. It's as simple as that. It's not a big job. It's about waking up and asking if I can love my friend in front of me. Can I love the fireplace in front of me? Can I love the tree outside of the window? Can I love the neighbor over there even though I don't know their name? The answer to each question is Yes Yes Yes!! Even if the neighbor is mistaken, their essence is divine. Come from love, not fear with each choice at each moment.

I found that faith, which everyone is born with, eventually turns into knowing and it becomes solid. When I was first coming into my knowing many other people told me that I was way out there. My healing happened when I knew my back was straight and I was done. Whenever I see anyone that is out of peace or out of alignment, it does not make me go out of peace or alignment. I don't feel that anymore. I am so thankful for my teachers and my horse that knew who I was before I realized who I was, and I was very grateful they held it for me until I was ready to rise to it. If it took a car wreck to be the trauma that brought me to my intent, I am thankful for it and yet, I would not choose to do that pain again.

The pain serves us. We can stop and say, I don't ever want to do that again. One little whoops can take us back into pain but why would we do that again? Why would we want to? I can hold for other people knowing that they too can come out of their pain. I know you can come out of your depression. I know you can come out of it because we have done it, we did it, and so can you. Jesus didn't say it's only me. He said what I can do, you can do, and there will be greater works done by you than me. It's simpler than most people think. Allow people to rise to it. Allow it. Be the example anyway, what other choice do you have? This is the reason this book was written for you 20 years later to help you know you don't have to hurt anymore.

Angel's Toolbox

Here is a simple meditation I did for years that changed my life.

Everywhere you go, see yourself and all things as the creative force of the universe called God/love. Because it is not easy to transcend humanness, I tell my Angels to 'Fake it till you make it'. It is important we look at our past and let go of it. Bless it, show gratitude for it because it creates who we are right now; our journeys give us the tools and compassion to see God in others and ourselves and why wouldn't we really want to be in love with who we are right now?

Testimonials

My energy level and overall sense of wellbeing has improved. I am optimistic about my allergies to make-up, clearing up — will know when I try it on again. [Note from AF: Used to be a model.] I am very motivated to continue with the liver cleanses and to now stop drinking coke as I saw for myself the damage it caused (caffeine, too!). I no longer have cravings for caffeine, because my energy is so much better. I am going to remind myself to "love me" everyday. Thank you, Cindy. I love you all. I offer these words of encouragement to others, "Trust it. It will change your life!"
—Wanda - Writer/Consultant - CA http://writementor.com

My eyesight is much improved. I have worn glasses since 5th grade and no longer need them! My hair is no longer falling out! My joint pain is much less and my wrinkles are gone! The feelings in my fingertips and toes has returned from numbness from chemotherapy! I have more energy. I am a "10". I know my purpose is just to love. I see now that I can feel like I am 20 again.
—Cris-CA Angel!

My physical health was good when I came but the Cleanse has given me a much greater appreciation of how everything in our experience is connected to our physical well being. I feel much better about maintaining health and getting stronger. The highest effect was on my emotional well being-being able to let go of negative feelings I had about myself which I hadn't realized were so strong, has really relieved a lot of stress and pain. Love is an incredible gift I will take with me always. This Cleanse has given me a closer connection to God and an acceptence of myself. A wonderful experience! —Dr. Dan- Indiana

This Cleanse experience has made me aware of all that was holding me back. How to let go of the emotions that make your body ill over time. It has been freeing to be filled with love and to feel now that I am a vessel of love to all around me! My physical self feels so pure and light. Learning the lessons of love and how to love yourself at each level is so empowering! Learning to nourish our bodies through our positive thoughts and good food had added so much joy to me, I can hardly wait to get home to share it with my friends and family. —Renee, Indiana-respiratory therapist

This is my second time to Angel Farms. Physically I feel lighter. My abdomen flattened! My sleeping feels more restful. I wobbled on the water intake over the year. I love the food and the environment at Angel Farms. Mentally I feel more at ease and lighter. I am comitted to love myself more. Love all the mind food and enjoying a break from my cell phone! Spiritually I have the most change. I am infinitely grateful for all of the lessons of love! I enjoy every teaching and am becoming more aware and connected to the Source! Thank you, Thank you, Thank you!!! —Martha Jo- Ca. Excellent massage therapist!

WOW! Everything is alive! I can't believe the difference in my body! My back isn't sore and my legs have calmed down! I have gotten some good information to help my body love me back. I couldn't believe the stuff that came out of me! Worms! Me! What! I was in need to talk better about life and myself. What a Concept! I am glad to lose 1 inch of my belly and I am 10 pounds lighter. YA! —Pepper-Baker, waitress, master cook!

If Cleanliness is next to Godliness, and Angels are usually next to God then Cleanliness is Angelic! Thank you, Angel Farms. —Tom-engineer-farmer

WOW! WOW!WOW! I feel incredible, whole, super graditude, grounded, patient!!!! I feel like I really get to live more than ever! WOW! What a Blessing! —Brother Blair-excellent father and farmer

Angels Farms is a place of divine restoration of body, mind and spirit with the added gift of realization that letting go of all the toxins in the body, aids in our releasing the toxins of our mind and spirit as well. For me it was the most profound overall healing experience I ever allowed myself to have. I'm also in deep appreciation to the care of Cindy Sellers and her staff, for their great healing and profound learning experience.....Blessings, —Bruce L. Erickson, Management Consultant on critical issues of sustainability and consultant to the World Health Organization, Geneva Switzerland.

So many wonderful changes! First, I am more me! Not nearly as scattered as before. Before I came in to do the Cleanse, my asthma was in full force. I had very heavy and labored breathing. On day 3, I put the machine I would have to use 2 or 3 times a day, away! I am now breathing regularly thru my nose. I have not had to use it again! I see better with much impoved vision.

Spiritually, I am more at peace and am looking forward to my daily journey and my co creation. I now am very conscious of my spoken words and thoughts and my relationships. I have lost weight and feel and look way younger! —Linda-Hawaii-personal assistant

My moods are even and calm and happy. My connection to Spirit is stronger. My addictions to nicotine and caffeine are no longer with me! The pain in my liver and gallbladder has subsided. My skin is clearer and my eyes are brighter. I will now always remember and know who I am! I love and respect my body temple, probably for the first time in my life! This is one of the most profound transformational healing programs that one can go thru. You cannot be healthy with a clogged colon. Release and trust, This Cleanse can and will change your life. Larry is really a very talented body worker. He helped me to release energy which was contracted in my body. As a body worker myself, I can confidently say that my session with Larry was one of the best I have ever had. The session with Cindy helped me to always remember that I am Loved and that I AM LOVE.—Paravati-Healer,California

I feel better than I ever have in my whole life! Before I came to Angel Farms I was consumed by anger, fear, and worry. I was feeling unloved and unloveable. Now I know I am loved, I am love, and that is my purpose to be here-to love. I am Bursting! Physically I had all sorts of aches and pains. I have had several injuries, on of them led to a joint replacement surgery. Since being on the Cleanse my body feels so much better and stronger. I believe now that is is clean and getting the nutrients it needs. During the Cleanse I lost millions of liver stones and some big gallstones. It is amazing to see the body release that and creat space for more love to flow. It feels great to let go of all the anger I was holding on to. I have lost at least 10 pounds and will continue to lose more because I am in touch with my body for the first time in my life! I am so grateful to everyone at Angel Farms. This is the best and most loving thing I have ever done for myself . They have such a caring and all encompassing program. I felt that my session with Cindy was completely integral to me letting go of everything and feeling loved and cared about all along. That was HUGE for me. It was a completely enlightening experience. I feel whole and complete. I cannot wait to go home and see my family and friends and shower them with love. —Jessica, Teacher, New York

I feel like a different person. My own person. My old self; my new self. . . on all levels, physical, emotional and spiritual. The Cleanse is life changing and life affirming. After two years of transition - with husband to divorced and single, moving house and downsizing, yikes, (My wardrobe had to shrink by more than one-half.), and watching my business take the economic hit of 2008 - I am fully shifted from my idea of what I was and ready for this rebirth and self that the Cleanse offers. Can't say it enough - Cindy is awesome, competent, confident, wise and loving, sparkling and funny, just what I needed to bring out those qualities in myself as I cleared out "old stuff" to make space for the new and, most importantly - I TRULY AM. Get here as fast as you can! It is not painful. It is for anyone who has a human body and eats food. You will find health and lightness and, hopefully, your true self.
—Ann Bridget Waters, Community Activist, California

I feel lighter, more conscious and ready to spread the love. I am trying to remember how I felt before this Cleanse but I am finding it difficult, because, I feel so good now. It's amazing to think that I was so conditioned to feeling tired, sore, weak and unempowered. . . so used to constant pain that I assumed there was no other way. Feeling like I do right now PROVES that my body is strong and that I have the power to heal completely. I feel like Angel Farms has opened a door for me - one that was never closed but that I had pushed away with thoughts of self-doubt, fear, pain and other disillusionments. Cindy reminded me thar the only real thing is love. And LOVE is what I am. This is the best investment you can make. HEAL YOUR BODY AND MIND.
—Laurel, Self-employed, California

After suffering from chronic stomach pain for many years, I now actually feel no pain whatsoever! My mental clarity is much better and the inflammation in my skin has cleared. Emotionally I feel much more grounded and happy, and until now, didn't really understand the impact my symptoms where having on my life. Spiritually, I have remembered how important yoga, and meditation is in my life. My runaway thoughts are so much more apparent."
P.S. I talked to Anna two weeks later and she said her symptoms have completely reversed. —Anna, Singer & Artist, Oregon

I came here with some trepidation. However I was welcomed with love and concern. As the process began I was worried about it, but after the 1st day I found that I could do this with ease, I

knew that only good could come from the process. As the days went by I noticed a tightening of my skin and some changes in the dark spot on my leg. And as I prepare to head home I can say this (I feel more like I do NOW then I did before!)
—Don, Port of Entry Agent, Utah

I arrived at Angel Farms, my health was a mess. The first thing I noticed, my hair started changing color. My ankle that had been black and scaly for the past 6-8 years, began to change colors. I have lost 15 lbs. And I don't have the major swelling in my legs and fingers and my toes and fingers are pink. Overall the Cleanse dumped a great deal of stuff from my system and I don't have any doubt that my heart, kidney, liver, and lymph system are working much more efficiently.
—Joel, Teacher, Utah

I feel clearer. I'm living in the now. I feel fearless. Better reflexes. I am more flexible. This Cleanse makes perfect sense why it works. —B. J. Penn, Hawai`i-Native Hawaiian Teacher & World Famous Athlete, www.bjpenn.com

This experience has been so awesome. I got closer to Jesus, and I have seen things come out of my body, and feel like I got my life back. The journey I went through doing my session with Cindy was out of this world. To see my self lose weight was so wonderful.
—Emily Naeole, Puna Councilwoman, Hawai`i

Physically I lost 10-15 pounds, I am stronger, faster and have more stamina and energy and my eyesight is better. Emotionally I am peaceful, stable, clearer, happier, and more accepting. Spiritually I am connected and more fully with Spirit and flowing. The session I did with Cindy left a flowing loving healing vibration that clears the pockets of the colon in the mind; peaceful feeling that still lasts to this day, that is not declining but accumulating.
— Kaliko Kanaele, Hawai`i Native Hawaiian Healer & Counselor, Tech at Angel Farms 3 years now!

After the Cleanse on about the 8th day I could breathe so much easier, I am coughing very little and recovered some pretty awesome, energy back that I lost prior to the Cleansing. I also sleep better and have stopped smoking! I believe ahead of me will be the experience and outcome with more understanding and joy and with greater certainty of life. So grateful too- meeting all their people just simply Awesome! It would help everyone in everyway to experience the Cleanse-

Everyone should have this experience not found anywhere else.
—Delancey, Native Hawaiian Healer, Hawai`i

I just have never done a Cleanse in my whole life. As I settled down I could feel all my anxieties come alive. I prayed and fell asleep. When I woke up I realized I am alive. As each day passed I felt better and better. I know I will be completely cured. My allergies are completely gone!! Psoriasis is nearly gone and that is a Miracle!! Parasites from 30 years, gone. I had diabetes for two years and is now gone. My heart attacks and anxiety of six years is gone. High cholesterol I had for two years is gone. (It dropped to 200 points in the 10 days! It was 345!) Fear from 61 years is gone! My thyroid that was out of balance 40 years cured. I was on 11 medicines and now I am on NONE!! I feel 45 and look it! My energy is back and it is never too late to regenerate. Grief and anger gone, eyesight still working on it. Weight loss 11 lbs. Hair growing back in. Rheumatoid Arthritis of 4 years gone! And I haven't even begun to exercise. It is all good and life is beautiful!!"—Kanela, Native Hawaiian, Retired, Hawai`i

I am feeling very sacred, valued, optimistic, and spiritually (as well as physically) cleansed. I am happy all day long, the small annoyances don't touch me at all. My body feels energized and my chronic muscular tension is lifting. My eyesight is improving. I am so done with the old me, I'm feeling gratitude, confidence and have found acceptance replacing judgment. Thank you angels for saving my spiritual life and bringing me home!!!—Cheryl, Artist, Hawai`i

When I first came into the Cleanse, I felt very uncomfortable with myself. I was struggling with my weight and my life. Throughout this Cleanse I realized I am beautiful and loved. Even though others may not speak the language of love, I can. When at school others may be gossiping, but it won't affect me because I am love, I am loved, and I have loved. —Lydia, Student, Hawai`i (age 16)

WOW! Physically I have lost 25 pounds and feel renewed! Emotionally, I am in a better place than I have ever been, spiritually I have been saved. I have found tools and ways to forgive, forget, not worry, and live in the "NOW". The greatest gift I could give myself is Angel Farms." —Steve, Sales Rep, Hawai`i

"Well I feel great and I feel so much lighter and slimmer and I don't get headaches any more. I don't get car sick and I love that.—Naia, Student, Hawai`i
328

Satisfied by the results, in particular, removal of a large nest of parasites. The effect was immediate of a large boost in energy, although large credit also must be given to the effect of spiritual teachings offered. These teachings were both "live and in person" by Cindy, and on recordings by Gregg Braden, N.D. Walsh, and Chopra. Besides satisfaction, emotions include gratitude to all the staff and feeling relieved of such great burdens.—Donna, Educator, Hawai`i

Physically I feel so much cleaner, stronger than I did when I started. Have been on a slide into unhealthy eating habits and a sedentary lifestyle for the past eight months. Accelerating over the holiday distractions, and come here to focus on caring for my body. Emotionally was exhausted, now it feels great to be grounded, hopeful, full of gratitude and joy. I felt blocked with fear and am now feeling surrounded by energy and light. Spiritually I arrived cut off from spirit. It was amazing to dive into spirit, love, and energy.—Carolyn, Designer, California

Physically I feel like I have the energy of a 15-year-old. No aches in my back and my joints. My skin feels so much better, and my whole inside feels like I have a new body of cleaned parts. Emotionally I feel grounded and calm. I don't have the anger at everything that disappointed me in my everyday life. If I do get angry, it goes right away and I don't hang on to it. Spiritually, I feel so much more in touch with the world in a positive light, and with myself.—Ron, Fisherman, California

I can walk again, I am relaxed and feel much better than when I came. I feel closer to God. -Richard, Retired, Nevada

Physically I feel very young, emotionally I am full of gratitude and new potentiality. Spiritually I feel a new path is opened to go deeper into presence, into the now. If you have chosen Angel Farms Cleanse, you have made the most important decision of your new life. —George, Songwriter, California

I feel very comfortable in my body. I feel so thankful that I'm not carrying around who I am not anymore. WOW! I feel emotionally available to myself. It used to take so much effort to not allow people and situations to upset me, but now it's automatic to accept whatever happens and love it. Knowing it to be in perfect arrangement. I don't feel my past influencing me any more. It is truly in the past. I had tears of joy this morning because for the first time I felt happy and excited to be hereon Earth. No more do I feel that I don't want to be here. I feel alive and ready to live. Show yourself how much you love yourself and give yourself the opportunity to release fear and live in love.—Lona, Student & Mother, Hawai`i

The Cleanse was a miraculous enlightenment though skeptical at first, I've become truly convinced of the benefits of this process. I feel more alive and aware - and I can tell that I'm getting a lot more out of my food. The team here is truly marvelous. It was a pleasure to interact with them everyday. I wholeheartedly recommend Angel Farms and the Cleanse a path to healing. —Wayne, Computer Programmer, Oregon

I am going to Live!!!!!! In love & in Joy. I felt a little low in energy & delicate. My body is not in any pain and I feel like I am not dealing with a burden of toxins. I feel more oxygen & blood in my brain. I am relieved to have emptied out & released all that garbage. My skin is clearer & softer - my eyes are clearer. Emotionally I am blissed out. I feel peaceful & calm, letting of fear is sinking in & having an effect. I feel in Joy to know I made the decision to come here & give this to myself & my health & to be in Love & Live In Love!! Spiritual — my guides & Angels are so Happy. I am grateful I took it to a whole other level. Where I Am God Is and Where God Is I Am.—Joyce, Homemaker, Hawai`i (Now on staff with Angel Farms.)

Physically I feel waves of energy similar to Goosebumps. My hands were stiff and jaundiced with tendonitis and nerve inflammation. Hands are now supple with massively increased circulation and motion. Tendonitis is gone! Headache I have had for 1 2 years is gone! Clarity of thought, memory returning! Fingernails look pink like a baby. Emotionally I am calm, centered, connected, and anger is gone and fear is gone!! Spiritually a door has opened!! Want to feel light? I am positively flying! Your illness is part of your path to experience the Divine. Free Yourself!!"—Jonathan, Builder/Photographer/Consultant, California

I am calmer and feel I now exist deeper inside of myself. I feel a softness and a warm peaceful glow. In letting go, I have learned to wholly love myself. I feel through this Cleanse that I have accessed the source of my doubt and fear. Through coming face to face with this source, I am able to bridge mind and body and walk in a renewed awareness. I have had a huge change and release

of anger over patriarchal religions, and have brought spirituality back into my life. I can no longer live hiding, always thinking about others details, I will no longer dread anything. I will no longer put myself down. I now live in the NOW. I have all the tools I need. This Cleanse has influenced and transformed me more spiritually and emotionally than I originally had thought. However, I have noticed many physical changes like I have a softer belly, my pelvic girdle is relaxed, my skin is smooth and glowing, My eyes lifted, my movement fluid, no sign of any B.V., Yeast infection or UTI! No more teeth clenching at night. I have recognized that most of my past physical dysfunction resulted from shame, guilt, feelings of inadequacy and fear, and anger. I have put down my sword and and now holding a chalice! Thank you , Angel Farms! This Cleanse is the best gift you can give to yourself. Your body is your vessel, you spend every moment of your life connected to it. Why not treat it with the utmost respect and reverence by taking the Cleanse? This Cleanse gets to the source and thus leaves you feeling so whole and pure.
—Joanna, Student/Body Mechanic Instructor/Healer, California

How can I describe it. Upon arrival I felt physically, emotionally, and Spiritually strong and healthy. NOW, I feel physically unstoppable, emotionally grounded, and Spiritually at peace with myself and connected with God in a new and invigorated way! This is a life changing event that will not only help you physically but on levels in your life you can not even imagine. Cindy took me to a connection with God that will stay with me the rest of my days. She also helped me to see how I can be at total peace with myself and to love others unconditionally-I was ready! AND I can smell after 47 years!!! A Miracle!!!"—James, Engineer, Colorado

I have given myself a gift by coming to Angel Farms, that gift was Love. Love truly is the answer to it all. I had an idea that fear played a large role in my past journey and I had no idea I was living my life from fear! No wonder I was so sick. I was poisoning myself every moment that I was not operating from a place of love. I saw with my own eyes what was released, what I was allowing to live in me, no wonder I hurt so much in the past. My body feels completely at "ease" for the 1st time in my life and love is the only healer.—Cagney, Teacher, Hawai`i

I replaced a gallon of diet soda and coffee a day with water and feel phenomenal!! I feel so at peace, in love and a part of the Creator."—Holly, Administrator, Pennsylvania

331

WOW!! I have been changing my food and supplements to obtain maximum health for years. My wife has been sharing with me her successes because she has been cleansing for years. She was so impressed with the program at Angel Farms because of the support of Cindy and Larry. When I saw her transformation, I was (on Board)! Even though I was very healthy looking outside, I have lost 18 lbs.- my skin is so much clearer-My eyes clearer-I feel as if I am brand new! My knowledge in nutrition can now be put to use 100% instead of that toxic colon trying to absorb nutrients in its toxic state. I'm grateful for this experience, it has enhanced my life. The gifts I learned on the Cleanse will serve me forever. Thank you Cindy and Larry Sellers for your sacrifices and dedication to serve Mankind."
—Robert, Personal Trainer and Nutritionist (for 40 years), Hawai`i

I had a lower back problem that has been almost completely gone. My hair has darkened and I have much better color. My voice-singing has improved. I have been on a spiritual quest for some time and this whole experience has amped that upped quite a bit. I will pass the great teachings on and learn to love myself even more.—Kevin, California

I can sing clearer, deeper, project my voice stronger and feel my diaphragm breathing and lungs while I sing. Colors are brighter every day! You know the chronic diarrhea I had for 20 years is gone! I am not running to the bathroom anymore (!) and my colon is strong! Good movements! I absorb nutrition and feel it since so much has been swept out of me. Thank You! I promote you! I am alive."—Vivanna, Hawai`i

I have a deep and true knowing that I have begun again and this time with my true life partner God. —Kris, Mother, New York

I feel free! Light and Fluffy! Free of anger and judgment. Reborn! —Alex, Gardner, Health Councilor, New York

My physical health is fantastic!!! Originally diagnosed with autoimmune my energy was totally drained, eyeballs were swelling and hemorrhaging, thyroid was malfunctioning and blood sugar was difficult to control. My eyes were sticky from lack of moisture. I spent thousands of dollars a year on supplements and treatments, just to try and be well. During the Cleanse I was able to eliminate the thyroid and blood sugar supplements as well as the adrenal support. My body has stopped racing inside and I have more energy that I have had in years! I feel alive and well! I now have a sense of calm not realized for many years-probably never have experienced this sense *of grounding. As always, Jesus is my guide. This is the best thing you could ever do for your life! Mahalo!! —Sheri, Administrative Assistant*

Vibrating in the heart juggling love and no-mind is a treasured space and Angel Farms excels at enhancing this. The couples counseling was the deepest, most compassionate I have ever had pulling out buried and doormat relationship challenges. Ah Cindy, if we lived in Japan she would be named a "Living Treasure". —Chuck (Idaho Free Spirit)

I feel as though I've released so much on many levels. Physically I dumped a ton of toxins and now free of nicotine for the first time in 40 years-yes 40! I feel more in touch with my body's needs and will continue to honor this marvelous temple.—Kathleen (ID Artist)

Go—It will change your life. —Karen (AZ Homemaker)

After Larry's session, I was so relaxed and in another space that I lost all track of time. I have never experienced body work that took me there like that to that extent before.—Jenny (ID Jewelry Designer)

Ready for each and every moment. I am eternally grateful to Cindy, Larry and the whole Angel Farms community and to me. Mahalo.—Duncan (CA Bodywork)

I came to be cleansed with my wife. I felt that this is about so much more. I received so much more from everyone. The acceptance and love from everyone was a gift that I hadn't expected but cherish. It's been a wonderful experience that will help me forever."—Phil (ID Contractor)

It has accomplished my goal of being a healthy person and a better person.—La Neice (ID Decorator)

This experience at Angel Farms will change your life forever in a miraculous, positive way. You will feel renewed and you will even amaze yourself! Cindy's session was Incredible! She graced me with her Angel love. I got really down to the core of major life issues. I realized I Am worthy, I am powerful, I am loved and I can speak my truths. —Satya (CA Makeup Artist)

I've lost lots of weight off my back - imagine - Guilt! Gone! My turkey neck is gone!! I feel and look much better! My face wrinkles are gone! I eat much less now and am nourished. My hands and feet were very white and now they're pink! Thank you liver cleanse. I also dumped lots of chemicals!!! The wonders of modern medicine... Learning that I was wanted and loved was an amazing miracle and shift in my world. Thank You!!!" —Ann (ID Mom)

I was a big coffee addict. I had been trying to quit coffee for 11 years. I now longer crave coffee! I'm amazed. It's now a non-issue, in fact, I no longer crave anything! Not pizza and beer, wine and cheese, cheeseburgers and fries, appetizers and martini's, etc. I didn't even think that was possible!! My skin is also improving. I had serious "sun damage" on my face that is disappearing. I've learned that it was actually not sun damage, it was a build up of toxins that my liver was unable to eliminate because it was so overworked. I now drink 1 gallons of water a day willingly!! I eat about 1/8 of what I used to eat and I'm full. I'm no longer angry or resentful of cynical. I'm HAPPIER. I'm more at ease. I'm more at Peace instead of frantically racing around always running out of time. I'm no longer in judgment of people's stuff. It's wonderful!"I now trust in the process of life. I have given up control. Ha! As if I ever was in control! Ha! Previously, I had a regimented schedule and was "time crazy." I even came to the cleanse with a list of things to do that "needed to be completed" before I returned home. Ha! That's funny to me now."
—Rhonda (HI Videographer Assistant)

I feel pure! My body feels lighter, my mind feels lighter and my soul feels brighter! Everything I know is changing and feeling good. My Temple is clean! I really want to keep on surfing, but I think I'll catch the next wave in for now! Thanks everyone, I love you!"—Arthur (HI)

I feel I am a work in progress. I feel so much lighter, physically as well as spiritually. My senses have sharpened; taste, smell, hearing and vision. I have been carrying a lot of this "stuff" for a long time, assuming it was just part of growing older NO!! Not anymore!! I look forward to renewed vigor physically, as new doors open. I have a future and it looks pretty rosy! My mind is clearer and my determination is back.... Never quit. —Jane (HI Botanist)

Many small miracles for me. I came to have one miracle but have had more doors open in my spirit as well as my body. I feel great in my body I never knew how good I could feel. Unbelievable what was cleansed out of my colon as well as my entire system. I have had a shift (much needed) with my awareness spiritually I seemed to have had an opening with the purging process of my body. Amazing

Program Cindy is a Natural Healer. Big MIRACLE is my loss of fear with the loss of all the parasites. My breathing is excellent now my right lung cleared its toxins. My right ear was damaged and I hear much better in that ear."—Kerri (CO Self Employed)

I feel 10 times better on all levels. I feel this was like a big reminder washing over me. I have had in my life (found out about), so many of the tools used here. I used so many in my life. But my fifties hit and kicked my ass. Menopause, loss of mom, kids growing up and leaving home, empty nest, tried to refill with another family and relationships. That was all about emotional manipulation and anger. I got lost, stuck and was drowning. Losing my essence. My life force draining away and didn't care too much physical discomfort had developed. Now I'm free of the past finally flying where my spirit has been waiting for me. Thank you.—Joyce (HI Farmer)

I FEEL more peaceful, I feel clean on the interior. I have learned techniques to bring me back to love and peace."—Bruce (CA Retired)

I feel much better physically and my emotions are higher than Ever. I feel and look younger. Turning point in my life. Spiritually I have grown and now realize the facts of love in life. Life is Love. —John (CO Retired)

I feel so much better physically and especially emotionally. My spiritual health has improved more than I ever thought possible. The lymph node that had cancer in it has gone down in half. I will continue to do my maintenance at home and get rid of it. Cindy is a wonderful teacher. —Dawn (UT GIS Specialist)

As a whole I feel fabulous, I love my body. I am pampering and loving it. I am, His is, no fear only love! I am a spiritual being having physical experiences totally. —Leana (ID Home Maker, Lover)

When I walked through the doors of Angel Farms I was broken physically, emotionally and spiritually. I had severe right knee pain, sciatic nerve pain, painful leg cramps, and numbness in hands when sleeping, chronic fatigue, and headaches on the physical side. Emotionally I was a mess, not to mention I had NO spiritual health. It all was drained from me about a year ago." "From day 1 my knee has not hurt at all. I've had no leg (muscle) cramps since thousands of liver stones were flushed from my body, allowing blood circulation through out my body. Numbness in hands that used to disturb my sleep are no more. My sciatic nerve on the right side REJOICED on Day 10's cleansing, when that pocket got emptied. As time goes on and I follow maintenance monthly, I know I'll heal inside even more. Everyone is complimenting me on the slimming down in my face and the darkening of my hair. I've lost 11 pounds in the cleanse period and a total of 9 inches in my chest, waste and hips.Spiritually now I know that God loves me and always did. I don't have FEAR no more and I feel happy to have let go of negative emotions that had ruled my life. I have been set FREE and I owe it all to Angel Farms!!! —Lorraine (HI Teacher)

When I was reading testimonials on the web site, I noticed a word that was commonly used, "light" everybody felt lighter. I didn't understand what that meant. I thought, weight? But, it is the perfect word filled with light. My mind is lighter, happier, joyous. My body feels, lighter, released from a crusty shell. My spirit feels lit glowing. I have learned that physical, emotional and spiritual well being and joy, starts with having a clean vessel otherwise we just spend our lives spinning wheels continuing to be splattered with mud. Nothing is more important in life than this. Do it! I came to Angel Farms in so much body pain and I left completely pain free. It changed my life forever. —Janet (ID Business)

I feel energized in the morning, less hungry, happy excited for the day. Lots of gratitude, peaceful, new outlook on life. See food differently and water. Excited to start living and to experience life to its fullest." —Nehemiah (ID Claims Manager)

I have been awakened! My gratitude level is a 10. I can say that I have been going without. I now will always go with in. I am excited to serve the world and shine my light that is within me. Most important recognizing where that light comes from. Mahalo ~ I am every positive quality that is in this negative in this universe. I can not want to begin this new journey. —Lori (ID Property Manager)

I am overwhelmed just now feeling like I have left old baggage and illness here! I am grateful beyond words for this experience! Physically I feel light and energetic, emotionally I feel a bit fragile, like I need time to digest the wonder. Spiritually I feel grounded and renewed the best place I have been since memory began... Thank you!! God Bless...What I did not expect to find.. A group of the warmest fuzziest kind of people ever. Generously open beyond words...Thanks, that makes the best memories. —Shelly (ID RN)

After 2 days my chronic back pain was about 95% gone, no more meds, I felt more positive & relaxed.—Mary (HI)

Vibrant, on-fire, at peace, in love, no more aches & pain or disease! —Barbara (ID)

After the 8th day I dumped all my medications for depression & anxiety down the toilet. I no longer feel dependant on chemicals to balance my brain. Physically I also lost over 20 pounds & feel lighter in general. Great peace to remove self from pain.—Mary (HI)

Change is beyond words on all levels!" I literally felt my body thanking me for taking this step. I am now aware that each and every event I've experience or participated in since Life immemorial have brought me to this point and time. I find myself going philosophical so easily these days. ON the emotional level, new tools, certainly added to my tool box, for example new definition of money to be open to the abundance, that is always present and to remove myself from blocking my birth right. Fear, Cindy these are very powerful for me to sat the lest, I can go on, on and on! On the spiritual platform, Cindy, words are just so lacking to give it justice or better yet to give it form. The ability to enter that realm or to visit and find yourself in it at all times is shuttering to my previous conception of what is spirituality." —Joseph (HI Real Estate Finance)

Awesome, I have increased physical and emotional strength as a result of the Cleanse! Mild fat for my expressed milk is an inch more since I have returned from Angel Farms! More nutrition for mom, more for baby! —Tammy (ID Neonatal Nurse)

I came because of a prayer, looking for an answer of how I could get my health back, I knew this is what I needed to do and it answered my prayer! I know this is just the beginning of my new Life. I can't wait to get home and start changing or continuing my new Life. I thought that I would know just how I would feel after 10 days, one way or the other, but that not true. My health is changing now, my edema is gone, my heart is slower and more regular, arthritis is better, gout is gone! Emotionally I am so grateful with the peace I have, spiritual I am at peace with God. I can't wait to serve with Love and try to touch other people and my family. —Bruce (ID Self-Employed)

Having come badly dehydrated I now feel incredibly hydrated throughout my body! I am slimmer and more alert. I came skeptical but open minded, hoping for a lot expecting little. I may not be leaving with huge changes like some. But I have tools now to make them happen. The love and care that was shown during the Cleanse was extraordinary. Even little changes in Life can be miracles and for those that I received while doing the Cleanse I thank you.—Marsha (ID)

Physically my body feels great, light and the body moves freely, posture greatly improved, no back pain, can bend/flexible, easily. Emotional, reminder to react from love and listen to my body when emotions arise. Spiritual, reaffirm why I am here, cleared out my fear to be my spiritual self. Be in the moment!-Keatrice (CA)

I feel incredible!! I feel the healthiest I have ever felt since I was pregnant with my son 37 years ago. I feel clear in my body and mind. I know I am a child of God!—Rosie (CA Financial MGMT.)

I feel so clean and renewed. Each day was a new experience and exciting to see the changes. Spiritually woken up again, renew! Everyone here was so kind and caring, Hoku - getting her eyes to sparkle, Gail so good at helping and smiling, Jorgina, WOW = sisters in diving - always loving and giving, Shelley no greater gift given to us than her gently service, Larry never ending presence and gift of hands, Cindy full of light and love, giving so much to so many. Thank you for caring, thank you for following your journey. Thank you, for you….Love always to remember. —Phyllis (ID Dental Assistance)

I feel very loved by my dear Jesus and that I could find peace in his arms anytime I want, Jesus loves me & finds me priceless so I know I'm a 10. It was interesting for me that as I let go of any fear, anger, etc. my physical became better and I was able to pass more. MY skin obviously tightened & feels so soft & new, I don't need as much lotion anymore! My left leg would have numbness quite often & I would change my shoes - thinking the shoes were the problem. I no longer have the numbness, even my hair feels softer & more vibrant. I believe my digestive system wasn't functioning properly, my colon always felt stressed - it feels so calm & peaceful now. I definitely have more energy now - I would always feel tired no matter how many vitamins I took. I'm amazed of the parasites, liver stones, worms & inner intestinal lining that was let GO! Its the beginning of a beautiful journey.—Carol (HI Secretary)

A "10"! Awesome! I don't know what else to say I came expecting a journey and what a journey it has been. I came because of deteriorating health, back pain, ligament issues, muscular problems. Aware of course of spiritual and emotional issues I have been working on. Today the bags and black circles under my eyes are gone, I sleep beautifully, I feel better than I can ever remember feeling. Muscles that have hurt ALL THE TIME, don't hurt. My back and legs feel better everyday. When I came I hoped to feel better, achieve moments, maybe, where I was pain free. Today I have so much more than just moments, I love myself for giving myself the gift of the journey. Spiritually and emotionally this was just what I needed - and so much more than I expected. I now know my purpose and that it is safe to walk there.-Janis (CA Boat Captain)

I have released my attachment to caffeine, diet coke, fast foods! I have learned how little I need to eat to maintain energy. I had lost touch with God before Angel Farms. I now have God totally filling every cell of me, I don't need any love from anyone or anything, I share God's love with all I meet. The hole used to full with alcohol, food, etc. I now have God filling, I am God Love, Sharing God's love is my purpose in Life.—Maggie (KY)

Where do I begin and what could I put down on paper, that angels haven't experienced? OR yet too. My physical condition is totally opposite of what I felt like when I arrived at Angel Farms. (God Bless you, Cindy and Larry, for following your gift, that God has handed you, both. My pain on a scale of 10, was an 10, and now on my 9th day is a 3. Emotionally, on a scale of 10, 1 being the least, my emotions are a 10, (Full of God and loving myself. Thank you Annie and God) Then, there is Spirit, my Spirit has always been stronger then this physical body which I had totally forgot to love and care for. I love with kindness, natural foods, rest, TLC in all, this Cleanse has been for me a rewarding gift from God. A learning tool for me to be shared with others, thank you angels Cindy and Larry. Thank you God, my guardian angels mounds of thanks to you Angels for being here also. Your faces have inspired my days of Cleansing. Love you all forever...—Annie (ID Retired)
I could not believe all the stuff that came out of me. I feel lighter the pain is less, I'm letting go of all my excess fat. My skin is clearer with more color, I am loving myself and the world, Life seems easier.—Delecia (WA Retired)

How can someone put into words of how it feels to get your Life back. To feel so realized and content with yourself and everyone around you is a magnificent feeling. My pains are almost gone (physically), my pain inside my heart is gone, my soul is reborn. I honestly believe that I was dying inside out, now I know I was. I never believed I could be taken from what I was to who I am. I lost all my bloated-ness I have carried for 10 years, my body is electrified, a trip of a Lifetime! Thank you Angel Farms...Focus and let yourself go into the security of the people who take you down the road.—Kelly (ID Self-Employed)

Subsequent to being diagnosed with Fibromyalgia fifteen years ago, there has been no day without pain in the muscles of my body, resulting in headaches or migraines, inability to sleep soundly or through the night, high level of anxiety, constant irritability and depression. By the second day of the Cleanse, I was sleeping soundly through the night, waking up energetic and without pain. I began spending my mornings swimming instead of willing my body to force itself up out of bed. By the completion of the Cleanse the headaches dissipated and there has not been any hint of anxiety, fear, irritability, or depression. I stopped smoking (after 34 years), gave up coffee and Diet Cokes which I used to drink in place of water. This is particularly impressive since these have been the staples of my morning and daily regiment for many years. NOW that the body is no longer subjected to constant pain, my mind is able to rationalize, refocus and re-prioritize. Circumstances or events that used to create anxiety or irritability no longer seem important or worthy of anger. I have a sense of calm and peace, no longer needing to over-analyze, defend, dwell upon or beat an issue senseless. I can now choose how and when to react with greater clarity. I can now accept that it sometimes be to be loving that it is to be right (this would not have been in the realm of possibility before the Cleanse). I can now let go and choose to be happy! How does one go from feeling unworthy, unimportant and insignificant to feeling empowered, brilliant and deeply loved in ten days? To leave the guilt, shame, regrets and all other entrapment's where they belong in the past and to reconnect myself as a Child of God, a wondrous and unique miracle with infinite choices, capabilities and possibilities was huge for me. Understanding that it is always okay to forgive myself and the knowledge that I will never walk alone will forever be my source of comfort and strength. Instead of looking at my life and asking "why me", I can now envision the promises of joy, peace, forgiveness but most of all LOVE and say "that is me.—Ann Marie (CA Banker)

My experience at Angel Farms was incredible, I was amazed at the effect on my body the cleansing had. The chart of the colon showed the areas of the body that drew the nutrients from that area. You could see daily how each area was effected. Cindy told me I had issues with my right kidney, that is the area we reached last, before we even reached it I had decreased my water weight. I am overweight and had a lot of swelling. It has gone down incredibly. With the continued cleansing program Angel Farm offers, I believe I will continue to shrink. My daughter was on the Cleanse with me and it was trans-formative for us. Our relationship had a shift and we were able to release prior garbage, that had effected our relationship. Spiritually Angel Farms program has facilitated me realizing how much love I have in me and I do not need to be afraid any more.—Kay (KS CPA)

This Cleanse has been a total remodeling of the temple that is this body!! My whitewash crypt is now a beautiful temple. All the dark ugly places in my body and my soul have been cleansed by the angel of water, air, light. This feels like the True Babtizism!!—Nirvana (HI Retired)

When I arrived swollen & uncomfortable from my past year of chemo & radiation treatment, I felt pain & stiffness and would get tired very easily. Each day of the Cleanse has changed this discomfort, each night has been a very relaxed and I have solid sleep. After all 10 days I feel rejuvenated and full of life's energy. I can think, breath and see everything clearly I know who I AM and look forward to staying this way. I feel the Angel Farms program has Cleansed all physical, emotional, and spiritual areas of my being. I am very blessed to have experienced this God Loving process. I also feel more strength in all of these areas and can't wait to practice them in my everyday Life! Do It For Yourself! Do It For Your Body! The experience at Angel Farms was inspirational I would encourage any person that wants to renew their health!! The education is outstanding, there is so much information, that you receive at Angel Farms! —Vicki (ID Major Accountant Specialist)

I am standing taller, my face fuller, skin radiant, circulation has returned to my hands and feet. My creativity and flow have improved dramatically, especially since the morning of day 8!! I am hopeful, have renewed faith in my future and the future of human kind. My belly feels great, breathing deeply is much easier, circles have faded under my eyes, my sense of smell has improved!" This is a unique opportunity to receive the blessed work of Master Healers! Take this opportunity to visit the fountain of youth where you will see real miracles OCCUR!—Jonah (OR Artist)

I came in thinking I was pretty healthy but just wanted to enhance my health, Little did I know!! The ache in my shoulder is gone, my stomach feels great, no more pain when I go without eating (I thought it that was just me)!! My hair turned back to its natural Black & I no longer have wrinkles on my face!!! Better than all that I've learned to really Love, no more giving it to God and taking it back. "I feel so refreshed, totally at peace, more in tune with God." I was wearing a brace for tendonitis on my right shoulder, the pain was so severe I couldn't sleep. It is gone!!!! I continually felt hungry, if I didn't eat I would bloat and would feel ill, that feeling is completely gone! My skin is clearer, smooth, NO more makeup. I feel GREAT!!!—Myrna (ID Retired)

Feeling lighter, brighter (lost 25 lbs.), breathing more freely, emotionally lighter, thinking has quieted, and I go to the bathroom more! In the beginning I was emotionally not centered or physically. In each day I felt lighter spiritually speaking & physically. Talking with you and the others who were doing the Cleanse made the process more soothing & relaxing, it helped me for that 90 minutes to go into myself to understand what I was holding onto & having trouble recognizing within me. The Cleanse helps you clear all your past judgments & emotional hold ups, through the years. It's once in a lifetime experience.—Monroe - HI - mechanic

Cindy's wonderful way of being, the support of others in the group, and watching growth & change, along with the reinforcement of books, tapes, it all comes together. You deserve to live in Health & Joy & Love.-A. Christensen (DC)

I feel spiritual and complete for the 1st time in my Life! The entire Cleanse is not only internal but spiritual as well. The Angel Farms Cleanse, is a way of Life. An education not to be found anywhere else. They really do show the Angels around you. Cindy & Larry truly are Angels. I Thank you so much. I love you Both you have truly touched me. "You will truly love yourself, for doing the Cleanse!—R. Denning (AZ Shaman) I deserve! If the docs have not been able to help you go to Angels Farms.—Joe (ID Reiki Master)

I began the Cleanse with hesitation, but was willing to try anything due to my pain. I was at the end of my rope. I had the pain for

8 months and had been flat on my back taking narcotics to get through the day for 1 month. When I saw what was coming out of me I was shocked and sold to the idea of cleansing the bowel. When on the 8th day I was able to walk with no meds I was blown away. Learning how my thoughts were creating my physical state had a huge impact on my healing. I know I will continue to heal as long as I remember the teaching I received at Angel Farms. No matter what your reasons are for talking ourselves out of the Cleanse, put them aside. "I believe that this is a necessary for everyone to have a vibrant body and good health. —Michele (HI R.N.)

Emotionally Energized, physically-90% better, spiritually awakened. I came here not realizing this wasn't about the food I ate yesterday, but in a way it turned out to be true!!! All the actually food that I was eating all created monstrous, abnormal things that came out of my body - It didn't hurt (not to scare anyone) but its out and I am so happy!!! Astonished!! Food of my heart, soul from the past, fears & emotions, self loathing, quitting, are gone my mind & heart is healed. Come enjoy! You are worth it!!!—Jackie (AZ)

I feel light but grounded - and in the process of re-entering my body. Yoga this AM - felt incredibly wonderful - ease, spaciousness, energetic connections and energetic strength, very powerful. An effortlessness & ease, in movement. I feel a little edgy still - extra sensitive (around a loved one) Bit I generally feel more "allowing and loving: - very "direct and honest", less hesitation - much more courage" in who I AM. I feel beautiful & powerful in the goddess way! "I might have to add this later....(my story.... But I'll try: "my experience, process at Angel Farms has allowed me to step to myself and meet my courageous heart! Angel Farms has facilitated my Blossoming into this courage that has always been there (of course - thanks Cindy!) and now I feel capable of the greatness I have been brought here to share and create and reflect in others!!" I have come home to myself!!!! Trust the process, stay in the moment-and whatever judgment comes up at Angel Farms - you will let it go!!" Know that a huge PEACE will come over you and your heart will know it - and your mind will finally come around too!—L. Lowell (HI art consultant) Physical 5 lbs. lighter, emotional happily adrift with new strategies and blindingly new perspective on the world. Spiritual, renaissance of tangible, constant spirit, self- love. My process in tangible and spiritual. A number of strategies to employ. When undesired emotions like anger/frustration arise, like evoking my third eye to awaken my heart, the exploding rose, the 'proof' effect. Eating habits will change and a greater understanding & comprehension of nutrition and food & food signatures. Deepak & Gregg B provided spiritual models I look to continue and more easily embrace, as well. Cindy's compassion/leadership was unequalled in value. Anthony's food was sustaining & inspirational. Larry's sessions was unique and memorable, despite my liquid state upon exit! Face our challenges head-on: Angel Farms will help the process. "Let the novelty of Angle Farms come to you, take what you will and don't worry about the details.—Greg (CA)

I feel more clean, more clear and much more open to love and positive experiences. I believe in myself and more than I ever have and truly feel like I can accomplish anything I put my mind to and focus on. My body looks and feels much better although I still have possibly some blockage still in my colon (that should come out tomorrow) I understand more about myself and how everything I say, think and do really matters - immensely. Everything I put into my body matters. All food, thought and actions have to be digested & create a specific affect. I matter and I am very important to this world! Its definitely worth it!!—Faith (CA)

Solid & clear! Forgiveness begins by not blaming anyone for anything! Amen = I AM! —Paul (HI)

I feel lighter, connected to myself and my essence. For the lst time, I know I am here and want to be! I deserve to be! My body feels and looks lighter - I've lost inches over many areas of my body face, arms, back, waist). My true self. I know who I am and not what I'm not! I know I belong on this earth and always did, I believe I deserve to love and love myself for the 1st time ever. I believe it on a very deep level in my BODY and my SOUL! "This is the hope you thought you'd lost, couldn't find, didn't think existed - that could heal you on a deep profound level. —Linda (CO)

I AM -I AM — I AM so healthy my breathing, I 'm clear with tons of energy. I sleep great my toenails & fingers are clearing up. I am so clear! Even my eyesight is returning, no need to use glasses! Thank you! I LOVE myself! —RJ. Hampton (HI)

I feel like I'm better prepared to greet the rest of my journey and that I can proceed with my entire being. There is no feeling like having your body, mind, & spirit in a clear & clean state. The moment that I heard of the work at Angel Farms - it sounded right for me! I didn't even have to hear much, I was having liver issues and my right shoulder wouldn't heal properly. Both areas are much relieved now and I believe they will continue to heal. It will be my goal to continue caring for myself. So I can give my all!!! Thank you for assisting me along the way!! Do it for yourself but do it! No gift is greater than being clear at the core.—Diana (HI)

The process of the Cleanse itself was quite challenging given my childhood history, but past profound was that I let go of the psychological & emotional toxins that occupied my shit & interacted with the very core of my cell membrane. I have flown many miles to confirm that "I AM" & in the "I AM" I will always love myself! So what I created embracing my creation co-creation with the universe can only serve to teach me, self nurture, voice, compassionate, loving, believing, letting go, forgiving, breathing with the universe... —Evelyn (NY Children's Counselor)

Physical - released so much sludge, a tangle of worms - results- I feel more connected to my body, I feel more connected to my spirit I feel I can trust my emotional body to stay harmonized. I have been in the deepest crevices of myself to really hunt out & expose & shine light on all the places that have limited me- this has been purging of disempowerment back to empowerment. I feel stronger - like I can not only stand on my own two feet but once again be in service to the divine self & be part of the solution, instead of the problem, here on the planet earth" Use this experience to allow yourself to go deep, become self referent and let go of all that "stuff"- emotional, mental & then physical that no longer serves. Allow, accept, let go & Don't judge yourself. —Alaya (CO)

Absolutely clearer in my thinking & feelings. My heart felt more open (about as wide as the ocean & more) as well as my attitude & intentions. I felt more of a connectedness and reverence to all life. More expansive and appreciative. More in love with myself. My biggest ha's-besides my black pubes!!! (Hair color changed on second day to black!) your affirmation reminder, dear Cindy, of Who I Am. I'd gotten so busy taking care of everyone else I had forgotten me. I'd lost my path. I had strayed. And you in your infinite wisdom and knowledge were able to bring me back to my path... "I AM" and most important, that I am not a failure or unsuccessful if I have to have the surgery. I had forgotten how to love me, and you showed me the way. Your guided me back to my potency, my clarity, and my own powerful inner wisdom-I am God, I am Love, & I love You! You helped show me that having surgery may be a part of my path, and if it is, then that is good after all, as we are all perfection in the eyes of love. "It's all good," as my daughter Sasha would say!! —Michele (CA Healer)

I finally could let go of my past. I tried for 20 years through hypnotherapies and counseling to let go of my dads abuse and mothers death. I gave up. MIRACLE!! My hair changed back to color. MIRACLE!! I was always tired and sometimes slept 14 hours a days and was still tired and run down. Now I have energy like when I was 15. MIRACLE!!! Numbness is my leg is mostly gone. MIRACLE!! I just feel love. Thank you God and Angel Farms.. You saved my life!! I realized that the only truth is to life is the NOW. How sick it makes you to not let go of the past anger and negativity. I learned how the Universe works and how we all connect in Love. The best and only thing we can do to change the world for the better is to love our selves first. So we can be shinning examples, so we can change the world from anger to love on a cellular level. I converted my belief that we are all children of God, some are just trapped in the dark because they don't know what they are doing. This was the hardest thing to let go of because of my past abuse. I learned about nutrition, how digestion works and in general how body, mind, and Spirit works. Thank you guy's a million endless times!! My relationship to my daughter changed extremely to Good!! I am REBORN.—Danny(HI musician and drummer)

Since I began the Cleanse I've noticed several things have changed. I've withdrawn from caffeine and totally stopped taking my hormones for menopause-yet I have no menopause symptoms anymore. My skin tone has definitely improved and my eves have brightened. My varicose veins have decreased in size, I've had some food allergies for 16 years and today I drank a smoothie with bananas in it and was fine, (I'm thrilled). As for emotional & Spiritual, I have been feeling a lot less defensive and a lot more tolerant & peaceful. I feel the Cleanse has helped me release the stored negative emotions I was harboring. —Denise (IL)

For me, the pressure in my body began around 12 years ago...frequent headaches, and tight back muscles. I read, researched, visited, and participated in more than 40 healing sessions over the past decade.. no gain-just pain. By the 9th day of this Cleanse, the pressure had finally subsided... and I feel more alive than I have ever felt before! Thank you-Thank you You are happy, healthy, and holy-and if you are not *feeling all three, then NOW would be a good time to do the Cleanse!—David (CA)*

Today, my last day of the Cleanse, I am excited to have lost 14 pounds in only 10 days. I feel as though my body has gotten a kick start and I know my ideal weight is just around the corner. I am also hungry several times a day; I noticed this 3 days earlier. For the first time I think my body is getting nutrition and actually is capable of burning it as fuel. I am impressed at how delicious soft foods are and the many pureed vegetables soups are definitely something I will continue at home. I have come to love reading the ingredients on everything. I had to wait months to arrange for this time off and I am so grateful I did! I can only urge others to do the same. Put yourself first and do this one important thing for yourself!-Francoise (CA)

I feel clearer, lighter, more joyful! I didn't come in with many physical issues. This Cleanse helped me experience a profound Spiritual and emotional awakening. A clean vessel can hold a lot more love and light! Go for it! This cleanse will change your life, give you more energy, more vitality, improve your health and increase your creativity and productivity at work.-Dr. Win (CA)

I feel more at peace, happy with myself, accepting of where I am in my life, energetic, more clarity, love of God. I feel so peaceful now and accepting of my skin problems that have depressed my in the past. I have reaffirmed my love for God and myself and my calling in life to show love to others, just as Cindy and Larry have done to the people going through the program with me. I have confidence that my body and health will continue to go through significant positive changes. This program is a life changing experience that will clean your Spirit, mind and Body!-Kelly (CA Healer)

Physically I came here with a life threatening challenge and I know it is gone! Gout problems gone, stroke level blood pressure now constantly with an ok range. Emotionally I am very focused on what I am about (Loving others) in their participation in becoming whole. Spiritually I now know at a cellular level that I am loved by God-What a gift to receive the gift of Faith. Life to me is a process. This was a 10 day holistic healing process. I can finally personally relate to Jesus saying " You must be born again to enter the kingdom of Heaven. and when you are walking around Heaven's Gate here on Earth what more is there? I have seen the light! The 0 to 8 conference with Cindy healed life time wounds that caused me to be stuck (signature from the past) this was such a moment of honesty it could not help but be absorbed by love.-Ken (Farmer-Idaho)

I feel Cleansed, God's love and the unconditional powerful love of Me!! I primarily arrived at Angel Farms to support my partner in his journey back to full love and health. To see him endure pain to let the "good stuff" in was difficult, but a must for his advancement. During the Cleanse I connected in love and life with the other Angels and our beautiful hosts, and appreciated life's purpose-Love, Love, Love, Love is all you need! If you love yourself or know you need to love yourself and don't, DO THIS-It will transform you into an angel (or give you wind beneath your wings, if you were an apprentice angel before.)-Jon (WA)

Swelling under my right rib cage is gone. The mucous of 2 years is thinning and loose-not like a hard object. The pain in my neck and head is gone, pain in my liver is gone. I am now more aware of the power of love and the destructiveness of anger. I feel less depressed and more hopeful. I learned to chew my food, and how improper absorption of nutrients into the blood stream, has affected my life. I have recognized the life long blessing of clearing the colon. Just do it! Clear Everything! Make Room for New!! —Pat (HI)

My intention started quite vain, younger looking skin, lose a few pounds, etc. Day ten of the Cleanse I find myself aligned with my higher self, my body tuned up from the inside out, my heart at peace and (my vanity put aside) my body light and slim. I thank my body, my organs, every night for giving me a sweet body, I thank Cindy, Larry, and Shara for reminding me of my Source, my creative power and giving me the opportunity to begin my life anew. We all need this, Thank you Thank you! —Nancy (CA)

The immediate visual differences in the iris, after my initial treatments, were remarkable. The study of iridology, while still discounted by the medical profession, is an important element in the diagnosis and repair of the body's organs. And the cleansing of the colon should be a culturally understood and regular practice. The omission of this regimen from our health program is inexcusable given the overwhelming evidence of its importance.-David (WA)
I was amazed at how easy the process was, particularly the first few days. I found that spending most of the time in meditation was extremely beneficial . As historical residue of my time here on earth was flowing out of me, historical events were floating into consciousness and being released. I have never been one to gain weight but in the past few months I had put on ten pounds or

348

so. Starting the program, Cindy read my irises and told me it was due to low kidney function and that I would expect to lose 10-13 lbs. in the course of the program; that it was water weight. And I did, much to my delight. Now my kidney function has returned to normal and I am able to be comfortable again. —L.D. (WA)

I have more energy and oxygen. My stomach is softer to touch. Powerful refocusing of core energy. I have done dozens of leading health programs. Angel Farms tops them all! —John-nutiva.com

I have more energy and better circulation. My sense of smell has returned after being gone for years. The dark circles under my eyes are clearing. I feel more calm and centered and closer to my Source. I can't remember when I felt this good. This gift is priceless. —Krisha (WA)

I feel physically stronger, my senses are clearer, my heart has healed-grief released, spiritually I feel close to God and all the Angels are very close.-Dianne (CA)

I feel much more centered, relaxed in my body and clear emotionally. It feels like my body has opened a lot during the Cleanse and cleared a lot of emotions. I would recommend this program here to anyone. It has the remarkable ability to heal on the physical and emotional levels and the constant input of spiritual wisdom is great! I cannot envision a situation in which someone would not gain significant benefits from this program on some level physical, emotional, or spiritual. It is Great! —Stephen (London)

The Cleanse is the greatest gift you can give yourself. It is the most important treatment for ill health.—Courtenay (CA)

All the pains I had on my left side are gone. The lymph node under my left arm has shrunk. Back pain gone & bladder is happier, I know I am love and have a choice. At Angel Farms I learned that my body is infinitely intelligent. This is so much more then a cleanse, it is a journey into wholeness and love. Oceans of gratitude flow from my heart!-Pollyannabush.com singer and teacher My physical health is the best its ever been! My emotional body is the clearest its ever been! MMMMMM Spiritual! I experienced a breakthrough in the illness I had been suffering from for 14 years, and that was the Least of what I gained. I'm grateful to the illness for bringing me here, so I could experience being free from fear for the first time in my Life. Thank you God and Cindy!!

Whatever doubts you may have, came from the same place as the illness that led you to think about coming in the first place. Let go of one and you will release the other!-Jaijomusic.com

Best thing I have ever done for myself! —Kristy (HI).

I went from great health to Optimal health. My sense of smell returned and I have had a deeper sleep at night. I am more rested when I wake in the morning. I am a better person physically and Spiritually from have gone through the Cleanse. Given the chance, the body has the amazing ability to heal itself. The Cleanse is that chance. What a beautiful blessing it has been to go through the Angel Farms program. We are very excited about our new clean colon and becoming clear physical vessels. Even more importantly, we are grateful to you for helping us transform into Angels and helping us transition from being absent to being present, from the torment of the past and the future, to the freedom of now, from judgment to acceptance, from worry to trust, from fear to love. —Darrell - Hawaii

Physically a lot less congested with mucus: much better circulation, I do not have cold hands and feet, now. Emotionally I am not stuck in the future or in the past. I know I am an Angel and a vessel of Love.-Joy-Hawaii This Cleanse is by far the Best thing you can do for your body (and I have been around) without the Cleanse everything else you do will not be able to be a 100%. Hang on-it Is worth it! Angel Farms is the missing link-never before have I experienced a program more life changing & in many cases-life saving. Very educational. Cindy & Larry Sellers Comprehensive cleansing program is absolutely the Best! —Rebecca - aquacranial.com (Maui)

Better, Better, Better, in every category & classification you can think of. Awesome! I let go of much unneeded obstacles. When I take a breath, it touches my brain! The gentlest and most restorative tissue Cleanse I have done. —Ty - aquacranial.com (Maui)

It works for me overall the aspects of the body-mind-soul. I will not push but be myself as and example, and I would say I have waited for this Cleanse all my life, that's it, I am hooked! My joints are limber and lighter"miracles" My emotions are evened out and i feel totally relaxed and at peace with myself. I am Spiritually recharged!—Minhoi (CA) Belly Dancer
I am tired but relaxed and willing to allow and trust the process,

I am strongly connected to guides and guidance. I heard about the Cleanse from Jill and realized I was ready for a major transformation that would Cleanse and establish me firmly in the body. —Carol (CA)

I came due mainly to parasites and the negative energy that was behind the parasites. I wanted to be free from this very difficult burden and to move forward with a positive loving mind, body, and Spirit. I am a new person, more in tune with my real self, and my heart is alive again. My body feels lighter, like I am walking on the clouds, and I feel more graceful. I am absolutely enthralled with the results. If any fears come up on deciding to do this Cleanse, look at them closely, and by all means, let Love be your influence. Love yourself enough to know that you are worthy of the best-and this is it. You will be extremely happy when you see it for yourself. —Chael (FL)

I feel vibrant, light in Spirit and in body. To get truly clear in my heart, this has been the most important step in the enfoldment of my journey. It feels wonderful to be clear inside. —Lynn (CA)

You would just be amazed at what is going on inside you that is hampering your health. I have increased mobility and my kidneys are functioning better. Emotionally I am feeling more centered. —Cheryl (CA)

Just coming to this (cleanse) resulted in seeing, looking, & loving myself so that I can truly help this planet. I feel whole and I know I can do anything and hold that space. This Cleanse changes your life, the way you look at life, feel love, feel God more, Just Do It. My skin looks beautiful, my hair darker, my eyes look brighter, the yellow is gone. Emotionally I feel stable, not moody, light and easy. Spiritually, I am feeling Oneness! —Jorgina (HI)

I feel ten years younger, I haven't felt this healthy since my 20's. Phenomenal transformation of health. We are systematically manipulated not to realize we are the "One". Once people see the bars they know they are in prison and what follows is the desire to be free. —David Icke-(London)

Much improvement in connection to Higher Divine Self. Pains seem to be gone from body. —Sworn (HI)

I am amazed at what came out of my colon. I feel lighter, especially my stomach area. I feel you do a great and amazing work cleansing the colon. You have been taught well. I feel that a lot of the schools have been too diluted with information & both gravity and pressure should be introduced.—Nadine (Nevada)

I realized that living in Fear caused me to accept choices in my life that were not made by me or, made by me, but where not choices that were made from love or from my heart. I came with low energy, cough always, fatigued easily, high calcium levels, kidney's stressed, pessimistic, bitter, judgmental, and at the end of my rope. I wanted my personality back. I Am Here. —Mike (Canada)

I feel Spiritually re-born. I am very excited to share my new self with my children and friends. When I came to Angel Farms I was very tired and feeling like I was finished with the fight. Angel Farms helped me see the light. I now walk away feeling full of energy and full of love. I am ready to see the world through my new eyes (No More Glasses) and to feel my love for myself and the love I have for everyone else. My search when I came here was for harmony and inner peace. To stop the voices in my head and to be able to walk with confidence. Cindy and everyone at Angel Farms has helped me to see myself for who I really am, to feel at peace and calm. I know the voices in my mind won't stop right away but I now have the tools to help me stay in the NOW, to relax and just be. In a clouded world of darkness when your head feels like it has a blanket covering it, Angel Farms is the Light, the love, the strength & encouragement to help clear you mind. —Stephanie (Canada)

I've had a multitude of fascinating, interesting, and important experiences in my life that have changed and moved me, but nothing as profound as this. If you are ready to shift at whatever-be it physical, emotional, or Spiritual, this guided process will bring you back to Yourself. -Kelly (HI)
I came bloated in the stomach if I ate or not, hemorrhoids, and bleeding rectally. Emotionally up & down, unbalanced. Spiritually Stable but could use some healing and clarity to focus on intent of my creation. After: I started to feel more alive in many ways. Less pain in my stomach. Emotionally: actually opposite. Spiritually: more clear, balanced and supported.-Anantha (HI)

Since my Cleanse, I am 10 lbs lighter, no longer need allergy medication or acid reflux medication. My artificial hip no longer even feels present. My mind seems crystal clear now and I have no addictions. When I first started I was very depressed, I was a chain smoking pot, smoking some tobacco, drinking and eating too much alcohol, bad food and coffee. Today, I am doing none of that and best of all I'm not fighting against any of it. I'll really have no desire for and mind altering stuff-after 40 years! My life is in my hands! Not only did my physical problems disappear during the Cleanse but many other thing were healed that I had no expectation of. —Fred (CA)

I came with negative thoughts, low self esteem, house clutter, under my waist body fat, felt heavy, fear, low thyroid, anger, sad, alone, rejected, cold. After: Loving, Peaceful, Energized, lost 7 lbs. lighter. Everybody has parasites, even me who did so many cleanses. Don't wait, Do it, All the body pain can disappear." —Christine (CA)

I felt much lighter with good energy and clarity of thought. The program helps you evaluate your eating and living habits. Being conscious of what I eat, how much and how fast. —Sean (WA)

Physically healthy with minor IBS (Infrequent) emotionally going through a transition period spiritually growing every day. Physically sessions went quite well. Feel that was a good sign of health prior to sessions. Felt lighter, more energy but needing a bit more sustenance to feel really good. Some more clarity and higher awareness. Feeling lighter emotionally as well as physically, is the biggest benefit for me. Chew and slow down while eating. Don't let yourself get over hungry. —Lisa (WA)

I have increased energy.... Feeling of well being... I just feel lighter in my mind and body. My skin looks better. I just feel much healthier as a result of the "Cleanse." I never listened to the inspirational tapes before and would like to incorporate them into my life. Just do it! In a relatively short time one can make a dramatic improvement on their body, mind, and spirit." —Sallie (CA)

I feel physically more awake, springy & clearer. The prostatitis symptoms are still here, but I believe that will soon be history. I know what to do now emotionally, I feel vulnerable, but without fear. I feel even more sensitive than usual. Spiritually? There are no words... I know. —Jim (CA)

Physically I am experiencing an awareness of my body that has not been there before. Love my soft tummy!!! Emotionally I feel at peace with myself, patient, I am aware of the energy from others, enjoying eating in a different light. Spiritually to me this was the most amazing part of the "Cleanse". To be able to go back to the womb and feel the emotions were truly awesome. The love in finding the path to God will be with me for the rest of my life. From the hallway to the door, I am there. Amazing. To feel healthy again has been what I've been looking for over 30 years. Now that I've gone through Angel Farms Cleanse I have my health, physical & emotional. I loved it all.—Terry (CA)

The biggest change I noted was in my hips a release of stiffness and pain. I also see shifts in my interest in food. I am not nearly as agitated about hunger. I haven't felt hungry and have experienced almost no interest in eating except when I really feel hungry. This is very different. —Molly (CA)

I came feeling fatigued and unable to visualize a compelling future. I felt that as old stuck intestinal matter left and parasites were going as well, that emotional and spiritual issues became clearer and could be released. It feels like the beginning of a new way of being in the world that comes from safety and love, and knowing fear is useless and draining. If you need that specific elusive answer for your evolution toward wholeness- do this Cleanse. Physically I feel clean, clear, not bloated, I am breathing with my belly breath without thinking about it. Emotionally my heart feels open and safe. I love myself in a new and exciting way. Spiritually I feel aligned with God's purpose for us to realize we are Love. —Carole (CA)

Aloha Ke Akua Mahalo Nui Loa!

This book is about my 20 plus years of experience at Angel Farms Ministries in Miracles and transformations! You too can awaken "The-Angel-in-You" at Angel Farms Cleansing and Rejuvenation Center. We offer THE 10-day Cleanse of the Body, Mind and Spirit. You will journey deep into yourself to Cleanse and remember your truth. You will discover the Powerful, Creative Being that you are, raising your vibration to a Clarity of Purpose and Peace in your Body, Mind, and Spirit. Our program helps people out of pain when they are ready to release it. Haven't you hurt enough? We can help you find peace and happiness again.

The 10-Day Cleanse
A journey, a shift, a re-birth and transformation.

It is a natural, age-old process, incorporating pure water and various herbs. We use natural gravity flow and FDA registered units, to gently flush and eliminate toxins that have been held in the body for many years. By removing the toxic material, the body is then able to absorb nutrition, and heal itself miraculously. The Angels have an excellent opportunity to see what has been released from their bodies at the end of the session each day, and not through some goofy glass tube! How are you supposed to see what that stuff really is? Kaliko says every day, "Better out than in." During The Cleanse we use Spiritual & Emotional Counseling, Inner Child Sessions, Hot Stone Therapy, Aromatherapy, Ozone Therapy, and Nutritional Counseling, Cranial Sacral, Temple Lomi Lomi, and much more. On approximately the 7th day the "Angels" do a liver cleanse in which they access their stored anger and release it. Thousands of stones are released from the body the next day, pain free of course, and the new blood flow is awesome. We have witnessed many miracles on the 8th day. The program includes an Orientation Meeting before each Cleanse to inform "Angels" of the day-to-day mechanics of The Cleanse. The Cleanse is followed by a Graduation Ceremony in which we film the miracles as they celebrate their new, awesome, selves.   We have thousands of miracles filmed.

Transitional therapy works hand in hand with the 10-day Cleanse. I take you back to before you were 8 years old, using relaxation techniques. This helps clear emotional issues that challenge your life now. This process is one of self-realization and empowerment, helping "Angels" know that their choices and challenges are not to be judged, but honored. This session is one of the unique therapies that only Angel Farms uses to clear old belief systems that really open the way to true healing.

This Cleanse is Written in the Dead Sea Scrolls!

Quote from dead sea scrolls "Think not that it is sufficient that the angel of water embrace you outwards only. I tell you truly, the uncleanness within is greater by much than the uncleanness without. And he who cleanses himself without, but within remains unclean, is like to tombs that outwards are painted fair, but are within full of all manner of horrible uncleannesses and abominations. So I tell you truly, suffer the angel of water to baptize you also within, that you may become free from all your past fears, and that within likewise you may become as pure as the river's foam sporting in the sunlight."

"Seek, therefore, a large trailing gourd, having a stalk the length of a man; take out its inwards and fill it with water from the river which the sun has warmed. Hang it upon the branch of a tree, and kneel upon the ground before the angel of water, and suffer the end of the stalk of the trailing gourd to enter your hinder parts, that the water may flow through all your bowels. This will free your body from every uncleanness and disease. As the water runs out of your body, it will carry away from within it all the unclean smelling things of fear. And you shall see with your eyes and smell with your nose the abominations, and uncleannesses which defiled the temple of your body; even all the fears which abode in your body, tormenting you with all manner of pains. I tell you truly, baptism with water frees you from all of these. Renew your baptizing with water on every day of your fast, till the day when you see that the water which flows out of you is as pure as the river's foam. Then betake your body to the coursing river, and there in the arms of the angel of water render thanks to the living God you are free from your fear. And this holy baptizing by the angel of water is: Rebirth unto the new life. For your eyes shall henceforth see, and your ears shall hear. Fear no more, therefore, after your baptism, and the angels of air and of water may eternally abide in you and serve you evermore."

After the Cleanse you are rare in the world. You have fewer worms, parasites, mucus, ropes, pepper stems, metals, chemicals, pills, liver and gallbladder stones, and other assorted lifetime accumulations than most people you know. Your sugar, blood pressure and cholesterol levels are normal! Your skin looks radiant and you remember your glow! It's okay to be the one you have been waiting for, if not you, then who; if not now, then when? You can do it later, maybe? What if later never comes?

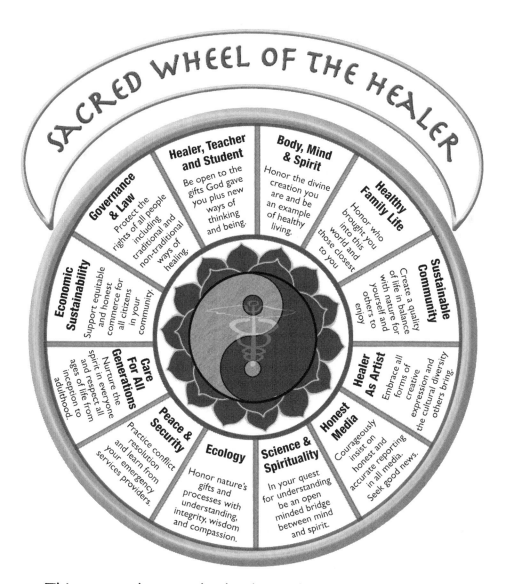

This poster honors the healers of the world who I have yet to meet and those wonderful healers who brought the miracles of their gifts into my life in a time of need...

Especially to Cindy Sellers and Angel Farms,
for her divine healing gifts!
This wheel was created to honor you.....blessings,
—Bruce L Erickson

Index

Angel Toolboxes
20, 32, 43, 64, 71, 89, 90, 95, 97, 100, 102, 104, 127, 141, 166, 172, 173, 181, 197, 201, 242, 262, 265, 266, 269, 271, 281, 285, 292, 293, 294, 298, 321

Miracle Stories
33, 39, 45, 49, 50, 59, 66, 101, 106, 120, 121, 140, 144, 146, 147, 148, 149, 150, 153, 156, 160, 206

Photo Attributions

Cover Photo: Larry Sellers, Rainbow falls in Hilo, Hawaii
White and Pink Plumeria Flowers: IStock RF photo
Single Pink Plumeria Flower: IStock RF photo

Cindy Sellers Cover Photo: Graduate Troy Jenson
http://www.troyjensen.com/nav.html

Page 25: Colon — from Doctrine of Food Signatures by Cindy Sellers

Page 28: Snowflake — Public Domain Image http://commons.wikimedia.
org/wiki/File:Wilson_A._Bentley_snowflake,_1890.jpg

Page 35: Kidneys — Royalty Free Dreamstime Image © Gunita

Page 36: Iris — Photo: Larry Sellers

Page 42: Female Reproductive Organs — Royalty Free Image
MedicalRF.com/Getty Images

Page 49: The Urinary Bladder —Public Domain http://en.wikipedia.org/
wiki/File:Illu_bladder.jpg

Page 53: Hepatic and Spleenic Flexture —Public Domain http://
en.wikipedia.org/wiki/File:Illu_colorectal_anatomy.jpg

Page 56: The Knee — Grays Anatomy Public Domain Image
http://commons.wikimedia.org/wiki/File:Gray352.png

Page 57: The Hip — Public Domain http://en.wikipedia.org/wiki/
File:Gray341.png

Page 58: The Feet — Public Domain http://en.wikipedia.org/wiki/
File:Foot.png

Page 61: Spleen — Public Domain http://en.wikipedia.org/wiki/File:Illu_
spleen.jpg

Page 68: Breasts — From Doctrine of Food Signatures by Cindy Sellers

Page 70: Thyroid — Public Domain http://en.wikipedia.org/wiki/File:Illu_
thyroid_parathyroid.jpg

Page 73: Diaphram — Illustration: Brad Lee Coffel/©Angel Farms

Page 75: The Pancreas — Illustration: Brad Lee Coffel/©Angel Farms

Page 77: The Lympathic System — http://en.wikipedia.org/wiki/File:
TE-Lymphatic_system_diagram.svg This file is licensed under the
Creative Commons Attribution 3.0 Unported license.
Attribution: http://commons.wikimedia.org/wiki/User:The_Emirr

Page 82: Iris — Photo: Larry Sellers

Page 87: Lung — Public Domain http://commons.wikimedia.org/wiki/
File:Lung_%28PSF%29.png

Page 94: Dollar — Public Domain http://en.wikipedia.org/wiki/
File:United_States_one_dollar_bill,_reverse.jpg

Page 98: The Heart — Public Domain http://commons.wikimedia.org/wiki/
File:Gray490.png

Page 98: Tomato — Photo: Royalty Free Image
Foodcollection RF/Getty Images

Page 108: Tongue — http://en.wikipedia.org/wiki/File:Tongue.agr.jpg
This file is licensed under the Creative Commons Attribution 3.0
Unported license. Attribution: Arnold Reinhold

Page 112: Movement of Food — Public Domain http://en.wikipedia.org/
wiki/File:Stomach_diagram.svg

Page 116: The Liver — Public Domain http://commons.wikimedia.org/wiki/
File:Liver_superior.jpg

Page 135: Parasite Photos from Cindy

Page 143: The Brain — Public Domain http://commons.wikimedia.org/
wiki/File:PSM_V26_D768_Brain_of_gauss.jpg

Page 145: Brain Cat Scan — Photo: Royalty Free Image
MedicalRF.com/Getty Images

Page 152: Neuron — http://commons.wikimedia.org/wiki/File:Neuron-
SEM.png This work is free software; you can redistribute it and/
or modify it under the terms of the GNU General Public License as
published by the Free Software Foundation
Source —Nicolas P. Rougier

Page 191: Liver — Public Domain http://commons.wikimedia.org/wiki/
File:Liver_superior.jpg

Page 194: Liver — Illustration: Brad Lee Coffel//©Angel Farms

Page 195: Gallstones — Photo: Larry Sellers

Page 203: Energy Field — http://www.bigstockphoto.com

Page 216: Aloe Vera — Photo: Larry Sellers

Page 220: Cayenne Pepper — Dreamstime Royatly Free Image
©Paul Paladin

Page 224: Comfrey — Photo: Larry Sellers

Page 226: Echinacea — Permission is granted to copy, distribute and/or
modify this document under the terms of the GNU Free Documentation
License, Version 1.2 or any later version published by the Free Software
Foundation; with no Invariant Sections, no Front-Cover Texts, and
no Back-Cover Texts. A copy of the license is included in the section
entitled GNU Free Documentation License.

Page 229: Goldenseal — Shutterstock/Royalty Free

Page 232: Noni — Photo: Larry Sellers

Page 235: Turmeric/Olena — Permission is granted to copy, distribute
and/or modify this document under the terms of the GNU Free
Documentation License, Version 1.2 or any later version published by the
Free Software Foundation; with no Invariant Sections, no Front-Cover
Texts, and no Back-Cover Texts. A copy of the license is included in the
section entitled GNU Free Documentation License.

Page 239: Garlic — H. Zell— http://commons.wikimedia.org/wiki/
File:Allium_sativum_002.JPG Permission is granted to copy, distribute
and/or modify this document under the terms of the GNU Free
Documentation License, Version 1.2 or any later version published by the
Free Software Foundation; with no Invariant Sections, no Front-Cover
Texts, and no Back-Cover Texts. A copy of the license is included in the
section entitled GNU Free Documentation License.

Page 286: Cell Structure — Illustration: Brad Lee Coffel/©Angel Farms

Icon: Angels Toolbox — Box illustration: Brad Lee Coffel/©Angel Farms

CDs, DVDs and Charts Available at
www.angelfarms.com

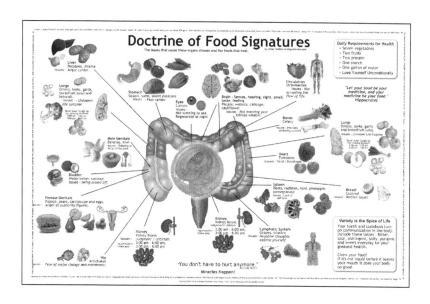

Angel Farms

www.angelfarms.com

R00200

Made in the USA
Charleston, SC
15 October 2012